Connecticut

UNBROKEN

THE TRIUMPHANT STORY OF A WOMAN'S JOURNEY

TRISHA BAILEY

Written with C.K. MULFORT

Foreword by Nate Burleson

Some of the names and identifying characteristics have been changed to protect the privacy of certain individuals.

For information regarding author appearances at live events or inquiries about special discounts for bulk purchases, please reach out to the Creating My Own Yes sales team via e-mail at BookSales@CreatingMyOwnYes.com.

First Edition

ISBN: 9798397698429

Cover design by Powerhouse Creations.

Manufactured in the United States of America

Library of Congress Cataloging-in-Publication

CONTENTS

ACKNOWLEDGEMENTS		5
FOREWORD BY NATE BURLESON		7
ABOUT THE AUTHOR		9
ABOUT THE WRITER		11
CHAPTER 1	**THE FIGHT**	13
CHAPTER 2	**HUMBLE BEGINNING**	28
CHAPTER 3	**COMING TO AMERICA**	43
CHAPTER 4	**NIGHTMARE BEGINS**	57
CHAPTER 5	**NIGHTMARE CONTINUES**	69
CHAPTER 6	**RUNNING FREE**	86
CHAPTER 7	**MY FIRST LOVE**	110
CHAPTER 8	**FINDING ME**	134
CHAPTER 9	**RISE OF THE EMPIRE**	152
CHAPTER 10	**LOVE HURTS**	170
CHAPTER 11	**SAME MISTAKES**	188
CHAPTER 12	**THE COMA, THE TRUTH**	201
CHAPTER 13	**LESSON LEARNED**	223
CHAPTER 14	**REMAINING UNBROKEN**	240
CHAPTER 15	**HAPPY ENDINGS**	261

ACKNOWLEDGEMENTS

I would like to thank God for the blessings he has bestowed upon my life, and for the strength he has given me to overcome obstacles. I would like to thank my best friend and confidant C.K. Mulfort, the author of this book for bringing my story to life. I would also like to thank my good friend Nathaniel Burleson for writing the foreword of my book.

I want to express my gratitude to my five children, Kashena, Natalia, Gabriel, Kayla, and Ocean. To all of my exes, thank you for the love, care, and the valuable life lessons you each have taught me. A special thank you goes to Galvin for igniting the idea of entrepreneurship within me. I am grateful to Onrique for being an amazing father to Ocean and for pushing me to prioritize self-care and seek the help I needed.

Thank you to my University of Connecticut family for giving me my first opportunity. Furthermore, I would like to express my gratitude to my girlfriends, guy friends, and family for being there for me every step of the way.

To my mother, Gloria Tomlinson, thank you for giving me life, guidance, and unconditional love. I appreciate every sacrifice you have made for me. To my sister Yolande, thank you for being my safe haven when I needed someone the most. Brian, thank you for showering me with love and allowing me to practice my mothering skills on you. Sean Wideberg, thank you for placing your trust in my words and believing in my dreams. To all the employees at Bailey's, thank you for providing our patients with exceptional care, filled with love and kindness. And to my darling T.D., I love you and I am grateful for you.

My grandma, Rose Jones, your memories live on in all of us. Your kindness continues to inspire me every day, and I will strive to follow in your angelic footsteps. This book is dedicated to you, Grandma—I love and miss you dearly.

FOREWORD

Every so often, we are fortunate enough to meet someone who becomes a true friend. However, even within that label, we may not fully understand the depth of their experiences or background. As I read this book, I am struck not only by how inspiring it is but also by how much I have come to learn about my friend. The skillful storytelling conveys her heartfelt experiences in a way that is both captivating and thought-provoking.

By titling her book UNBROKEN, Trisha Bailey has captured the essence of her remarkable story in a single word. Her journey speaks to the experiences of those who have faced trauma alone, while also resonating with a diverse range of readers. Through her unique perspective on a woman's journey from hardship to success, Trisha effortlessly connects with her audience, inspiring them with her heartfelt experiences. Her open heart and wise insights provide a better understanding of empathy and kindness, appealing to women of all races, single mothers, those dealing with trauma, and individuals seeking guidance in their entrepreneurial pursuits. Trisha's ability to face obstacles head-on is evident throughout the book, providing readers with inspiration and motivation to overcome their own challenges. Additionally, the book is written in a compelling style that reads almost like a work of fiction, keeping readers entertained and engaged from start to finish.

I have had the pleasure of knowing Trisha for a few years now, and she never fails to impress me with her business acumen, intelligence, and sense of humor. Her contagious laughter never seems to stop. We met through a mutual friend who could not stop talking about how amazing this woman was. So, when he asked me to host her 45th birthday party, I felt honored. Since then, we have had many engaging conversations, shared laughter, and collaborated on successful business ventures. When she walked into the party, I could see her happiness and positive energy radiating like fire on a candle. It was evident that Trisha's unique personality had drawn in all her friends and family members towards her.

One of the more impressive traits of Dr. Trisha Bailey throughout this book is her ability to balance keeping it real while also offering guidance. Moreover, her dedication, compassion, and empathy, even for those who have hurt her, is what gives this book so much depth. In this book, she skillfully navigates complex aspects of life and presents them in a way that is accessible and relatable to all readers. Whether you are a mental health professional or a barista at Starbucks, I believe this book will be an invaluable resource.

Through our interaction, I have gotten to know her personally, listening to her story from her days in Jamaica to where she is now. That is why I am so excited and honored to introduce you all to a phenomenal woman. As you read through these pages, I encourage you to keep an open mind and be willing to challenge your assumptions about judging a book by its cover. Whether you are examining the complexities of love and relationships, the challenges of living in a rapidly changing world, or the nature of human identity, Trisha finds a way to write with honesty, sensitivity, and a deep sense of compassion for the human condition.

Trisha's insights may challenge some of your thoughts, but I am confident it will inspire you to think more deeply about the trauma you've experienced and the journey in which you are traveling. I commend Trisha for her contributions to the betterment of people in all facets of life. That is why I am so excited and honored to introduce you all to this phenomenal woman.

— Nate Burleson
American Television Host

ABOUT THE AUTHOR

Life for many entrepreneurs has not been a crystal stair, and for Dr. Trisha Bailey, there is no exception. From the dirt roads of Jamaica to dominating the medical field, Dr. Bailey has proven herself to be the epitome of the word entrepreneur. Her gritty background makes her no stranger to hard work, but it is her passion and kindness that has led to her success, making her the wealthiest Jamaican woman to date.

At thirteen years old, Trisha Bailey migrated to the United States from Jamaica, leaving behind a family, hoping, and praying for her success. While many people may view her past as dark and traumatic, Trisha Bailey has taken those experiences to help create her own yes by strategically facing the obstacles in her journey head on. She was the first to graduate college in her family when she received her bachelor's degree from the University of Connecticut in 1999, where she lit up the track as a star athlete. She would then obtain a master's degree in business administration in 2005 and a doctorate in management in organizational leadership in 2010.

Dr. Bailey has taken over the home medical equipment industry as the only Black woman in this arena, establishing pharmaceutical and durable medical equipment facilities across the country. In 2021, she was a finalist for HME (Home Medical Equipment) Woman of the Year! An award that recognizes a woman around the world for their leadership in the market. Additionally, Dr. Bailey's achievements include being named the 2023 JP Morgan Chase and ONYX Magazine Woman of the Year. In the spring of 2023, Dr. Bailey received an honorary doctorate from the University of Connecticut and Bridgeport University.

Dr. Bailey has made a significant impact in the real estate market, owning properties across Jamaica and a wide range of commercial and residential real estate in both the United States and Jamaica. Notably, she holds the distinction of being the first Black woman to own commercial real estate in the esteemed areas of Vero Beach and Edgewood, Florida. Through her exceptional business skills and decision-making abilities, she has joined the ranks of billionaire women entrepreneurs, reshaping the course of history. Recently, the University of Connecticut honored Dr. Bailey by naming a cutting-edge facility, the Bailey Student Athlete Success Center, after her. This recognition serves as a reminder of Dr. Bailey's hard work, achievements, unwavering dedication, and her ability to inspire and uplift others.

ABOUT THE WRITER

C.K. Mulfort is a Haitian American writer hailing from Florida, known for his diverse portfolio covering books, screenplays, teleplays, and stage plays. From a young age, Kenny's imagination was filled with vibrant stories that unfolded in his dreams like cinematic movies. Inspired by these vivid visions, he honed his storytelling skills and transformed his musings into written works of art.

In the spring of 2007, C.K Mulfort discovered his passion for writing when he made his directorial debut with the stage play entitled "*A Walk in My Shoes*," a project that showcased his exceptional writing talents. This marked the beginning of a prolific journey as a writer. Mulfort proceeded to write, produce, and direct four stage plays during his university years. In 2009, he received his well-deserved degree in Journalism from the University of Florida.

C.K Mulfort has been using his intriguing experiences mixed with his interesting mind to write captivating stories. On December 10, 2020, he released his debut novel, *"The Other Side of a Mirror,"* a gripping psychological thriller that leaves readers on the edge of their seats. Notably, his talent has garnered recognition in esteemed competitions, having reached the finals of the Scriptapalooza screenwriting competition in 2010 and 2013 for his riveting scripts, respectively. Mulfort continues to blaze a trail of creativity and captivate audiences with his distinctive storytelling ability. With each new venture, he takes readers and viewers on a remarkable journey through the depths of his imagination.

UNBROKEN

CHAPTER 1

THE FIGHT

"That burning feeling of wanting to kill for the sake of survival is where my mind fled to, and had it not been for God, there would have been no return."

The stillness of the night cast a shadow under the moonlight and snuck through my bedroom window. The shadow placed an eerie veil over the room where evil could easily lurk, ready to strike at any moment. I couldn't help but feel tension draped over my entire body like a weighted blanket. If that weren't bad enough, the overwhelming silence drowned out even the faintest of sounds. I couldn't hear anything. Neither the familiar background noise of *Frasier* playing on the television, nor the loud snores of my faithful dog, Mandy, lying beside me.

Thump…Thump…Thump…

My heart pounded in my chest like a drum beating against my rib cage. Its frantic rhythm matched the pace of my racing thoughts, sending shivers down my spine. I sensed my heart trying to warn me of looming danger, but my mind couldn't grasp it.

So, there I lay, frozen in fear, as the relentless thumping continued to torment me. It must have been well past midnight when I awoke from a dream, only to find myself stepping into a living nightmare. It wasn't the first time I had woken up in a panic, but this time was different. I felt exposed, as if something remained just beyond my reach, waiting to strike. The memory of that night would continue to haunt me for years to come. It's a constant reminder of the day I believed my life was about to end. Yet, despite the fear holding onto me, I would do whatever it took to make sure I never felt that way again.

That night, fear coursed through my veins, and if I said otherwise, I would be lying. So much so, my intuition collided with the growing panic, and deep within the thickness of it all, a strange hypersensitive feeling began to take over. It was one of the few times I remembered being truly scared. Yes, fear is a normal and natural response that arises when we are threatened, but I always felt like I was different. It was as if I possessed an immunity to negative emotions that could influence my thoughts, emotions, and actions, leading me to behave out of character.

I have always prided myself on my ability to remain composed and resist impulsive actions, even in the face of overwhelming emotions. Fear, in particular, has never had a hold on me. This innate characteristic has been with me since childhood, where my remarkable bravery was evident to others long before I recognized it within myself. It is this absence of fear that has shaped the person I am today. Therefore, to hear me confess that "I'm scared," it is a statement not to be taken lightly. And on that night, I was terrified.

TICK! TICK! TICK!

The paralyzing ticks of the clock hanging on the wall taunted me with its endless tick-tock, each second feeling like an eternity as I lay in bed. Even if I wanted to run out of there, I couldn't. The silence surrounding the room had already begun to suffocate me like a heavy weight pressing down on my chest. That turned my bedroom into a prison cell as time became its guards. Outside my window, the crickets fell silent, as if sensing the gravity of the moment. There were no sounds within the walls of my home, no creaks, clicks, or hissing. No voices beyond my bedroom door and certainly no pitty-pat footsteps running around. Even the house itself seemed to hold its breath in anticipation. At that moment, I felt like the only person left in the world, and the thought was both eerie and troubling. All I could hear were my own slow, steady breaths, a soothing rhythm that offered little comfort in the face of the unknown.

The bedroom door slowly opened, followed by his loud footsteps approaching. They echoed in my ears like a church bell on a quiet Sunday morning. Even with my eyes closed, I could envision his devilish grin behind me as he stripped off his clothes that smelled like weed and day-old cologne. I remained as motionless as a corpse, curled up in a fetal position with my eyes shut tight. The icy temperature met the warmth of my blood in a more frigid room than I was used to. Chills covered my entire body as the churning in my stomach intensified. Even with the plush comforter draped over me, the coldness seeped in. However, the temperature wasn't the only thing cold in the room that night.

"You up?" His deep voice was slurred, shattering the silence as his unwelcome hands slid up my legs—from my ankles to my thighs.

I dreaded every second of it, clenching my pillow, pretending to be asleep. My body stiffened like a log, and the more his calloused hand grazed my skin, the tighter I squeezed the pillow, until my nails dug deep into my palms. My heart raced faster as the ability to breathe became a difficult task. The fears of yesterday lingered in my mind, threatening to take over and pull me back into that dark place I had worked so hard to escape from over the years. I had poured my heart and soul into creating a life filled with triumph, love, and joy. Yet here I lay, confined to my bed while a wicked and deceitful man invaded my body with his unwelcome touch.

So often, people would ask how I ended up with someone like him. Someone so detached, cruel, and completely different from me in every way. My response was always the same. *"I didn't notice at first!"* But looking back, I wondered if that had just been an excuse I came up with to hide my own lustful desires or to rationalize a terrible decision. As the days turned into months and months into years, I witnessed the evil in him appear regularly. I should have seen it, but perhaps I was too in love to do so. Or maybe I was waiting on a change that would never come, like some happy-ending fairytale bullshit.

He was always emotionally indifferent, but I figured he needed someone to love him. And I felt like I could be someone to help bring joy and richness into his life. His ability to be unavailable and cold-hearted at the drop of a dime… well, I mistook that for some sort of mid-life crisis based on his unflattering position in life. Therefore, I did everything to help propel his passion for music, hoping he'd be happy. That only worsened things and pulled him into a world where it was okay to disrespect women, to view them as objects rather than human beings. That world gave him an ego so big that even he could not contain it, allowing him to feel invincible. Staying out until the wee hours of the night partying, drinking, and doing whatever else only God knew became part of his routine. Sometimes, he'd return home a day later as if it were nothing. The sad part was that no matter what he did, I foolishly made sense of it and accepted it as normal.

"Trisha? Babe…?" he whispered.

I allowed the silence to serve as a response, but that wasn't enough for him. He wanted more. As I lay there, I felt him tugging on the seams of my black panties, starting off gently and then forcefully. The more I remained still, the more his frustration grew. I took a gulp of air, hoping he wouldn't hear me. Beyond my control, a tear slid down my cheek, onto the satin pillow. Inch by inch, his hand traveled along my body, down my back, across my ass, and onto my thighs. The warmth of his body creeping up on me made me uneasy. The overpowering odor of his breath, tainted with the pungent smell of weed, disgusted me to the core. It was an assault on my senses that left me feeling disgusted. I cringed at the thought of him touching me any more than he already had. I might as well have been a rock mired on the side of the road, motionless and detached, waiting for the moment to pass.

"Babe! You up?" This time his voice was much sterner.

I sighed softly, refusing to move a muscle. I wanted him to leave me alone and walk away. But that didn't stop him. Instead, he began nibbling on my ear as his right hand reached into my panties and touched the spot that wanted nothing to do with him. Every night he did the same thing—come home, wake me up, and expect to have sex no matter how I felt or what I was going through. Yes, I was his wife, and I understood that it was my role to please my husband sexually, but at the demise of my health? My sanity? How was that fair to me? Sex with him often left me feeling withdrawn and objectified, as if I were nothing more than a hole for him to cum inside of. Yet, I still surrendered to the deafening silence as if I were a child in a game of hide-and-go-seek, waiting for it to be over. That didn't matter as he flipped me over, climbed on top of me, and pried my legs open.

"Get off of me!" I shouted, mustering all my courage.

He grabbed my wrists and pinned them to the mattress like shackles. I was stuck, and the more I fought to break free of his hold, the tighter he squeezed, nearly cutting off the circulation to my hands. I repeatedly tried to get him off me, but it was a miserable failure. That was strange because I had always considered myself a strong-willed fighter. That's how it is when you're raised in a tough home, especially when you're trying to understand the world around you. That toughness prepared me to fight physically and mentally and get back up when I fell. It gave me the strength to fear only the person I saw in the mirror. That bold attitude was predicated on the inherited environment that molded me into the woman I became.

Growing up in Jamaica, I had to fight a lot, and most of the time it was unnecessary. I fought boys, girls, and on one occasion, an adult. Fighting became part of my DNA; oddly enough, none of the fights I engaged in were my battles. I was the person in town that my sister, cousins, and friends called on whenever someone wanted to fight them. Unlike me, they were always getting into some sort of trouble, and each time it happened, I was there to clean it up. Not just for one of my cousins—for all of them.

Fight after fight, I swiftly became known as some sort of enforcer no one wanted to deal with, neither boys nor girls. Even with my skinny petite frame, I was ready to take on anyone. I wouldn't say I was proud of it, but it was who I had become—a ruthless fighter determined to win—figuratively, literally, mentally, and physically. As kids, we were permitted to fight if we needed to defend ourselves. The crazy thing was that sometimes the kids' mothers would jump into the fight, and when that happened, my aunts would be right there to handle things. I believed they allowed us to fight because it was their way of creating an environment where we learned to defend ourselves.

One fight stood out among the others because it taught me a valuable lesson. It's been over thirty years, yet I vividly remember it like it happened last week. My mother, who lived in the United States, sent my sister and me customized pencils we considered to be very special. Not only because they were sturdy, colorful, and had our names engraved on them, but they were also from America. For my sister and me, anything from the U.S. was something we cherished as if it were gold. Then again, we didn't have much growing up, so we loved everything we were fortunate to own, including those pencils.

It rained that day. I remember because I had to be very cautious on my way to school, walking around the mud and jumping over puddles to avoid dirtying my clothes and shoes. One of the local girls from school, LaKeisha Thompson, decided she would steal my sister's pencil. Yolande was devastated, and although she knew LaKeisha had taken her pencil, she continued to search for it in hopes that she'd get it back. Like most younger sisters, Yolande was an irritating and talkative "pickney" (a term used for children in Jamaica), but she was never one to stand up for herself. Yolande was much too timid to do so. That's the funny thing about self-control; it's oftentimes a limited resource because the part of the brain exerting that control eventually tires out. And for my sister, there was no exception. After waiting long enough for LaKeisha to return the pencil, my sister decided to stand up for herself.

"Wey mi pencil deh?" Yolande asked.

LaKeisha laughed in my sister's face when she asked for the pencil, boldly denying that it belonged to Yolande. To make matters worse, she arrogantly walked away with her head held high, as if she were a queen. Despite my sister's desperate pleas, LaKeisha adamantly refused to return the pencil. Overwhelmed with sadness, Yolande came running to me in tears, telling me the entire incident. So, once again, I found myself standing up for someone who couldn't defend themselves, just as I had done on numerous previous occasions. And like the other times, I had to handle the situation.

Our little town was much like a family, for better or worse. Despite the occasional spats, we were loyal, loving, and protective of one another. In my town, we all knew enough about each other, and I knew what I needed about LaKeisha Thompson. Even down to the exact route she took to get home from school. That was easy because she'd taken the same path every day for years. Her route ran through a stretch of huts disguised as homes surrounded by a dirt road littered with trash and rocks. Nothing about this route was pretty.

Once school was over, instead of socializing with my friends, I ran home as quickly as possible, changed into my shabby clothes, and threw on a pair of worn-out shoes. That was the only rule I knew about fighting—if you're going to fight, take off your school clothes and put on your playing clothes. Don't fight in your good clothes—not ever! So that's what I did. After the rain cleared, the sun beat down relentlessly, leaving the air dry. The road, once slick with mud, had begun to dry up. I dashed outside, hoping to catch LaKeisha as she made her way down the dusty path. Now, as shocking as preparing for a fight may sound, it was also completely normal—my typical whoop-ass tradition.

I ran down the hill, breathing heavily, and there she was, walking my way, laughing and playing around with her friends as if she'd done nothing wrong. The fire in my eyes intensified the closer she got; she had no idea what was coming her way.

"LaKeisha! Gi mi sista back har pencil," I demanded.

"No! Dat nuh fi har," she shouted. LaKeisha continued to argue that the pencil didn't belong to my sister as I stood there, staring at the pencil that had Yolande's name written on it.

"Dat pencil deh fi har. 'Er name pon it. Give it back now!" I demanded as I stepped into LaKeisha's face— eye to eye.

Part of me hoped she'd do the right thing and return the pencil, because honestly, I took no pleasure in fighting. None whatsoever. However, at times, it was necessary. Especially when you had someone like LaKeisha Thompson trying to make you believe the lies coming out of her fucking mouth. It drove me wild and left me staring at her with a fury growing in me like mighty ocean waves.

After all the bickering about the damn pencil, I had grown tired of it and just wanted to beat her ass. My heart raced to an irregular beat, and I was breathing heavily from all the fussing. Suddenly, I lunged toward her, wrestling her to the ground, trying to snatch the pencil back. Just ten seconds was all it took to retrieve it. I took a deep breath, basking in the fact that it was over. Or so I thought.

"Git out fi mi way, bitch!" she muttered as she stomped off.

And just like that, my brain shifted to a gear beyond my control. I became a cold, unemotional demon, my softer side taking a back seat to the anger steering my next move. Calling me a bitch had always been a trigger for me. I don't know what it is about the word, but it has gotten me in trouble with a few people. Or perhaps I should say it has gotten a few people in trouble with me. Rage shot through me like a missile and unleashed itself without considering the consequences. That was the case when I was eight years old, standing in front of LaKeisha Thompson, and that is the case today.

I felt a fire burning in my eyes as my jaw clenched, the tension bustling in my muscles. It took away my ability to think straight, allowing everything to move in slow motion. Then, a flash of bright red streaked across my vision just before I grabbed hold of her and flung her to the ground. I climbed on top of her and began punching her with no regard for life—even pounding her head against the muddy dirt road. Every movement felt like a series of still images, my fists swinging across her body, morphing her face into a contorted expression she'd never worn before. I could still see her screaming, but the ringing in my head drowned it out.

I saw the pain in her eyes as her soul disappeared from the fake ass persona she had forged to fit in a world of indifference. Yet that still didn't stop me. My fingernails repeatedly slashed across her face, painting it red. If that weren't enough, blood began oozing from her eyes as my thumbs savagely dug deep into her sockets. I couldn't stop myself. I desperately wanted to, but whatever had taken over did so with vengeance. This act of violence wasn't cruelty, though. It was mercy and justice combined. The aftermath of the assault left scars on LaKeisha's face that would be a permanent reminder of the brutality I inflicted. It was a lesson taught to me by the women in my family. Nevertheless, I started to wonder, if I was constantly fighting everyone else's battles, who would be there to fight mine when I couldn't?

"You know you want this dick! Stop acting like that," he said, bringing me back to the present.

That night, he held my wrists with his right hand and used his left hand to slide his erection inside me. Forcefully. My mind and body, with one accord, refused to welcome him in. So much so, that my body was far from lubricated, making the friction unbearable. The room became darker and colder as he continued thrusting himself inside of me. I felt myself shivering from the fury that was taking over me. The pain of him fucking me while trying to squirm away increased. It felt like my skin was ripping. Looking up, I saw his eyes were closed, and it was as though he couldn't hear me. He fell into a trance-like state, as if he were a drug addict taking a hit of heroin. His need to climax was more significant than anything I was going through mentally, physically, and emotionally. It was so deflating to have someone who supposedly loved and cherished me invade my body in the manner he did.

"Bitch, stop moving. Damn!" He squeezed my wrists harder.

I took a deep breath and began counting, hoping an answer would come to me by the time I reached twenty. That's what I did in situations I desperately wanted to escape. I did it back when I was thirteen, and I did it that night—anything to help distract me through the moment. Sometimes, the only way I knew to survive was to behave in ways that made me uncomfortable.

One.

Two.

Three.

My mind sputtered into darkness. The moment paralyzed me so much that I couldn't even cry. It was as if I were watching a movie, and someone suddenly pulled the plug.

Everything I knew about myself, including my confidence, went out the window that night. Without question, the woman lying in that bed was a stranger. She wasn't the woman I had come to know all these years—that determined fighter with a loving persona that everyone knew me to be. Instead, I'd become a despairing woman who thought it would best to give up rather than to fight. A woman who begrudgingly accepted mistreatment and dishonest behavior for far too long without putting him in his place. So, while imprisoned under the strength of a man I had grown to love and hate, I waved the white flag and surrendered to his demand.

Four seconds. Five seconds. Six seconds.

The moment had grown tiring as he penetrated my body forcefully, scarring my soul and spirit as much as he scarred my body. So badly did I want to push him off me, but I knew where it would lead. More fighting. Physically, I couldn't take it anymore. However, mentally, I was still far behind, cataloging all the what-ifs of the situation. What if I laid there, quiet as a mouse, and allowed him to fuck me like the two-dollar whore he saw me as, just to get it over with and avoid the fight? Or what if I fought back, and this time he decided he had enough and beat me up worse than the last time? Even worse, what if our fighting woke up my children and they walked in, bearing witness to the trauma? There were so many questions and not enough answers.

"Get off me!" I screamed.

After a few moments, a voice screaming in my head demanded I get up and be the fighter I knew myself to be. So, I did just that. I fought and squirmed from his hold, but again it was a miserable failure. He dropped his entire weight on me, pinning me to the bed while holding my wrists. He wouldn't stop, and the more I begged and pleaded, the more aggressive he became.

"Stop it! Just let me fuck!"

Finally, my right hand slipped from his hold, and I quickly reached for a wine glass sitting on my nightstand. It all felt surreal as time seemed to slow down, yet I could feel the speed of my heart racing more than I was used to.

No more thinking. Grab the wine glass. Smash it into his head.

Pieces of the sharp, thick glass went flying across the bed. I knew there was little impact the wine glass could cause, but I didn't know what else to do. Certainly, I couldn't just allow him to continue beating me. In most cases, my anger triggered his violence, but fear welcomed my rage at that moment. That burning desire to protect myself for survival, by any means, was where my mind fled, and had it not been for the grace of God, there would have been no return.

As a child, I wasn't used to nights where I'd lie in bed listening to the sound of my aunt and uncle fighting. Nor had I ever witnessed a man land forceful punches across his wife's face like how it happened to me. What I saw in his eyes was terrifying—a cold, dark, emotionless stare that reflected my pain and terror. I never imagined what took place that night would come from the man I loved.

"Get the fuck off of me!"

I swung the broken wine glass all over the place like some sort of crazy person, desperately hoping he would back off. Despite the pain and fear he had caused me, I had no intention of inflicting harm on him. How could I? I mean yes, I was a fighter, but using a weapon to severely injure someone to the brink of death? No, that was not in my nature. On top of that, he was still the man I had chosen to spend my life with—my husband. All I wanted was to protect myself in that moment, or better yet, for the whole shit to come to an end. However, he didn't see it that way. He perceived it as a threat and therefore reacted with increased anger, becoming more determined to harm me.

"Please! Please, don't do this. I'm begging you not to do this to me. I love you, and I don't want you to hurt me. Think about our son, and my kids," I pleaded. Despite my attempt to calm him down with words, he tried to grab the broken glass from me, but I kept swinging it back and forth, refusing to let him pry it out of my hands. Who knew?

If he somehow grabbed it from me, there was a chance he'd kill me with it.

Suddenly, the wine glass slashed against his forearm, opening a gaping wound. The rusty, metallic scent of his blood wafted toward me as it oozed from his arm like a leaky faucet. That awakened the monster in him. Disregarding his pain, he shoved the glass to the side, grabbed me by the hair, and flung me off the bed like a lightweight pillow. He slammed me to the floor so hard that I lost my breath for a long agonizing moment. Part of me tried to get up and run away, while the other part wanted to fight. That internal battle to fight or run left me stuck, unable to escape his wrath.

A flash of bright light appeared, as if a truck drove right through the bedroom and quickly disappeared. Blood came pouring from my mouth like a waterfall. At that moment, I realized that his fist had crossed my jaw, nearly shattering it.

An explosion of pain came rushing all at once as I tried to process what had just happened, and before I could, he did it again. This time, it came across my right eye, shattering me to pieces. Finally, tears came pouring out as if it were the first time I had ever cried. I was weak, less than nothing. No one would treat a stray dog like he treated me. That look burning in his eyes was different. Not just rage but pure evil. I had never seen a face with eyes like that before, neither from him nor anyone else I'd ever been with. I genuinely believed he was the devil himself, neglecting everyone in the world just to be here with me. Alone! It had to be because I refused to accept that God could create a human being like him. Over and over, his knuckles bashed my face to the point it felt more like soft tapping rather than heavy punches.

The rock-like punches landed on my head, across my shoulders, and over my entire body. Physically, I fought back, but I'd be lying if I said I remembered what I did to save myself. Perhaps I kicked him? Punched and scratched? Who knew? Maybe I just curled up, hoping to protect myself. Beyond the blood, flashing lights, and brutal pain, I couldn't remember much of anything else.

From the silence came a faint buzzing then ringing sound. It was sharp and pierced right through my head. The more he pummeled my face and body with his bare knuckles, the louder the ringing in my ears got. He'd stop, sit on me, and berate me with insults when he got tired. "You fat, ugly bitch! You ain't worth a damn! Piece of shit bitch!" For nearly three hours, I yielded like a helpless child to the torture of this evil soul. The smell of his sweaty musk mixed in with his weed-infested breath surrounded me.

At last, the punches thrown at me finally tired him out, yet the nightmare was far from over. Time stopped and lingered, with a thick and heavy silence covering us like a heated blanket. I looked up and stared at him with my jaw clenched tight and my fists balled. I wanted him to witness that the fighter in me was still there. That's when he tried to take my ability to breathe, placing his calloused hands around my neck, squeezing so tightly that my muscles began to contract. I no longer had control of my hands, feet, or any part of my body. It might have been just fifteen seconds, but it felt like an eternity. Looking into his eyes, it was clear he was squeezing with all his might. He even spat directly in my eyes as he tried to squeeze the life out of me. Over and over again. If that weren't bad enough, he blew snot out his nose and smeared it all over my face.

"What now, bitch!"

That was enough to give me the strength to fight back and ultimately push him off me. However, I admit, there was a sudden realization that I could die, and the more I fought back, the more the thought became real. So much so, that I almost took comfort in the idea of death because I couldn't take this anymore. I just wanted it to be over. Then, I began to imagine what the better version of myself would have wanted me to do.

Fight! As scary as the thought of him killing me was, the vision of one of my children finding me dead in a pool of blood frightened me the most.

I couldn't let them see me like that and be forced to deal with the trauma for the rest of their lives. In all the fights I'd been in, there was always damage to my body. However, damage to the mind always took longer to heal. Returning to empathy or possibly happy memories required a level of patience that I somehow lacked. In my mind, the damage caused by those moments needed years of healing. So essentially, getting beaten up was, in reality, being beaten down. Before that night, I had been through all sorts of shit, and although I couldn't undo the trauma that I had been through, I knew I didn't have to be defined by it. I could overcome it. That's how I have arrived here today, at this moment, telling you about how I formed my path to creating my own yeses and how I remained unbroken.

CHAPTER 2

HUMBLE BEGINNINGS

"As kids, sometimes we may be unaware of the sacrifice and the hard work someone puts in for us. It's not intentional, but it happens..."

Plip, plip, plip... the raindrops danced on my rooftop, their gentle patter growing louder with each passing moment. Snuggled in my makeshift bed, I would listen to the soothing melody and smile joyously. The bed, a humble sanctuary that had cradled me through countless nights, consisted of a worn-out foam mattress resting upon a weathered plywood platform. Yet, regardless of the conditions I was forced to live in, the rain had an unwavering way of allowing me to believe that everything would be alright.

Plip, plip, plip...

That melodic tingling sound has always been a soothing sound for me to embrace, like little therapeutic fingers tickling my brain. Living in Jamaica—especially in Woodland—it seemed to rain frequently. I didn't mind it, though, because I'd stare out into the unknown as a little girl, watching the raindrops trickle down my windowpane. Most of the time, I heard the rain more in my soul than through my ears. It ignited a sense of warmth throughout my body that made me feel safe. Almost as if I were being hugged from within.

More than anything, those nimble, gentle raindrops taught me life lessons I've carried throughout my life. Like the liquid goodness from the heavens bringing health to the world, I too believed that's why I was placed on Earth—to help those who can't help themselves. I watched the rain enrich the sweet brown soil that grew abundant crops on our farm—the same way I did with my children, pouring love into them so they could grow plentifully. The brown hue of the tree trunks deepened once touched by the rain, allowing me to understand that change was possible no matter the condition. The green grass and flowers turned glossy, reflecting light from above, impossible to ignore. Like the raindrops, I knew God's light dawning on me would take place no matter where I landed. Indeed, rain taught me valuable lessons.

I was born in St. Elizabeth, Jamaica, one of the oldest parishes on the island. My mother and I moved to Kingston, where I spent some of my early life. However, I have little to no recollection of the period that I spent living with my mother. In fact, had it not been for my mother telling me, I would have assumed that I had always lived with my aunt. After receiving no support from my father, my mother was forced to leave me with my grandmother and aunt in a town known as Woodland—the rural mountainous terrain of Jamaica's southwestern coast.

My grandmother's house sat on the highest peak of Woodland, nearly two miles from the main road. You could almost see all of St. Elizabeth from her house, stretching out far into the ocean. Most of my family stayed with my grandmother, including my sister, Yolande. But as for me, I stayed about a mile down from my grandmother's home with my aunt, Verona, and her husband Breddah. Anytime I wanted to go to my grandmother's place, I had to walk through a stretch of bushes along a makeshift dirt road.

In Jamaica as a toddler standing outside my aunt's house

My aunt's house was far from sturdy and definitely not spacious. In all honesty, it was more of a hut than a house, measuring at most two hundred square feet—and that's being generous. The house was constructed of shaky boards and weakened concrete. We didn't have a kitchen or a bathroom, nor did we have access to electricity or running water. Life was as basic as it could get. Heck, I didn't even own any toys because we couldn't afford them, or we simply weren't allowed to have them.

In our tiny hut, I stayed in the back with my cousins, Jody-Anne and Howanie, while Aunt Verona and her husband lived in a room divided by a thin metal sheet. Sometimes, if it rained hard enough, it would squeeze through our roof and splash against my skin. It didn't happen all the time, but it wasn't out of the norm either. We placed cardboard and cloth on the floor to absorb the rain or dirt that got inside.

Long before I was born, my aunt's husband, Breddah, and other men in the town had built the house. And like many of the huts surrounding the community, they were colorful, often uneven, with walls that slowly deteriorated. My cousins and I were afraid to jump or run around because there was a chance we'd probably ruin something. Of course, there was no such thing as privacy, either. We showered in the back with a bucket of water we gathered from the rain. Yet, as deplorable as it may sound, those were some of the happiest times of my life. It was a place that I called home, indeed.

The surrounding area was beautiful, with trees full of fresh fruit, wild greenery, and gardens covering the mountain with breathtaking views. Legend has it that one of the reasons our house sat on the highest part of the mountains was because it supported the plantation my family developed in the eighteenth century. It was the only part of the mountains where crops flourished. My family is part of the Hitchman family, a prestigious name known to many of the people of Jamaica. I don't know much about my family tree, but I do know that it is decorated with an eclectic group of people. My great-great-grandfather was an Irishman who married my great-great-grandmother, a Chinese woman with Jewish blood. Somewhere down the line, melanin was added to the mix. I could stare into the mirror at my almond-shaped eyes and see how far my Chinese roots ran through my family.

Those who saw my living conditions when I was in Woodland could consider my childhood to be impoverished. Perhaps it was. However, on the inside, looking out, I never saw it that way because of the richness of love surrounding me. We didn't have the glitz and glamor that others sought to have. No functional toilet and no air conditioning. Stray animals wandered the area searching for food. Yet, I didn't feel deprived, never wanted more than I had, and never felt like I was missing out on anything.

Then again, I didn't have much to compare my condition to, because everyone in the town lived as we did. It's not like I was reading books filled with fantasies and made-up realities that were almost impossible to imagine. Nor was I watching *Lifestyles of the Rich and Famous*, thinking, *"Why can't that be us?"* Besides, without electricity, I couldn't watch TV. That helped me see the world in a different light, because there was no need for comparison. We were all enjoying our lives with what we had and who surrounded us—even through the storms. The rain reminded me of that every time it came pouring down. That's why I loved the sweet serenade of rain tapping against the windows. It spoke a truth that offered love and comfort rather than the brutality of a cold world.

In 1987, Hurricane Gilbert landed in Jamaica, and it was one of the most devastating storms to date. I remember looking up at the dark and gloomy sky as the heavy winds swung the trees back and forth, followed by the pouring rain. Concern covered everyone's faces—except for mine. I was in awe. I was just ten years old, and as terrified as I should have been, I welcomed the sight of the storm.

Part of me wanted to go out and play, but my aunt would have none of that. Instead, she grabbed me, and we all gathered beneath the bed in fear as we listened to the loudest and scariest bangs and thuds throughout the night. Gilbert, a Category 5 hurricane, tore the roofs off almost every home in the town. After the storm passed, I saw considerable damage everywhere. Trees were knocked down. Our outside kitchen was destroyed. Deplorable dirt roads were turned into mudslides. And, while most of the homes were destroyed, ours stood strong with no damage. That was one of the first times in my life when I could firmly connect God to the pouring rain.

Being born into a poor family, I was exposed to this self-sacrifice at an early age, understanding that it's not always just about me. Instead, it was about everyone. The more I learned this, the more I started practicing it. At a young age, we all had to play a role in our home. My aunt's husband, whom I looked up to as a father, made sure of that. He said it was our way of ensuring survival. Today, I still practice that exact principle in my household. My children and family all know that everyone must account for something in the house for us to function beyond just survival. If it worked for Breddah, I knew it would work for me.

Breddah had an empathetic spirit and masculine strength that made him simply divine to me—soft and gentle with an ever-present half-smile across his face. There's no way to say it other than he was different. In Jamaica, I always felt like there were two types of men. The first type consisted of men with youthful souls who loved to play with kids. Everything about them seemed open and welcoming. They told terrible jokes over a game of dominoes with a beer in their hand. They were never ruffled by societal expectations of a man, always wearing a smile like a uniform. Then there were those who reminded me of robots—lacking emotion and functioning like a programmed automaton while suppressing their anger. For the most part, they all cared for their families. Protecting them and providing for them economically as best as they could, yet their emotional availability for their children and wives was often absent. That caused some of these men to walk around with a chip on their shoulders, dealing with some emotional damage. The only thing left of them was bitterness and confusion.

Breddah, however, was neither of those men. He was his own man. Despite his friendliness, he didn't say much. He wasn't a man of many words, but his presence and love were enough that he didn't need to be talkative. He was a total enigma, and I never understood why. He had reasons to be bitter, just like some other men, yet he moved like the king of his castle with all its riches. He held his head high, never rattled. Stress somehow rolled right off him like raindrops on a window surface. Being around him was always so refreshing, like being on vacation.

Breddah spent most of his time on the farm, raising livestock and managing crops. Although he mainly worked on the farm, it was like a serene hideaway, giving him peace, joy, and gratitude. In return, he gave the land attention and care. His hardworking calloused hands nurtured the ground from which golden seeds became luscious fruit and hearty vegetables for our family. Indeed, that farm was as sacred as any corner of God's creation.

Every so often, I'd go out to the farm with Breddah. I could tell he loved those moments just as much as I did. I considered it to be my happy place. Standing on the farm was like some form of meditation and not just a source of our family dinners. We would walk miles through a stretch of woods just to get to the farm, and each time we did, I noticed something different. That's the thing about life. No matter the route you take in your journey, you'll always come across something new to take in or to tackle.

Breddah and I spent hours planting seeds in the gardens and picking out the ready-to-harvest carrots, potatoes, and cabbages. Even the aromas of the soil, grass, and manure were pleasant. Those were some of the happiest, most impactful moments of my childhood.

My aunt Verona always said, "The small details of what you do today magnify what you receive tomorrow." Even my little cousins, Jody-Anne and Howanie, who could barely write their names, had to do their part. Whether it was feeding the donkey or cleaning up around the house. As for me, my day began around four thirty in the morning. While the others slept, I was outside in the back, starting the fire. We didn't have a faucet or well, so sometimes I would have to run down a mile, through the bushes, to fetch water from the millions of raindrops collected in large buckets. Barefoot, I went back and forth to grab water until I had gathered enough for the house.

Running was about all I did. I swore, anywhere I went, I ran. If I had to go to the shop, I ran. Going to school, I ran. Whenever my aunt or uncle asked me to get something outside, I ran to get it. Running gave me a feeling of power in a life where I had none. Sometimes I believed I was running toward something rather than away, hoping to find shelter in a world that often left me confused. Besides, running was more efficient than walking. It allowed me to get things done much faster.

By the time I returned to the house with buckets of water, the sun would be peeking over the hills as the wood blazed with hues of orange and red. My aunt would be out back, standing over the burning fire as she prepared breakfast and tea for us.

"Thank you, Trisha."

Even though it was my role to help around the house, Aunt Verona made me feel special whenever she expressed gratitude. She was one for a life lesson, teaching a multitude of tiny things each day. Aunt Verona made me smile from ear to ear because she was extraordinary in a quite ordinary life. Indeed, my aunt was a remarkable woman I could model myself after, so much so that I called her "Mama," because she was like a mother to me. That's not to say I didn't have a relationship with my biological mother, because I did, but with my aunt, it was different. She taught me so much about life, and much of what I know as a woman nowadays came from observing her humility and strong work ethic. Aunt Verona also demonstrated a type of compassion and love I rarely saw in others. She was a woman everyone admired and what I envisioned as an angel on earth. No one sparked my understanding of what it meant to be a woman like my aunt did.

Like many women in Woodland, Aunt Verona didn't have much to give. Yet, her values and the life lessons she taught were worth more than anything I could receive. I watched her sacrifice everything to ensure the fulfillment of our lives. Every Wednesday night, she would gather the crops her husband had harvested and thoroughly wash them.

Then, she would load the donkey with the produce and take the twenty-five-mile hike into the city at four o'clock that Thursday morning. Sometimes I'd get emotional thinking of all those miles she walked on her journey from Hitchman Hill down to the market. She did this each week just to make sure we had something to eat. And by the time she returned home with pounds of meat and groceries, the sky would be as dark as charcoal, the stars shining brightly, and we'd be fast asleep. She did this every week regardless of how she felt, what was happening in her life, or whatever the weather conditions provided. She and my grandmother showed me the meaning of sacrifice.

As kids, my cousins and I were unaware of the sacrifice and hard work of my aunt. It wasn't intentional, but it happened. It wasn't until that one day, when I took the hike down to the market with her for the first time, that I understood just how much she sacrificed for us.

"Aunty, mi waan come," I suggested.

"Nuh sah! Trisha, yuh kyaahn du it," she laughed.

"Mi kyaa du it. Please, make mi come wit you."

She tried to warn me by explaining that the route was rough, hot, and long—and it was not meant for everyone. But I was young, energetic, and passionate about helping everyone—including my aunt. So, in my mind, there wasn't anything I couldn't do, but damn, was I wrong.

Forty minutes into the walk, I regretted my decision as sweat poured down my face. My feet were burning, and keeping up with the pace of her brisk stride was a struggle. Oh, how I yearned to stop and turn back, but I couldn't. We had to reach the market before everyone else, and we still had three long hours ahead of us. Besides, my aunt and grandmother had taken this journey countless times before, all for the sake of our family, so the least I could do was endure it this one time.

When we arrived at the market, my aunt sprang into action, selling, buying, and bartering the crops we had brought along with us. Our trips to the market were not to be taken lightly because they were essential to secure our food for the week. This was just a testament to Aunt Verona's unwavering commitment to our family's survival. As I said, we all had to do our part.

I was the oldest child, so naturally, much of the responsibilities, including caring for my cousins, rested on my shoulders. Every morning I woke them up and helped them get ready for school.

"Git up and git dressed!" I'd demand.

Getting them ready for school was a constant headache, because although they were young and full of energy, they moved like molasses. Not only did I have to get them ready for school, but I also had to make sure they arrived on time. The school was three and half miles away, and we had to walk the entire distance. That meant it would take roughly an hour to get there, and if we weren't on time, the teachers would punish us with isolation or severe paddles to our hands and behinds. Most of my beatings as a child came from school. I hated it.

So, every morning I would send my cousins off to school nearly an hour early to make sure they arrived on time. However, without fail, I would always catch up to them and usher them to their classes. I couldn't really blame them, though. They were just kids, and while I was also a child, I had a different demeanor. On the surface, one might have assumed I was no different from them— standing no taller than five feet and as thin as a starving child. But in reality, I possessed a level of responsibility and maturity beyond my years, even though my mindset remained playful and childlike.

I moved with a sense of urgency, constantly on the go, and conducted myself with a maturity beyond my age. I never wasted a minute of my time doing nothing. That's simply how I've always been. This approach led to fewer mistakes and less foolishness in my life.

However, the truth is, I didn't really care about all that. All I truly desired was to have fun. Even to this day, my inner child yearns for laughter and playtime with my friends, as it brings me immense joy.

I recall a time when I was seven years old and visited my uncle, Colin, in Kingston. His daughter, Lesa, had an abundance of dolls in her room, which I considered a privilege. There were big ones, small ones, white ones, black ones, and even colorful ones. It was the first time I had ever seen such variety, with different shapes, colors, and styles. Then, she offered me one, and of course, I said yes, choosing one of the smaller dolls, thinking it was a more considerate choice.

However, she said, "No! Yuh kyaahn get dat."

What? With all those dolls, she wouldn't let me have a little one? I couldn't believe her. So, I took it anyway, hoping to teach her a lesson. But I didn't know what to do with it. It's not like I was used to playing with them. Back in Woodland, we had to be resourceful with what we had to have fun. We would braid or plait tall grass to make it look like a child and use stones and mud to create toys. The land that God had given us was our source of entertainment and enjoyment.

Growing up, I didn't have many friends, and making new ones didn't come easy. I could never open myself up enough until I met Tasha Ingram. Tasha was a childhood friend I had grown fond of over the years. She reminded me a lot of myself—quiet, reserved, and loved laughing at the silliest things. She liked what I liked, thought as I did, and found joy in running just like me, which made us nearly inseparable. Because of Tasha, I learned that the value of friendship is not something you say, buy, or sell. Instead, it's something earned through steady steps that's built through trust. This was yet another lesson I had learned on my own.

Until I moved to America, I hadn't seen much of my mother. She lived two-and-a-half hours away in Kingston and came around three to four times a year, bearing gifts, like Santa. While in Kingston, she spent most of her time at the boutique she owned, selling fashionable clothing. I could count on my mother to provide my sister and me with some of the nicest clothes. She also made sure that my grandmother and aunt had enough money to make sure we never went a day without eating, either.

Like myself, my mother didn't know her father growing up. All she knew was that he ran off to England to be with his other family when she was just a child. One day, when she was twelve, my mother arrived at her grandmother's house and saw the face of a dark-skinned man working on the roof. Something about the man piqued my mother's interest while tugging at her emotions. By the time my great-grandmother went to introduce my mother to the man, he was gone. After that day, she would never have another chance to meet the man she saw on the roof, leaving her with that single memory of a man who may have been her father.

As a child, my mother and I had a lot in common. She, too, was raised by her mother, grandmother, and aunts. She moved around the island, even as a teenager, living with different family members. When she was twelve, my mother went to live with her older sister in Mandeville because she refused to deal with the rules my grandmother had set. She was a rebel in her way. By fifteen, she was off to Montego Bay to live with her other sister. And by the spring of 1986, she moved to New York to live with her sister, Joyce, to chase the American dream.

Now, I don't know much about my parents' relationship or why they separated, but like my mother's experience, my father was nonexistent in my life—whether it was his choice or not. Weirdly, it's as if they never had a relationship. I never saw photos of them, never heard stories of them, and of course, I never saw him. If I didn't know that it took a man and a woman to have a child, I would have assumed that I didn't have a father. But I guess when he left my mother to fend for herself, he also decided to walk out of my life, leaving my aunt, grandmother, and uncle to pick up the pieces.

It's quite a mystery that I never asked my mother much about him, either. Of course, there were times when I'd see other kids with their fathers at the market or church and wonder if one of them could be my father. I'd stare at the man, expecting to see some resemblance—maybe his eyes, nose, or even something about his gait. Occasionally, I imagined one of them coming over to me, picking me up, and hugging me like only a father could, saying, "I miss you!" I never told this to anyone because I understood I had no control over the situation. I could only think about it or try to move past it. Besides, as a child in my family, you didn't have the right to ask or say anything regarding grownups' business.

That said, I have a vague memory of my father that I cling to like a picture in a wallet. It's the perfect memory of him because it's the only one that I really have. I must've been four or five years old, and although I could vividly remember the day, I still can't make out his face. One Sunday, my mother decided to take me shopping, and boy, was I excited! I loved shopping with my mother—especially in Kingston. That's where everyone went for whatever they were looking for—clothes, nightlife, women, men, or a brand-new car. Anything at all! So, what child wouldn't be happy shopping with their mother in Kingston?

My mother always bought the finest things because shopping was and had always been her thing. She had to have the best-looking outfits, the prettiest shoes and purses, and the nicest jewelry. You name it, and my mom had it. She was rather vain that way. We had done this plenty of times, but on this occasion, it felt different. As a child, I could feel people's energy, especially my mother's. If she was happy, then so was I. And if she were upset, I'd soon become sad, even if I was happy before I saw her face. That's just how it was with my mother back then and how it is for me now with the people I trust and love.

As my mother and I walked through the crowded market, a man of medium build, his hair cut neatly low, quickly approached us. Immediately, I felt the coldness in her hand as I held onto her. I sensed how strange their interaction was as she stood face-to-face with the man. She barely made any eye contact and she slightly frowned. Her shoulders drooped down as if she had a long day. I turned to the man; his dark skin reminded me of a man I'd seen several times in my dream, matching his dark brown eyes perfectly.

My mother wasn't always smiling, but the dry look on her face that day was strange. If that weren't bad enough, the sun had vanished behind a canopy of clouds, allowing rain to come down. Not heavy enough to leave us drenched, but enough to ruin our plans. Didn't matter anyway because the man approached with a face that lacked expression. For a moment, they looked at each other like gunslingers before a duel. Based on my mother's facial expression, she wasn't expecting to see him. And from what I remembered, his eyes were emotionless, and although he smiled, it still felt peculiar.

My mother held onto me so tightly that she nearly stopped the blood flowing to my hand, pulling me closer to her. Everything seemed to go mute as they discussed something beyond my comprehension. The next thing I knew, my mother grudgingly pushed me toward him and released my hand. I looked back at her, and her eyes were focused somewhere else, avoiding eye contact. Perhaps it was her way of not letting me see her shed a tear. Or maybe that's what I told myself to make sense of it all. However, I was a child, and as a child, I never questioned anything adults did. So, I remained quiet, wondering why my mother had left me with this stranger.

The man's hand, weathered by years of hard work, held onto mine as he walked by my side. I saw everyone else's faces who greeted him as we walked by, waving and smiling. They all looked at him with gleaming eyes, as if they had the utmost respect for him. He was charming with a captivating persona.

Moments later, he led me into a shop where he ordered ice cream for us. Ice cream wasn't something I regularly ate, so it was a welcome surprise when I did—always bringing a sweet rush and a smile. Beyond eating ice cream with the man I believed to be my father, there wasn't much to recall. To tell you the truth, I remember the flavor of the ice cream more than I did his face or what he said to me. Vanilla.

Despite having no string attached to my father, I chose to hold onto that memory of him because, in that moment, he embodied the man he should have been. Or perhaps the man he could have been if not for whatever unfortunate circumstances had shaped his life. I didn't want to harbor negativity or resentment towards the man I barely knew. Like the cleansing power of rain, washing away dirt to reveal a fresh and pristine surface, I wanted to extend that same grace to my father. I understand that in life, we all need moments of self-renewal, shedding negative thoughts to become better versions of ourselves. That moment came with my father. After all, he was my father. Still, it's disheartening to realize that nowadays, I might not even recognize him if we were to cross paths on the street. That's assuming he's still alive.

CHAPTER 3

COMING TO AMERICA

"For most people on the outside looking in, they were right. However, despite all the odds and obstacles, growing up on the west side of Hartford allowed me to appreciate life even more."

Oh shit! I was on a plane. Like, I was actually *on a plane* flying for the first time. I kept staring at the cotton clouds outside the window in disbelief. They looked like they were moving, flowing like waves in the ocean, and at the same time appearing to stand still. I saw the sun fading in the background amidst infinite hues of white, close enough for me to touch. That was the day my mother moved my sister and me to America. From the moment we arrived at the Kingston airport until we landed in New York, Yolande and I were completely in awe. Funny enough, it was one of the few times we bonded as we anticipated what awaited the journey ahead.

In contrast to my sister and me, the airplane felt like home to my mother. She had flown so many times, she'd lost all fascination with the experience. Then again, she probably never felt much excitement about flying anyway. Not many things impressed my mother. She was cold and tricky to read at times. I felt it was because she had to be tough to avoid being at the top of the world one minute and then cut down the next.

She didn't have to tell me, but my mother had been through some fucked up shit by the time my sister and I arrived in America. I caught glimpses of her pain through the window to her soul. Through her eyes, I saw a woman yearning to heal but always deciding to cover it up by working—or just about anything to appear normal. Even as an adult today, I learn more about my mother which has painted the picture of our tumultuous mother-daughter relationship. Abandonment issues. Financial troubles. Not to mention family woes. Gloria Tomlinson had done life on her own for so long that she sometimes forgot other people existed in her world. Through it all, there were moments when she dealt with it for my sister and me, sacrificing her own worth to ensure we had a better life. After all, the only thing left for a girl used to pain was a woman who couldn't be hurt. And that was my mother.

Now, don't get it twisted. There's no question that my mother was full of love; she just had a funny way of showing it. She rarely smiled and didn't say much either. In fact, many of the people she knew questioned if she even liked them. They also knew my mother would offer her last dollar to a stranger in an instant, and if she could, she'd wrap her arms around all the souls who needed to be loved. I always respected her for that.

My uncles told me she was constantly judged because of her captivating features that seized everyone's attention—especially men. She was always poised and graceful, from her fashion sense to how she strolled through town with long strides, her posture perfect, and her shoulders squared. Her brown, almond-shaped eyes were like mine; in their depths was a remarkable story. She was always dressed in the finest clothing, as if she'd stepped out of an *Essence* magazine. Her glossy hair was fine and black as the midnight sky, stretching down to her back. Let me tell you, my mother was always flawlessly intact. She had perfect honeyed lips that always spoke the truth. Indeed, she was a woman ahead of her time, and she knew it. So, she carried herself proudly, exuding a bold goddess persona and clear form, regardless of the circumstances in which she was born.

I only know this because, over the years, strangers and family members have told me about my mother from back in the day. The women would go on about the clothes and shoes she wore, and of course, her bold independence. According to them, my mother was a woman who marched to the beat of her own drum. Men explained that the synapses in their brains would come to a standstill, making it impossible for them to move a muscle whenever she walked by. My mother was something else and noticeably a cut above normal where the rest of us existed.

The sun had nearly disappeared, casting a delicate golden light on the horizon as I stepped onto the land of opportunity for the first time. The bustle of people rushing past me in the airport was overwhelming, yet I couldn't help but feel a rush of excitement and anticipation coursing through my veins. It was as if the world was opening up to me, calling me to chase my dreams and carve my own path. At that moment, the thought of creating my own "yeses" in a foreign land, where anything was possible, felt like a tangible reality I held close to my heart.

It was September 30, 1990, which happened to fall on a Sunday, and I was finally going to live with my mother to see her in the same light that others did. For so long, I had vague memories of her, heard all the stories, and saw many pictures, but now I would experience her in all her glory. Thirteen years old, that's how old I was when my mother moved my sister and me from Jamaica to Hartford, Connecticut. Again, I was just a kid, and as such, there was no pleading with any decision adults made. Some parents granted their children a voice equal to theirs. That wasn't the case for me. Like most Jamaican parents, my mother thought it was best to be a stern disciplinarian who required her children to be obedient, respectful, and submissive. Nothing else. For me, there was no such thing as having a voice, so I packed my bags, hopped on the plane, and headed for the land of freedom and opportunity.

Now, here's the truth: before coming to Hartford, my sister and I thought of America as a utopia. A place where the roads were paved with gold and glitter filled the sky. The air was so fresh and clean that breathing it boosted our serotonin to unmatched levels. Everywhere we went, it smelled like pinecones in a bed of flowers. We assumed everyone walked around smiling, and anything you wanted, you could have. In my eyes, everything about America was simply astonishing. For goodness' sake, was I ever wrong! When we left John F. Kennedy Airport, I saw dark puffs of smoke bleeding into the clouds. There was an excessive harshness of honking and yelling. Disheveled people wandered the streets in a zombie-like state. Everywhere I turned, an ambulance or cop car sped past us, sirens blaring. The air reeked of cigarettes, beer, and garbage. But the worst part was the cold. It wasn't the type of weather that would quickly freeze your blood, but it was enough to bring chills to my entire body.

With every outdoor breath came the whitest puffs from warm lungs, just as white and dense as the clouds outside the airplane window. In Jamaica, we never experienced that type of weather, so I had to adjust quickly, just like I had done with so many other things. The more we drove through New York, the more cynical my image of America became. Broken, rundown cars were scattered along roadsides, and trash littered the streets. People walked past those things as if they were decorative fixtures. There were gigantic buildings as high as the blue sky, but outside those buildings were people looking for a place to sleep. They all looked bleak and famished. Where the hell was I?

Indeed, nothing I saw outside the airport looked like anything I had imagined. Even the food was different. The day we landed, we stopped at my aunt Joyce's house in the Bronx. Aunt Joyce is my mom's oldest sister and the main reason we moved to New York. I had not seen Aunt Joyce in quite some time, but like any other day, she offered my sister and me a snack. In Jamaica, fruits and vegetables were what we considered snacks, so it was expected when she handed us apples. We loved eating them. In fact, we loved consuming fruits of any kind, but there was just something about an apple that did it for me. As kids, we would run from tree to tree, picking them off the branches and eating them fresh in our hands. Not only apples, but also oranges, mangoes, bananas, and of course, guineps. So, if anyone knew what a good apple tastes like, that would be me.

I salivated at the thought of biting into that crisp sweetness and hearing the satisfying fresh crunch. But when I took a bite, I was severely disappointed. Despite its red and shiny exterior, the apple turned out to be rotten inside, with a mushy texture. Its flavor was tart and unpleasant, akin to toxic pollution seeping through the skin. Yuck! It was truly disgusting. To think that such a coveted place like the United States could offer such a repulsive fruit wasn't easy to understand. How could that have been happening in America?

Everybody who left Jamaica seemed to return rich, smiling from ear to ear. Or at least that's what it seemed like to us because we didn't know what rich looked like anyway. Nevertheless, I knew right then that the rotten apple represented something more than I could comprehend. I was no longer in Jamaica.

My mother worked tirelessly to get my sister and I to America, because like all immigrants who migrated to the U.S., she believed moving us here would offer a better life. I always respected her for that because I knew she didn't want us traveling the path she had journeyed all those years. Despite that, I wondered if she ever stopped to think about what my sister and I wanted. Not that it mattered anyway since we never had a say in anything as children. It's not like I didn't want to be in America, because I did. But I would be lying if I said my heart and soul weren't still back in the mountainous terrain of Woodland.

Occasionally, my mother would see my face and immediately know I missed being back in Jamaica, but she never said anything. Neither did I. I'm sure my sluggish, moody behavior and mute personality gave it all away. I had only been in Connecticut for a few hours when I began to yearn for the nostalgic scent of wood burning behind our house, the lively presence of my cousins, the sound of men playing dominoes, and the sight of penny wallies soaring through the air, resembling beetles with their flickering lights. What could I say? I wanted to be with my family and friends, living the simple life I had grown accustomed to without having to start over. I wanted to be in my safe place, helping my uncle harvest the crops. Or back inside the concrete walls of our dilapidated home that had been my shelter. I longed to be surrounded by everything and everyone I knew as my source of comfort. Instead, I stood in front of a basic brick building, trying to figure out how to call it home.

"Welcome home!" my mother said as we stepped out of the car.

Finally, we'd arrived at our apartment in Hartford, Connecticut, not to be confused with East Hartford. Everyone told me that leaving Jamaica would be the best for my sister and me, but I knew it wouldn't be easy, either. I saw the struggles from miles away, like the headlights on some faraway train. Yet, at that moment, I couldn't recognize how the transition would impact me throughout all my days. I felt like Eddie Murphy stepping out of his limousine in *Coming to America*. Actually, more like Arsenio Hall wondering where in the hell we were. Still, my sister and I couldn't have been more disappointed. So much so, that I was sure there was another America. There just had to be! The apartment in Hartford was even dirtier and more rundown than the ones I saw in New York.

On the west side of Hartford, at the corner of Laurel and Farmington, were the Willoughby apartments. That's where we lived. The area was split between poor black people and hardworking, blue-collar folks hoping to keep their heads above water. By 1990, there was a spike in the poverty rate that nearly doubled to 27.5%. Small restaurants began to close their doors, and hotels all over the city had cut available jobs to the point of going out of business. Hartford ended up looking like someone tried to light it on fire, but it just never caught.

Police sirens screamed in the distance as their cars sped down the streets, adding to the tense atmosphere. On every corner was a bodega surrounded by groups of boys looking to cause trouble. Crackheads overran the sidewalks, their eyes widening with desperation as they sought their next fix or a place to rest. This was the slums, where poverty and suffering were common, yet it seemed like just another day to those walking around.

As a newcomer to Hartford, I couldn't help but to be puzzled by my surroundings. Coming from Jamaica, I had expected the land of opportunity to look different. The neighborhood was far from picturesque, with its dilapidated buildings and sketchy characters lurking around every corner. Despite all of that, my mother seemed to see something different, something beautiful in the chaos. She was determined to make the best of our situation, and despite the poverty and danger that surrounded us, she was proud of what she had accomplished. It was hard not to admire her resilience and determination, even if I didn't quite feel the same way about our new home. My sister and I had no choice but to follow my mother's lead and "love" it as well.

My mother worked at the bank as a teller and her husband worked as an exterminator, spraying buildings and restaurants with insecticide to get rid of bugs and rodents. Indeed, they were living the American dream. The day I landed in New York was the first time I met my mother's husband. I didn't recall him ever coming to Jamaica to meet my family. If he did, he certainly wasn't memorable. She had met him in Jamaica, then she decided to bring him to the States, where they later got married. My mother actually called him up and asked him to marry her. Without a second thought, he said yes. If you ask me, she desperately wanted a husband, not because she feared being alone, but because she needed someone to help raise her children. Regardless, I always wondered how she came to select him.

In school, some kids referred to the area where I lived as the "hood." I didn't know what it meant until someone explained that the hood was a place embraced by criminals and people who had given up on life. It was a low-income location where the government spent millions on handouts. For most people on the outside looking in, they were right. Despite all the odds and obstacles, growing up on the west side of Hartford allowed me to appreciate life even more. Besides, I came from Jamaica, where I was doing more with less. And if I could make it in Woodland, then I knew I could make it in Hartford.

We lived on the second floor of the rundown, three-story, brown brick building with dingy windows. God, did it lack personality. I wouldn't have been surprised to learn that the place had been built in the early 1900s, which probably was the last time anyone did any sort of maintenance on it. The apartment was infested with rats and stray cats trying to get to them. The brown door leading into the apartment was raggedy—as if someone had repeatedly pounded on it with a hammer. I didn't know much about poverty then. Still, I sensed that all the residents living in the area were pretty much on the same playing field as the people of Woodlands in Jamaica. However, unlike the people of Woodland, the Hartford people all wore looks of despair on their faces. You know, the look of someone overworked yet barely receiving anything in return? Yeah, that look. They wore that expression every day and did it well, masking their pain and anguish with a coy smile and a slight head nod.

It was a quarter to midnight when my mother walked us to the front door of our new home. Entering the apartment for the first time,

I was neither pleased nor disappointed. Instead, I was stuck in a moment of emptiness, not knowing why. This was it? The moment every immigrant dreamed of, and there was supposed to be nothing more exciting than seeing your long-held dream become a reality. Although I was in the thick of it, I couldn't be fully in the moment for some strange reason. I was just a child, but I could feel a dark spirit approaching me the farther into the building I went. The darkness that extinguished my excitement replaced it with a paralyzing fear that nearly snuffed out my willingness to step into our home. The strange part about it all was that I didn't know why.

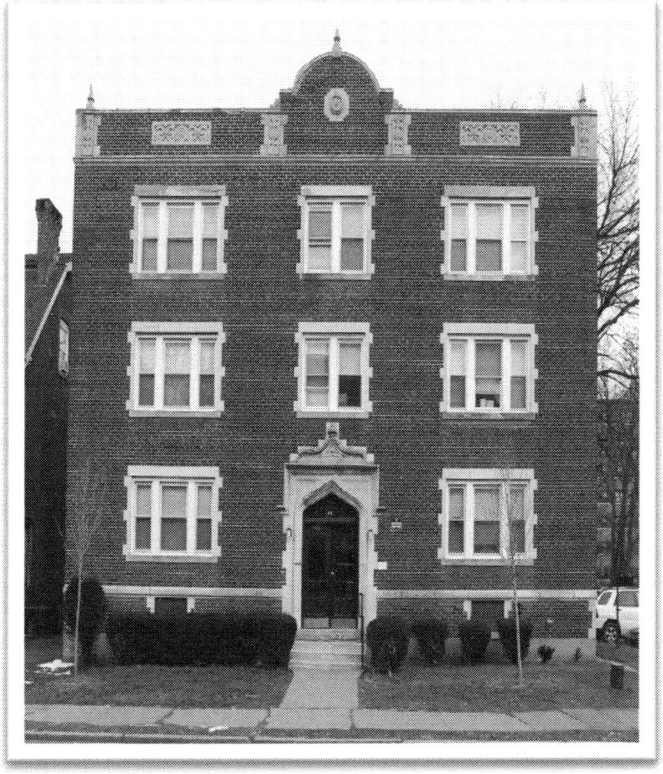

352 Laurel Street – Hartford, Connecticut

My arrival to America in 1990.

Smiling as always at the tender age of 13.

My mother and her husband lived in a one-bedroom, and although it was bigger and nicer than my aunt's hut back in Jamaica, it didn't feel as homey. All the doors squeaked and were tricky to shut, just like the doors in Woodland. Clothes cluttered the house, along with random appliance boxes, furniture, and whatever else you could think of. Honestly, it felt like we lived in a garage sale. Like most Caribbean households, we had a China cabinet against the wall in the living room and a worn-out sofa that turned into a pullout bed. That's where my sister and I slept. The refrigerator and countertops were crammed into the tiniest claustrophobic kitchen imaginable. We shared a small bathroom that always had plumbing issues, leaving us with cold water during frigid winters.

Going to the bathroom in the middle of the night was often terrifying because you never knew what to expect. Gunshots popped off in the streets, people arguing, and sounds of couples having sex were all too easy to hear through the thin walls. Police sirens often blared throughout the neighborhood. Cutting on the lights was just as startling, because the roaches would immediately scurry away once I did. Listening to their pitter-patter as they ran away like thieves in the night was disgusting. But after a few weeks in the house, it all became normal.

That was one of my exceptional traits—getting used to things quickly. I got used to my mother not being around as much. I got used to not having my father in my life. And I got used to being responsible for taking care of myself when no one would. There was just so much "getting used to," and I did it effortlessly. Except for one thing.

On my arrival in America, I was a young girl full of innocence. I discovered my interests and passions through zigzagging pathways filled with countless turns. On this pathway, everything seemed to gleam with love and joy, allowing me to see the world's goodness in a single gaze. There were no such things as murders, sex, drugs, or any of that shit I would later discover as an adult. I may have been thirteen when I arrived in Connecticut, but due to my naivete, I had the mental capacity of a five-year-old. If I'm honest, maybe even a three-year-old. In my mind, everything was colorful, safe, and covered with love. No one could do wrong, because everyone walking the Earth was guided by their faith in God. In addition to my childlike mentality, I was very small and short. I couldn't have weighed more than seventy pounds soaking wet. Therefore, I always felt out of place around other kids, but never enough to put fear in my heart. It was yet another thing I had to get used to.

Stepping into the unfamiliar halls of my new school, I felt like a fish out of water. Everything seemed bigger, louder, and faster than what I was accustomed to. Yet, there was also a sense of eagerness and opportunity that I couldn't ignore. I had arrived in America with my family only a few hours ago, and already, my life was taking a dramatic turn.

Despite my lack of enthusiasm for school, I found myself pushed forward by my mother's determination and my own curiosity. I was amazed to discover that my new school had placed me in eighth grade, two grades ahead of where I was in Jamaica. It was like being thrown into the deep end of the pool without knowing how to swim. The classes were more challenging, but I also found that I was more interested in what I was learning. Math, science, and writing suddenly became fascinating subjects that I wanted to explore further. I may not have been the top student, but I was no longer doing the bare minimum to get by.

As I walked through the hallways, I couldn't help but feel a sense of awe at the opportunities that lay ahead of me. America was a new world full of promise and potential, and I was ready to explore every inch of it.

There I was, sitting in a classroom surrounded by faces that looked nothing like mine. Even worse, they didn't sound anything like me, either. The girls had lighter skin, long dark hair, and curvy bodies. The boys looked like grown young men with part-time jobs after school. Most of them barely spoke English around me, only Spanish. Spanish? I had never heard anyone speak any other language besides English or Patwah, so I was shocked, thinking I didn't belong there.

Naturally, I freaked out, not because of the language itself, but because I thought I wouldn't be able to talk to anyone. As if that weren't bad enough, I was the only black girl in the school. There was another girl with dark skin, but she didn't speak English either. There was a total language barrier between my classmates and me, and because of that, I would remain quiet and keep to myself. Every day throughout junior high. I was lost and confused while trying to adapt to a new world. While doing that, some of the kids found it fit to pick on me. Oh, they spoke English when it was time to insult me… and insult me they did. God were they mean.

Nowadays, hearing stories of students being bullied deeply affects me because I was once that kid. Like many children today, I was compelled to hide my anger and bury it deep within myself. Time and time again, I chose not to show my bullies how much their actions had hurt me. However, I was unaware that by suppressing my anger, I was only causing harm to myself. That anger grew and festered inside me, like an infectious disease, until it became unbearable, leaving me with no choice but to either explode or implode.

However, as much as I wanted to lash out at everyone, I knew I couldn't. I was the child of an immigrant, and because of that, I could never cause problems, especially not at school. So, I did nothing. Instead, I became mute, blocking out every hurtful thing said about me. In my mind, I ended the bullying when I chose to go silent. If I didn't say anything, they had nothing to bully or ridicule me about.

During my middle school years, I didn't say much to anyone. I spoke to only one teacher, Miss Keaton— my eighth-grade math teacher. Unlike the others, Miss Keaton showed me compassion and made sure I understood my assignments and fit in with my peers. Everything she did was intentional to ensure that I wasn't left out of place. I'm certain Miss Keaton could sense my discomfort, and because of that, it was her purpose to genuinely care about me and my success.

On the other hand, my English teacher, Mrs. Jenkins, was the complete opposite. She seemed to take pleasure in making my already miserable life worse, forcing me to read out loud in front of the class so she and the other kids could laugh. They would scream things like, *"Ew! She farted!"* and my teacher would spray me with air freshener. I didn't know which was worse, feeling embarrassed or hurt. However, this taught me a valuable lesson: my dignity was the only thing I had, and though it may have been assaulted and mocked, it could never be taken away. As terrible as the bullying and shaming was, the worst part was yet to come. The darkness I felt on the first day of my arrival to Hartford would reveal itself, marking the beginning of a life I never expected.

CHAPTER 4

NIGHTMARE BEGINS

"Every night she would tell my sister and I to kiss him goodbye. It was a daily routine I'd come to hate."

Understand this—for most of us, nightmares are just our minds playing tricks on us, giving meaning to the unseen. They are figments of our imaginations that we easily forget when the light of day comes. But for others, nightmares are not the substance of a fictional world or an interpretation of a disconnected dream. They are the reality some people are forced to live in. The twisted shapes dancing across my vision were not mere hallucinations, but a manifestation of a darker truth I could not escape, no matter how hard I tried. Night after night, I found myself thrust into a world of torment where my fears seemed real, and my anxieties infected my brain like a deadly disease. And had it not been for the idea of chasing a dream, perhaps I would not be here.

One of the many things about walking in my shoes is that I encounter so many people from all walks of life. Some sought assistance, others desired to partner with me on some sort of business venture, and occasionally, someone wanted to establish a genuine friendship. However, whether it was a relative, acquaintance, or stranger, they all showered me with praise for every accomplishment I've achieved. Their words echo a familiar remark of, *"God has truly blessed you." "I envy your life." "I aspire to be like you." "Can you mentor me?"*

Some even requested something as simple as touching my hands for a chance at my good luck. Externally, I'd laugh and pretend to bask in their admiration, constantly nodding my head with a smile drawn across my face. Yet, internally, an endless flurry of emotions churned in my mind. It's a side effect of my chosen life and the success I've worked so hard to attain.

For the longest time, those heartfelt words pierced my mask, and I longed to escape to a peaceful place. Not because it was too much to bear but because of the struggles and all the other shit I faced to reach this point. Many of them didn't see the pain I endured or the confidence I lost, hidden beneath a blanket of cheerfulness and high energy. They don't comprehend my fragile mind, weakened by experiences many cannot fathom. Despite the success I built, there were times when I felt powerless and anything but blessed.

I don't hold it against them, though, because most of them aren't aware of the struggles I've endured. To them, I'm just another person with a seemingly perfect life. They only see the end result, not the tears, blood, and scars I still carry. If they knew the depth of my hardships, our conversations would undoubtedly take a different turn. I've encountered soulless individuals who sought to shatter me. Their evil gazes aimed to crush my spirit, but I refused to let them win. Those criminals had eyes as dark as the night sky and as void as an abyss. Some concealed their hatred under a guise of false affection. I often found it difficult to meet their gaze, fearful of being pulled into their wickedness. Yet, at the tender age of thirteen, I was confronted with such a being for the first time, and surprisingly, it happened within the confines of my own home.

Facing trauma is like venturing into a dark forest, where danger lurks behind every tree. Despite it all, taking the steps to overcome it and reaching the light illuminating the other side was all I could do. But it's cruel that the very people we trust the most—friends, family, and even lovers—are sometimes the ones to inflict the deepest wounds. In the blink of an eye, the image we have of them can shatter into a million pieces, leaving us to pick up the fragments of our devastated hearts. Life is unpredictable like that. It can change course in a single moment, whether by design, accident, or stupidity. We live in constant fear of the unknown, raising our guard to protect ourselves from threats we cannot even imagine. As a child, I learned the hard way that life can be unforgiving, yet that same lesson paved the way for me to create my own path and learn to say yes to myself.

This is the part where I tell you about my stepfather, and how his immoral and evil behavior helped shape me into the woman I am today. Oddly, when I tell you how, you may be thoroughly confused. Then again, truth is rarely pure or simple.

Before I moved into that one-bedroom apartment, my nights were peaceful. There was a sense of safety that covered my soul, preserving the blissful innocence of my childhood that I once knew. For most of my life, my dreams consisted of laughter with my cousins and friends. Peenie wallies glowing at night, and images of sweet memories from my childhood. But on the second day, everything changed. I stepped into that apartment on September 30, 1990, unaware of the shit brewing on the horizon.

Despite being a child, I felt a sense of security in my mother's fondness for her husband, my stepfather. I had heard whispers of him in Jamaica, but it was in Connecticut that I finally laid eyes on the mysterious figure known as my mother's other half. A sense of neutrality surrounded him, meaning he was neither good nor bad. He was like a shadow hovering in the background—almost as a soulless human being. If you ask my mother, she'd tell you all the great things about this monster and how he treated her like a queen, worshiping the ground she walked on. She loved him dearly. Sometimes I thought she loved him more than my sister and me. The truth of the matter remains unknown, but it certainly felt that way.

At first glance, my stepfather may have appeared to be a man of few words, exuding a charm that could easily fool anyone into thinking he was trustworthy. But behind the masquerade stood the sinister truth—he was a monster, the devil himself. I believe he had been dealing with his inner demons for so long that he learned to embrace them. It didn't help that he uprooted his life to the United States, where he sought refuge in the arms of my unsuspecting mother and concealed his disgusting ways.

Only minutes after meeting him, he welcomed me into his fold as if I were his own flesh and blood. It felt unnatural and strange—nothing like the men I grew up around in Jamaica. In their presence, I felt like a valued human being, which was something I completely lacked in the company of my stepfather. My time with my uncles was a treasure trove of valuable life lessons. They were true models of masculinity that unknowingly taught me the art of life. From farming through all seasons to appreciating a good beer. They even showed me the importance of taking responsibility for my actions, which has stayed with me throughout my life. This also included the need to be a hard worker and a protector of my loved ones. I was never a tomboy, but I certainly learned to balance my feminine and masculine energies, all thanks to my uncles.

The role that Breddah and my uncles played in my life was significant enough to make me believe living with my stepfather would be no different. I couldn't have been more wrong. It soon became apparent that he was far worse than any nightmare I had ever imagined. He was a creep and a loser. Regardless of his appearance, he was a stranger with secrets hiding behind lies and deceit. At first, he didn't scare me or appear to be malicious, but eventually, his presence left me feeling numb. His dark brown eyes were as empty as his hollow promises, and his energy was as bland as a blank sheet of paper. Despite this, he had a way of manipulating those around him, using his charm and charisma to influence my mother and perhaps make her feel comfortable enough to leave me alone with him.

I remember a particular day when my stepfather was getting ready to head out for work, and my mother insisted that I refer to him as "Dad." After all, he was Yolande's biological father, and my mother felt it was only natural for me to address him in the same manner as my sister. At the time, I didn't object to her request. I was just thirteen years old, a naive teenager sheltered from the world and brought up to follow the rules. So, obeying my mother's every command without a second thought was all I knew. Looking back, I realized that my mother was trying to create a perfect family unit, a façade that masked the harsh realities of our home life.

It didn't take long for me to realize that something was terribly wrong with the way he looked at me. The way his eyes lingered on me sent an instinctual jolt that coursed through my veins, awakening every nerve in my body. It was as though he saw me as his prey and was calculating his next move. In my mind, my stepfather was a monster from another world, sent here to deprive me of my childhood while destroying my budding womanhood. Gone was the welcoming spirit he initially presented, and he replaced it with an unsettling energy that made my skin crawl. He used that look like a weapon, making my worst nightmares seem like child's play.

On Sundays, I'd sit in church, watching my stepfather pray, and I couldn't help but wonder if his words were falling on deaf ears. A part of me hoped that the God I worshiped, who stood for love and forgiveness, was too pure to read the twisted thoughts going through his mind. Maybe there was a different God out there, one that could handle the darkness occupying his soul.

His presence was suffocating, his influence overwhelming, and he pushed me to do things that were beyond my understanding. That's the thing about fear. It has a way of isolating you, making you feel alone and helpless. For the first time in my life, I knew what it meant to be truly fearful. However, it was at that moment that I realized I had a choice: to cower in fear or to stand up to it. As a child, I often backed down to him and berated myself for it for years. But not anymore. I knew I had to find the courage to face my fear head-on.

It was my first day of school in America. My stepfather and mother drove Yolande and me to school. Yolande was in fourth grade while I was starting middle school. Despite the familiar feeling of starting a new school year, I was completely alone in a sea of unfamiliar faces. Unlike the close-knit community of my school back in Jamaica, the students didn't eat together or learn in the same class. It was a strange new world, but one that seemed to function, nonetheless. However, the lack of familiar warmth in the classroom left me disoriented and feeling out of place. As I looked around, my new classmates' eyes bore into me, as they wondered where I came from, like I was some sort of exotic creature. Maybe it was because I was the only black student in the class, or perhaps my Jamaican accent confused them. To add to the confusion, my eyes took the familiar shape of someone from China, causing further speculation.

Generally, I made friends walking home from school. So, when my mother picked me up the next day, I insisted on walking home. To my surprise, she obliged. Besides, I was a big girl and needed to do big girl things like walking to and from school. I have always liked being independent and hated to inconvenience anyone, including my mother. On the way home from school that day, my mother mapped out the way home, driving the route several times until I knew the way.

She coached me as we drove along. "Remember this, remember that street name. Turn here." She continued until the directions were etched into my brain, or so I thought.

"You got it?" she asked.

"Yes." I assertively replied.

In Jamaica, I had been the leader, confidently guiding the other kids to school using the back and side roads that I knew like the back of my hand. I was convinced that I had it all figured out. But then, I found myself in Connecticut, and the reality was quite different. I soon came to realize that the routes I knew so well back home were of no use to me here. The next day, my mother insisted on driving me to school.

"Mek sure yuh come home right afta skool, yuh hear?," she said as she dropped me off.

"Okay."

It was a Wednesday, which meant school let out early, at 1:15 p.m. That was when I began my journey home. I was on the same route my mother had shown me. You would have thought I'd taken this route all my life based on my confidence and the pep in my step. I looked for the breadcrumbs that would take me home—street signs, trees, distinctive houses, and landmarks. Ten minutes in, and I felt I was just a few blocks from the apartment.

God was I proud of myself! Before I knew it, I began noticing things I hadn't seen the day before—towering apartments, quaint shops, and a traffic light located at an intersection that looked totally unfamiliar. My once straightforward path became a maze of left and right turns, each leading me back to the starting point. The road not taken became overwhelming, leaving me alone like a soldier on an empty battlefield. Despite the success I had navigating the town of Woodlands, my sense of direction failed me in Connecticut. After hours of wandering, I stumbled upon a rusty windmill in the heart of downtown. A wave of realization hit me like a ton of bricks—this wasn't part of my mother's route. That's when I knew I was lost.

As the sun set and the dark sky took over, I found myself still wandering the unfamiliar streets of Hartford. Time passed quickly, and I had no idea where I was. Hell, for all I knew, I could have been walking around on the streets of New York for hours. And before I knew it, the world seemed much bigger than I had anticipated, and I wasn't sure how I would find my way back home. Despite this, I wasn't afraid. My innocence protected me from the harsh realities of the world, and it allowed me to believe that everyone was inherently good.

"Excuse me. Yuh know where Laurel Street is?"

"What'd you say?" the man asked, trying to interpret my thick Jamaican accent.

"Laurel Street. Mi lass and a try fi reach home." I explained.

At the time, a man named Emanuel Lovell Webb sent shivers down the spines of Connecticut's communities, especially its women. The former security guard was a suspected serial killer on the loose. He was said to be a tall, dark, stout man whose appearance was uncannily similar to the man standing before me. I wasn't aware of this information as I approached the man on the corner. I don't remember the man's face, but I'll never know if he wasn't in fact Emanuel Webb.

"Oh my God, girl, that's way on the other side of town," he said after thinking about it for a moment with a look of surprise. "What you doing way over here?"

"Going home."

"You know what? It's too far for you to walk. I'm going to put you on the bus, and I'll tell the bus driver to drop you off at Laurel Street."

Little did he know that walking was second nature to me. Back in Jamaica, I had easily covered over fifteen miles in a single day on foot. But as he pointed out, it was already eight or nine in the evening, and the thought of shuffling home on foot for several more hours was daunting.

The man firmly grabbed my hand and led me to an isolated bus stop along a busy road. During a haze of confusion and troubled thoughts, his presence shimmered as a glimmer of hope. With unwavering patience, he stood by my side, offering comfort as we waited for the arrival of the bus. His actions didn't startle me, as I had always believed in the innate kindness and compassion that dwelled within us all. To extend a helping hand and show love towards one another was a fundamental principle deeply ingrained in my being. So, in my mind, a stranger helping a young distressed lost girl find her way home was just a testament to that innate compassion that I thought we all embraced. No matter the circumstances. That's what I had witnessed in Jamaica and what I expected to see in Hartford. However, as time went on, I came to realize that the familiar shores of Jamaica had faded from view, and I had entered a new chapter in a land far from the home I once knew.

After a few moments, a bus with flashing lights pulled up, and the man grabbed my hand and placed me inside without uttering a word. He whispered something to the driver that I couldn't hear. I was still slightly mesmerized by my first bus ride experience. As soon as I sat down, a foul odor assaulted my nose, reminiscent of wet, mildewy clothes and week-old piss. Yet to my confusion, none of the other passengers seemed to mind. A peculiar atmosphere saturated the bus. Everyone exchanged pleasantries, but the anguish in their eyes was evident. In the rear, a group of noisy kids engaged in lively banter while others either read newspapers, slept, or immersed themselves in music with headphones on. Toward the front, not a single passenger talked or smiled. They all just stared blankly ahead.

"He's gonna tell you when to get off, okay?" the stranger told me.

I felt like a fish out of water as I sat there nodding confidently, pretending to understand. I knew nothing about riding on a bus, and as the bus rumbled along unfamiliar roads, my mind was racing with questions. *Where was it going? Would it drop me off at home? Would my mother see me when the bus came to a stop?* So many questions, yet no answers to be found. How could I have gotten so lost in just two days in America? I felt like I was drowning in a sea of uncertainty, with no lifeline to cling to. The journey home felt like an eternity, and my anxiety grew with each passing minute.

Finally, the bus stopped in a part of town I'd never seen before. I knew I didn't belong there, and the knot in my stomach tightened as I wondered what would happen next. Would I ever make it home?

"Okay, little girl. This is your stop," the driver told me.

"Mi don't know this place. Dis a Laurel Street?"

"Yes it is. Now come on. I gotta get going."

Reluctantly, I got off the bus as if it were on the edge of a mountain. I found myself in an area worse than where I lived. Trash was everywhere, music blasted all around me, and it was dark because most of the streetlights were knocked out. Every powerline had a pair of shoes wrapped around it, and when I looked up, I saw that I was on Lawrence Street. Not Laurel Street.

As the night wore on and the clock ticked closer to ten o'clock, fear began to bubble up inside me. Not because of the potential danger lurking in the darkness, but because I knew my mother would be beside herself with worry. The mere thought of her panic and distress caused me to feel completely paralyzed. Then, a figure emerged from the shadows, strolling down the deserted street. He had a wild, unkempt beard that looked like a shaggy coat draped across his face.

"Excuse me. Yuh know where Laurel Street is?"

I began to share my grueling experience of getting home with a kind stranger. He not only listened with compassion, but also walked me back to my doorstep as if he were my guardian angel. After wandering the unfamiliar streets for nearly nine long hours, I finally reached home at a quarter past ten. My heart raced with fear, expecting the worst from my mother's wrath. So, as the bearded man knocked on the door with me by his side, I braced myself for what was to come. To my surprise, my mother opened the door and immediately embraced me with open arms, holding me so tightly that all my worries seemed to vanish. Her warm hug was the first comforting thing I had felt since leaving Jamaica. There was no yelling, no punishment, and no scolding. It was a moment of pure relief and gratitude that I would never forget.

"Gwaan give yuh fadda a kiss," my mother prompted.

My stepfather, who worked as an exterminator, had decided to postpone leaving for work until I returned home safely. Every night my mother would tell my sister and me to kiss him goodbye. It made me cringe. That night, I went to kiss him good night, and I immediately saw him looking at me in a way I hadn't seen before. I was just a kid, and I couldn't make sense of the look he gave me. Then, as I pursed my lips to kiss his cheek, he turned his head and mashed his lips against mine. His tongue slithered into my mouth as his thick mustache prickled my nose.

One…

Two…

Three…

Four!

He held onto me with a disturbing passion, indulging in some twisted fetish that made my stomach churn. The taste of his recent dinner, curry chicken and dumplings, lingered in his mouth and invaded mine. In a sudden frenzy, he clutched my waist, pulling me in as if I were the woman of his wildest fantasies—tight and firm. My body froze in disbelief, as if my very spirit had detached from my body in an effort to escape. When he finally let me go, his face remained empty of any expression or emotion. I could sense from his blank, dark eyes that this invasive encounter was to be my new reality.

A flood of conflicting emotions overwhelmed me, leaving me lost and uncertain. Was it shock? Fear? Or simply a sense of helplessness that consumed me? My mother, who was in the kitchen with her back turned to us, was oblivious to his actions, and I was too cowardly to stop him. It felt like I was stranded in the middle of an ocean, drowning with a boat just a few feet away. My rational mind couldn't comprehend why he touched, kissed, or gazed at me like a slab of meat. Regrettably, I stood there like an obedient young girl, depleted of the fight and resilience that had once defined me.

Before that night, I had never kissed anyone, and although I was just a little girl, I knew what he did was wrong. I felt it in the pit of my stomach. Lord knows how utterly disgusted and disturbed I was by his actions. However, he was my mother's husband, the man she loved deeply, and the man she chose to care for my sister and me. Besides, I had no power or voice in the household as a child. So, I just waited for him to stop swirling his tongue in my mouth as if it were trying to escape out the back of my throat.

Perhaps it was a mistake, a misinterpretation of affection. But my hopes were thrown out when I learned I was not the only one to endure this sickening behavior.

The image of a dark cloud loomed over us, a symbol of the impending storm that was sure to come. I was just two days into my new life in America when the nightmare that would become my reality plagued me like a relentless swarm of termites, devouring every piece of my childhood.

CHAPTER 5

NIGHTMARE CONTINUES

"While some of the girls were practicing how to kiss a boy in the mirror, I was mastering the art of drawing animals on worn-out pieces of paper."

October 2, 1990 fell on a Thursday—it was my third day in America. On that day, instead of waiting for my mother to pick me up from school, I took it upon myself to walk home alone. Again. This time, though, I paid close attention to where I was headed. Besides, it didn't hurt that my mother went over the route home four times that morning!

I slung my backpack over my shoulder and hurried out of the classroom, eager to make my way home. *"Meck sure yuh go straight home!"* My mom's voice echoed in my head. I dared not make a stop at the corner store or lollygag along the way. As I took the journey ahead, all the familiar houses and landmarks that my mother had pointed out provided comfort along the way. Before I knew it, I was standing in front of the white double doors of our apartment, feeling a sense of pride and accomplishment.

I stepped into the apartment, and immediately, I sensed a dark presence lingering in the air that provided a sudden and brief sensation of coldness. It was also disturbingly quiet, creating an unusual and slightly uncomfortable feeling. As I made my way into the living room, the sound of footsteps coming from the bedroom broke the silence. It was then that I realized I was alone in the apartment with my stepfather.

"Trisha? A yuh dat?" my stepfather called out as I walked in.

"Yeah!" I joyfully responded.

My stepfather worked the overnight shift, which meant while we were sleeping, he was working. During the weekdays, he left the house at 10:30 p.m. and returned just as Yolonde and I were headed to school. So, when I arrived home that day, I figured he'd be there. I just didn't expect to experience what would happen next.

"Hello." I approached and kissed him on the cheek.

As children, we were taught to greet our elders with a kiss on the cheek as a gesture of respect. It didn't matter who they were, their age, or their gender; we were expected to follow this rule. Failing to do so could result in consequences. At the time, I didn't question this tradition because it was simply the norm, and I saw nothing wrong with it. However, with the benefit of hindsight, I realize how naive I was as a thirteen-year-old, still possessing the mindset of a much younger child, perhaps even a two-year-old. Although the custom was deeply rooted in my culture, I now understand how it could be confusing for some children and potentially leave them vulnerable. Parents worldwide emphasized the importance of safeguarding their children's bodies and privacy, cautioning them about the boundaries of personal space, particularly their daughters. *"Don't let anyone touch your private parts,"* is what many preached. Personally, I have no recollection of ever receiving that message, and if I did, it simply didn't register as something that would be relevant in my environment. That's how oblivious I was to the potential dangers, hurt, or confusion that could arise from something as seemingly innocent as kissing my stepfather on the cheeks.

As usual, I sank into the couch and began working on my homework, just as my mother had instructed me to do. It was a routine I was familiar with from Jamaica, but in America, that routine was more intense and focused because the pressure to excel was greater. Besides, watching T.V or playing with toys held no interest for me. And hanging with neighborhood kids was definitely out of the question. At first, being alone in the house had never bothered me, but that all changed when my stepfather made me feel trapped, like a prisoner in my own home.

While working on my homework, he sat on the sofa, right next to me, and stared at me. I spotted him in my peripheral vision, looking at me with a smirk on his face. He didn't say a word. Still, I didn't think anything of it. He was so close that I can still recall the smell of his Irish Spring deodorant with a hint of musk.

"Wa yuh a do?" he asked.

"School work."

At first, he would say inappropriate things about my body and my looks, and even the way I walked. But then his action turned into something more sickening than I could imagine. He inched closer to me, allowing his right thigh to press against my left leg. Then, I heard the sound of his belt unbuckling, followed by the slow unzipping of his pants. A cold chill rushed through my body, nearly leaving me numb. Even as I recall that memory, it echoes loudly in my mind—skin-crawling and demoralizing, like nails screeching against a chalkboard. My stepfather, the husband of my mother, a man who was supposed to protect me, took his penis out of his pants like some mischievous kid. Then, he moved a tad closer and began groping me, his erection sometimes brushing against my skin. I didn't really understand what he was doing to me, but I didn't like it. I didn't move a muscle as I kept my eyes focused on the homework sitting on my lap. Lord knows I couldn't look his way. Not only because I was scared but also because, as kids, we were taught to not look adults in the eyes.

It didn't matter, because before I could make a move, he grabbed my left hand and placed it on his erection, forcing me to squeeze it with a tight grip. That lasted for seven seconds. Then he took his hand off mine and commanded me to stroke his penis up and down. My jaw clenched from the anger and frustration that had plagued my body. However, there was nothing else I could do besides internally cry as I begged him to stop.

I was helpless and stuck, holding onto his erection like it was my only way out of this nightmare. Everything around me seemed to be moving so fast that my heart couldn't keep up. I can still feel his warmth in my hands as he devilishly smiles at me. He was lucky I didn't have a knife nearby. Then again, I wouldn't have done anything with it because I was terrified. One of the very few times I ever was. Still, I'm not sure if I was more afraid of what my mother would do to me if she found out than I was of what he would do to me at that moment.

"Go head," he murmured.

I tried to pull my hand off his dick, but he quickly recovered and placed his left hand on my right hand, gripping his erection tighter.

"I don't wanna do this…" I innocently murmured.

He could not have cared less about what I had to say. He just kept insisting that I touch him against my will. My heart pounded relentlessly in my chest, a desperate rhythm of fear and anguish. I wanted nothing more than to scream, yet the sound did not come out as easily as they did in my mind. I was stifled by the suffocating grip of my torment.

I even tried to play it off as some sort of game at some point, attempting to think nothing of it. But how could I not? Beyond the fact that he was a man I expected to receive guidance, shelter, and protection from, he was also my mother's husband. It may sound silly, but I was able to convince myself that maybe, just maybe, this was what people did in America. However, deep down, I knew what he was doing wasn't right. I felt it in the pit of my stomach, and it was an awful and immoral feeling that covered my soul like a filthy blanket. Even though I was a little girl from a sheltered background, I knew his actions violated my privacy and were ultimately wrong.

At that stage of my life, I was oblivious to the details of kissing, sex, and all matters related to sexuality. Completely clueless! It was the very first time I encountered any form of arousal, and the sensation was far more confusing than any other emotion I had previously encountered. Fear didn't compare because, with fear, there was always the possibility of escaping. But this particular feeling held me captive, and I couldn't explain how or why..

Furthermore, what could I do? Fight? His two-hundred-pound physique would have shattered my seventy-pound body. Scream? That would be a miserable letdown because no one would have heard me. So, I allowed my ability to cry to serve as my only action at the moment. I was overwhelmed by tears as I sat dead in the pit of an unfamiliar world. A dark world where evil lurked and purity was ravaged. This was the sort of darkness that only a monster could create for an angel.

One. Two. Three… I slowly counted, hoping my stepfather would have stopped somewhere in between. But no! That sick son of a bitch continued sliding my hand up and down his filthy erection, forcing me to touch all of him for what felt like forever. I tried to block out the sensory memory of his smell, which reeked like sweat and piss, stuck to the palm of my hand. Even worse, I can still hear him groaning in my ear the more he used my hands to stroke himself, inching closer to his climax.

Fifty-four. Fifty-five. Fifty-six... As I continued counting my way out of the agony, my body trembled uncontrollably, and my thoughts spiraled out of control.

Seventy-two. Seventy-three. Seventy-four…

I couldn't believe what was happening, and I began to question if this was normal. Was I overreacting? Was this something that other girls in America went through too? Of course, God wouldn't allow it to happen if it wasn't supposed to happen, right? My thoughts circled in my head like a swarm of bees, and before I knew it, I had fully normalized a situation that no little girl should ever have to experience.

You ought to know that I was a late bloomer when it came to anything dealing with the opposite sex, especially when you exclude the trauma inflicted on me by my stepfather. For goodness' sake, I was fourteen years old when I started my period. While some of the girls were practicing how to kiss a boy in the mirror, I was mastering the art of drawing animals on worn-out pieces of paper. I didn't even know how to describe the feeling of liking someone. Me? Like a boy? That was barely a thing. That wasn't the case for most of the girls around town. Hell, some of them had boyfriends before they got their periods. I can't say that my feelings for anyone were anything more than admiration. It was no different than me seeing a dog on the street and wanting to pet it, but never enough for me to take it home.

However, during my time in Jamaica, there was a boy who captivated my attention. It wasn't a head-over-heels infatuation, but rather a fascination that took my mind to a place of wondering. Whenever I got the chance to see him, the world seemed to somehow embrace a greater sense of serenity and radiance, and my heart fluttered in a bizarre manner. To be honest, I got more pleasure from gazing at him than anything else, even though I didn't know his actual name. Therefore, I named him Carlton. Where did the name come from? I have no idea. However, it felt appropriate and resonated with me. Surprisingly, despite never exchanging a word with Carlton, I managed to gain enough information about him through observing his interactions with others. It was as if an illusion of familiarity had been created between him and I that gave me a peculiar sense of truly knowing him.

Carlton and I went to different schools, and although I wish we hadn't, it didn't matter because he was always in my thoughts. Every day after class, I felt sparks flare as I came running down the crossroad, hoping to see him. Funny enough, I never wanted more than to just see his face. So, when I walked down the dirt road, always gingerly as possible, I would walk next to him without saying a word. Not even hi! He didn't say anything, either. I never really cared to speak to him because it's not like I wanted anything from him. And even if I did want to say something, I wouldn't know the first thing to tell him. *My name, possibly?* No. *How was your day at school?* That wouldn't have worked. *Do you want to play with me?* Yeah right!

I was speechless around him, so basking in his presence was good enough for me, because there was something about Carlton that drew people to him. Not just the kids, either. All the grownups adored Carlton like he was their very own. So poised, calm, and always blooming with a kindhearted spirit. Even at that tender age, he looked like he was destined to become someone of greatness. I guess it didn't hurt that he was good-looking too. He had the most appealing features of any of the boys I'd come across. Smooth dark skin. Deep-set eyes to match that radiating smile—especially when he laughed. His hair was neatly cut low, and his clothes were consistently neatly pressed.

Carlton, like me, was often quiet and reserved. Yet, his affectionate personality captivated me and put me at ease. I was too young to know about the emotions that could spark between a boy and a girl. Still, I knew the tingly feeling coursing through my body when I saw him was undoubtedly something I had no control over.

It's weird, but I love how he made butterflies flutter in my stomach and caused me to feel light on my feet when I gazed at him. It was the first time I felt any sort of emotion for someone I didn't know. Yet, I couldn't make sense of it. How could I? I was just nine years old, and he was fifteen. Therefore, I thought of him as a grownup. So, I walked alongside Carlton, pretending to be someone that he admired, and that was good enough for me. Hell, I didn't have words for Carlton, so I chose to be the unspeakably shy, innocent-looking girl I was.

That had been my first experience with someone of the opposite sex, and I could barely consider it an experience. So, when confronted by the man my mother referred to as her husband, it became evident why I was left confused and deeply troubled. Time marched forward, sticking to its relentless schedule, while I was left stranded with this monstrous figure disguised as a man. My gaze remained fixed on the doorknob, desperately yearning for my mother to step through it at any moment. However, she didn't. At least not before I began to feel his sticky, wet, warm fluid running down the back of my hand.

Disgusted, I turned away from the sight of it, but I could feel it quickly turning cold as it slithered along my wrist. It smelled like urine and some sort of washing chemical. I was too scared to move, and I just sat there as it dripped off my wrist, uncertain of what I would do next. It's not like I knew what it was. It simply confused me.

He buckled his pants and walked away without saying another word. I remained still until I heard the bedroom door close, and when I did, I quickly ran into the bathroom to wash all his fluid off my hand. It was gross and left me boiling with anger. *God, why was I so naive and stupid?* Yes, I was a child, but I should have done something about it. The fact that I didn't do anything allowed me to blame myself for what happened. Not him! It was all on me. Nevertheless, I could not even begin to understand the magnitude of the situation. Or even worse, what would happen next.

I stayed locked in the bathroom, crying my eyes out as I waited for my mother to return home from work. Finally, after what felt like forever, I heard my mother walk through the front door. I stepped out of the bathroom and dashed over to my mother as if she were a black knight there to rescue me. I wanted to say something about what had happened to me, but I didn't know how to or if she would believe me. I mean, how could I, as a child, convince my mother that the man she loves forced me to touch his fucking dick?

Plus, I didn't know how to verbalize what had occurred or articulate the word "penis," as prior to that day, I had never encountered a need to do so. Even worse, I was scared that my mother would get mad and punish me for what he did. Knowing my mother, I believed that would have probably been the easiest way for her to handle the situation. So, I didn't say anything, acting as if nothing had happened, controlling my emotions like some sort of robot. It didn't matter anyway, because before I could even say a word, that monster exited the room and greeted her with a passionate kiss. At that moment, I knew I wouldn't be able to say anything even if I wanted to. My voice was muffled in that instant, leaving silence to fill my soul. My blood chilled, the coldness bringing the synapses of my brain to a standstill. Some of what I experienced was pain and sorrow, but I learned to cope with it and found comfort in the idea that it was all temporary and would never happen again, even when it did. However, it's the overwhelming guilt and the profound sense of loneliness in my own reality that plagued me during sleepless nights.

The abusive encounters with my stepfather only helped remove the shades over my eyes, allowing me to see a side of the world that I had not seen before: a cruel dark place filled with people lacking emotions, waiting to take advantage of the weak; a place where those who didn't fit in got left behind, and those who supposedly did, made victims out of everyone else. I witnessed a lot of fear and anger around me with people apparently turning inward and only considering what they want, what they need, and what they desire. Therefore, some people have lost the capacity for empathy.

What was once bright and colorful became dull and unimaginative. The smell of roses now took on the stench of hot garbage and dry piss. Sunny turned gloomy, and warmth turned cold. Nothing was the same. I was just a little girl, learning to become a strong woman who could care for herself and others, but damn, did I quickly realize how much age didn't matter in this world. Kids were being murdered at the age of five. Little girls were giving birth to babies at eleven. Boys were going to jail at ten. And I was being raped in my own home at thirteen. That was the reality I had to understand quickly—that no one was above the dangers of this world. Not even me.

I've always believed that maturity isn't necessarily linked to age, but rather, it's forged through pivotal moments. These moments force us to confront our fears and challenge our perspectives. For me, that pivotal moment occurred when the little girl in me disappeared, leaving me to fend for myself. For years, I struggled with who to blame for my situation. My stepfather? My mother? Or perhaps myself? The answer was unclear, and the resulting conflict took a toll on me. As his lewd behavior continued, I lost my sense of worth, and it affected every aspect of my life. My relationship with my sister became quite rocky, to the point we'd fight over the smallest things. Whose turn to watch TV. Whose turn it was to clean the room. Anything!

Through the ordeal, dealing with my stepfather, my mother and I experienced a rift as well. I would act out and that would cause her to find other means to punish me, which later escalated to physical beatings. At times, it felt as though I could do nothing right. Sometimes, even when Yolonde did something wrong, I was the one who got in trouble. Despite all that, I would have rather fought my sister every day or taken a beating from my mother than have to kiss my stepfather on the cheek every night before he went off to work. I couldn't say anything because of my mother's attempt to create the myth of a perfect family. However, that only made me more rebellious. I hated it! Every time my lips touched his scruffy, bearded face, I cringed internally. It was like adding sprinkles to a melted ice cream.

I couldn't tell my mother and sister what was happening, but at the same time, I didn't understand how they couldn't see what he was doing. Consequently, I had to force myself to eat because stress had taken hold of my appetite. Sleep became nearly impossible because the thought of him doing something to me in the middle of the night infected my mind. So indeed, I was a prisoner. Even attending church became a challenge as the very man who was molesting me was the one bringing us to a sacred place, where I would witness him praying and rejoicing in the name of the Lord. It was a confusing and contradictory experience.

Soon, going to school would become a struggle. I would constantly stare at the clock hanging above the teacher's desk, watching the seconds slowly turn to hours. Sometimes between the ticks of the clock, as I sat in that classroom, I felt most at peace. It was as if time had stopped and taken away my ability to think of the torture my stepfather had put me through.

I didn't do much talking in school. Some of my classmates and teachers even thought I was mute. Most of the time, if someone spoke to me, I'd respond with silence or maybe a bashful head nod. As a result, I occasionally struggled with my classwork, and it was oftentimes revealed in my grades. Finding the motivation to do anything was difficult, and because of that, schoolwork became boring. Instead of focusing on the lessons, I was busy worrying about what would happen when I arrived home after school. Would he be there alone? Could I fight him off if he tried to do something to me? What if I didn't go home at all and just walked around? Maybe I could tell someone? All the questions in the world, and yet, no answers.

When the last bell of the day rang, I immediately felt my brain sending error messages that activated my fear. My thoughts became so scattered that normal functioning was impossible. With each step I took, my feet felt like bricks, and my heart raced to an unfamiliar beat. This was not a one-time incident, or two times, or three. No! It was more like an everyday occurrence that lasted a couple of years.

It took roughly thirty minutes to get home from school, and sometimes, I could stretch it to an hour if I walked slowly. But that wasn't enough because that would still leave me there, alone with him, for almost an hour. Maybe two. I had to come up with a plan to save myself. That would be the first of many where I had to create my own path. My own yes! I started picking my sister up from school and walking with her instead. In my mind, there was no way he'd do what he was doing to me if my sister, his actual daughter, was also in the house. And boy, was I right...and wrong at the same time.

The first time I entered the apartment with my sister, I watched his face turn pale, lacking any sort of emotion. It was as if I had ruined any and all plans he had conjured up in his mind. He sexually assaulted and molested me for several months when all I had to do was bring my sister home with me. I could not believe it. I wanted to kick myself in the ass for not thinking of that before. There were days when I would cry along the way home simply from the thought of it. I never knew how far he'd take it either. It was usually touching, some kissing, and of course, the flashing of his private parts. But never actual intercourse. Until that one day when it all changed.

Two years had passed, and I was still dealing with the bullshit of my stepfather, not as much, but one time was too many. Tiptoeing around the house while being very meticulous on where I found myself in the home became the norm. I felt like I was living in some sort of haunted house. Anytime he caught me alone, he tried to force himself on me or place his dick in my hands or mouth. He made it clear, as he often did, that if I told anyone, I could be sent back to Jamaica and my mom might lose her job. So, I remained silent. However, deep down inside, I felt like my mother knew what was going on with me. I didn't have proof or anything, but I could not fathom the thought of loving someone so much and yet not noticing their misery, their pain, or their suffering. Denial! That's what that was. Perhaps my mother didn't want to accept that the man she was sleeping with every night was molesting me. So, her not admitting it was a way for her to deny her failure to protect me. Or even worse, her realization that she married a monster. Besides, she would never acknowledge it was her fault because nothing was ever her fault. That was a reality she wasn't prepared to face.

One fateful night, I had a vivid dream where I mustered the courage to confide in my mother about the horrors I had been enduring. And in that dream, everything felt remarkably lifelike. The scents and sights were intense, and even the sensation of my mother's hand gripping onto mine as I led her to the couch felt real. It's as though we had transcended the realm of a mere dream and into real life. There, I gazed into her eyes, feeling the tears welling up in my own eyes just before I revealed the truth about the unspeakable things my stepfather, her husband, had subjected me to since my arrival in America. Then, I did it. I shared in excruciating details of how he forced me to perform unthinkable sexual acts that no child should ever endure at such a vulnerable stage of life. The consequences of those actions left me deeply scarred, both physically and emotionally.

Seated on that worn leather couch, I bared my soul to my mother, even telling her about the fear and intolerable loneliness that surrounded me in our home. With every word, I held onto the hope that my mother would grab me in her embrace, and together we would shed tears of our shared pain. I believed she would offer countless apologies, then meet my gaze with unwavering empathy, and reassure me that neither he nor anyone else would ever inflict harm upon me again. But I was wrong. Her eyes turned stoic as she stared at me in utter silence. Without uttering a word of comfort or extending any form of support, she coldly released my trembling hands and said, *"Trisha, stop lying!"* Before I knew it, she disappeared and left me behind, broken and forsaken. At that moment, tears streamed down my face as the realization sank in that I would have to face the ordeal alone. Even in my dreams, I could feel each drop falling onto my lap. The dream felt so vivid that I questioned whether it was just a figment of my imagination.

We moved into a three-bedroom on the south side of Hartford by the time I was in high school. My mother and stepfather had one room, my sister and I shared a room, and we had a back bedroom where we stored various things. The place wasn't lavish or anything, but it certainly had more character than the place on Laurel and Farmington. In that back room was where I spent most of my time. It was the only place in the house where I could be myself without the bickering of my mother, annoyance of my sister, and, of course, the assaults of my stepfather. Or so I thought. As we settled into the apartment, it didn't take long for him to continue with the molesting. He became more aggressive and bolder with his actions, forcing me to play with his penis while my mother or sister was in the house. And just like all the previous times, I'd cry my eyes out, but this time I had to do it quieter or else they would know what was happening.

As night fell to reveal the stars like a gathering of penny wallies freed from a jar, I laid in my bed wide awake with a sense of warmth springing from the cold. There were times I sensed imminent trouble coming my way, whispering in a way the ears could not hear. It was like some sort of supernatural sense that God gave me. Yet, I didn't often listen to that voice.

In the dead of night, while my family lay fast asleep in their beds, I slipped out of my bedroom and made my way to the secluded back room. That's where I spent most of my time. I considered it my sanctuary for deep contemplation. Little did I know that this night would be different. My stepfather didn't go to work that night, and I wasn't aware of that. So, between my footsteps across the floor and the ominous creak of the door, he must've been alerted of my presence. And there he stood, an eerie silhouette framed in the doorway, his piercing gaze fixated upon me, evoking a sense of threatening uncertainty.

"Wa yuh a do?" he murmured, smiling devilishly.

That was the most he ever said. Sometimes he wouldn't say a word as he approached me. As always, I remained silent, refusing to acknowledge his presence. Instead, I turned away from the silhouette standing there and prayed to God that my stepfather would leave me alone. But he didn't. He stepped into the room and shut the door, allowing the night to cover the room like the closing of black velvet curtains. Noticing the danger ahead, I quickly stood up and tried to get out of the room, but he stepped in my way. A long pause lingered between us as he stood there, seemingly thinking of his next move.

In complete darkness, it can take someone's vision a minute to adjust, but with my senses being so alert, it only took me a few seconds. Even before my eyes witnessed him take off his pants, I could see him doing so in my mind. As if it all were some sort of déjà vu. The sound of his pants hitting the floor was so unnerving that it pricked my eardrums. This was unlike any of the other times I had heard him take off his clothes. Then, he walked over to me, butt-ass naked, with his erection inches away from me.

"Touch it!" he instructed.

No! I refused to grab ahold of his erection and decided to stand up for myself instead.

"I'mma tell mommy."

I was known for being a fighter, but now I was quickly becoming a woman in control of her voice, and it was all thanks to him. No longer would I subject myself to his abuse and mind control over me. I had to stand up for what was right, expressing myself in a way I hadn't done before. Plain and simple, I was sick and tired of his shit. His entire presence was like some sort of infectious disease that I needed to get out of my system.

Little did I know that my words would have zero effect on him. He just stood there staring at me as he chuckled. With a stern matter-of-factly voice, he explained how my mother wouldn't believe anything I said, and if she did, I would regret it. I didn't want to believe it, but everything he said that night was true. No matter what I hoped to happen, I knew he would still be the man that my mother adored. Besides, love does have a way of making a fool out of us, and sometimes at the expense of those we truly care about.

Frantically, I made a desperate attempt to escape the room, but he grabbed a hold of me, yanked me back in, and then threw me to the ground. I landed, causing a loud thud, my body trembling with fear and despair. In the past, his despicable actions forced me to touch or perform unspeakable acts to his erection. But this time, as he stood over me, completely naked, an eerie sensation flooded the room, allowing me to know that this encounter would escalate to another level.

I tried to fight him off, but I was much too small to match his strength. So, I gave up, and accepted the inevitable. The second I did that, it happened. He stripped my panties off and climbed on top of me. I can still remember his heavy and musty body weighing down on me as he aggressively forced himself on me. I wanted to scream, but, again, something wouldn't allow me to do so. I just laid there with tears falling from my eyes as he shattered my virginity. I was helpless. I was scared. And I was…ashamed.

Ashamed of myself because I was this so-called fighter who could take on anyone, and here I was, surrendering like a little bitch! Indeed, I couldn't do shit to stop him, so I began counting in my head, hoping that maybe, just maybe, it would take me away from this moment. Over and over, he penetrated my body as I lay there, lifelessly. A severe pain throbbed between my legs as he continued to have his way with me, but I did not want him to know, determined to not let him know he had broken me. Besides, I hoped by remaining quiet, he'd feel guilty, hurt, or sort of negative emotions that came with these types of acts. However, he didn't. He just kept right on, pushing himself further into my body. By the time I got in the hundreds, I slowly began to lose count. Instead, my eyes drifted outside the window, stuck on the moon. I stared at it for so long that I didn't even notice he was done and had left the room, leaving my gaze stuck outside the window.

CHAPTER 6

RUNNING FREE

"Everyone was chasing some sort of high that allowed them to find sanity while placing them in a world they were not used to. For me, that came from running."

"On your mark! Get set! Go!" The sound of the voice blaring over the bullhorn sent a surge of adrenaline through my veins, electrifying every nerve in my body. I felt I had been born to run, and the starting gun was the trigger that ignited a hidden spark within me, one that I hadn't known existed.

As I stepped onto the track, the world around me faded into the background, leaving only the white lines and rhythmic pounding of my feet against the pavement. The rush of wind through my hair and against my skin, the beating of my heart, and the sheer thrill of the competition were enough to make me forget all my troubles. I was now in my happy place, my escape, and borderline my home. Only after the birth of my first child, when I would hold her in my arms, would I come to know such euphoric emotions.

Within the chaos of life, many of us searched for an escape, a way to transcend our mundane reality. Some sought refuge in drugs and alcohol, while others chased after wealth through questionable means. But for a select few, seeking unwarranted attention was the only remedy for their emptiness. Each individual was on a quest to attain that unique high, a state of mind allowing them to temporarily run away from their troubles and live in a different realm. For me, my high came from running. It made the familiar become unfamiliar, and the strange become captivating. Colors appeared brighter, thoughts became more profound, and the atmosphere was saturated with positivity.

It's amazing how the simple act of running could give you such freedom and safety. At times, I felt as if I were escaping from the mess I faced in my reality. I needed to have my toe to the line, parked in my stance, awaiting the sound of the gun blasting into the air. That's where I found comfort. And for a while, that was the only time everything around me would fade into nothingness as the silence became my blanket. Within the bosom of that silence, peace surrounded me. I only felt my heart thumping profusely against my chest as if it would jump out. Chills ran through my body just before I took off, and within those hundred meters, I was free and safe.

Time seemed to slow down to a crawl. Every little detail around me came into sharp focus just before the hearing *"On your mark! Get set! Go!"* which shattered the stillness. The crowd erupted into cheers, the runners around me stretched, and the trees swayed to a gentle rhythm, shedding their autumn leaves in a mesmerizing dance. Despite being in complete control of my body, I couldn't truly feel my hands and feet until that moment when the starting pistol went off. Those are euphoric moments when I recall the sweet aroma of the rubber track beneath my feet as the wind pressed against my face and the power of my movement hurled me toward the finish.

For those suspended moments, all worries, traumas, and stresses faded away, leaving only the pure joy of running. Even when my body screamed for me to stop, that euphoric energy kept pushing me forward. Winning didn't matter as much as the sheer thrill of running, of feeling my body surge with power and grace. There were days when I ran simply because I needed an escape from feeling trapped within the walls of my home. But every time I hit the track, I knew I had found a way to break free and experience the pure, unadulterated joy of movement.

20 Pershing Street Hartford, CT

By the time I reached the tenth grade, my mother and her husband had moved into a home on Pershing Street— a few miles up the road from our first home on Laurel Street. Our home was a simple white, two-story house topped off with a slanted ceiling covering three bedrooms and two bathrooms. And, of course, my sister and I shared a room while my brother, Brian, who was just born, stayed with my parents. However, unlike our apartment on Laurel and Farmington, this one was in an actual neighborhood. It reminded me of a home you'd see in a sappy 90's romantic comedy. Nothing glamorous, but certainly better than the four-story brick building we had moved from.

It was conveniently located just a mile from my school, an easy walk for me. As a shift was occurring in the lives of everyone in my life, I too was trying to make sense of everything in mine. I vividly remember my first day as a freshman at Weaver High School, barely fourteen years old. The new environment was a challenge, but after weeks of adjusting, I finally felt like I belonged. For the first time in my life, I had developed a sense of identity that didn't require me to reflect on myself from someone else's perspective. I didn't even want to go to high school.

I was so anxious about starting over that I remembered asking my eighth-grade math teacher, Miss Keaton, if I could stay at my old school instead of transferring to Weaver. Miss Keaton, who had a heart of gold, encouraged me by saying that high school would be an amazing experience. At that time, I couldn't believe her. How could I? I had left behind a peaceful life in Jamaica only to find myself in a world that felt like a living nightmare.

My stepfather's abusive behavior, along with the bullying and chaos in the streets, made it even worse. I had just started to adapt to the madness of the crazy world and accepted it as normal when I had to start all over again in high school. I didn't know what to expect there, but I felt like I was sinking deeper into my own personal hell. Nevertheless, I knew time would move on and I had to do the same. Somehow, I had to figure out how to make the best of the situation; otherwise, there was no telling where I would end up.

Freshman year at Weaver High was when I began to come out of my shell, blossoming into a woman and less of an awkward mute. The school was somewhat of a melting pot of races and cultures, many of which lived below the poverty line. African Americans, Jamaicans, Hispanics, other Caribbean people, and a white girl filled the hallways and classrooms of Weaver High School.

To the surprise of many, I didn't have any friends. Nor did I have anything to take up my time. No part-time job. No boyfriend. No extracurricular activities. Nothing! I was a shadow simply walking through life. Yet that didn't stop time from moving on, and if anything, I had to find a way to keep up with it. One thing was for sure, I wasn't heading home once the bell rang. No way! I wandered the school aimlessly, wasting enough time to arrive home when my mother did. I was shocked to see other students roaming around campus after the last bell as if there were more classes I didn't know about. That was different for me. Witnessing students participate in sports, hanging around hallways talking, and even sitting in organized after-school meetings for social clubs left me quite intrigued. I knew I had to be part of something. How else would I be able to keep my sanity? Or better yet, save me from the torture at home?

It didn't take long, though, because somehow, sports inadvertently became the answer to my question. I practically tried out for every sport there was. That's where I made my first friend, Tamara Jenkins, a senior on the volleyball squad. Me? A ninety-pound freshman with a thick accent, friends with a senior? Internally, I felt accomplished, smiling like a newborn. Tamara ultimately took me under her wing like a pet or child when I joined the volleyball team. She was the sweetest and most rational girl I'd been around. So much of who Tamara had allowed me to uncover a profound aspect of myself. I found great admiration in her bold and uninhibited demeanor, consistently venturing beyond conventional boundaries while maintaining a strong sense of structure. Her steady passion for her interests was truly inspiring. Witnessing her in action provided me with a newfound confidence that would prove invaluable on my own journey.

Volleyball was the first sport I started playing, and I barely knew anything about it. I never played the game in Jamaica, nor did I see anyone else play it. However, that wouldn't stop me from going for it. I considered myself to have a high athletic acumen that could serve me well for anything. That's the thing about me. My mindset would not allow me to believe there is something I could not do. Nothing! If someone else could do it, then I knew I could as well. Not only would I do it, but I'd excel at it, too. Perhaps gymnastics might have proved to be wrong. That's the second sport I tried to participate in during high school, and "try" is an understatement.

In my mind, it looked pretty easy. Watching the girls flip, bend, jump, and twirl their bodies in every way made me think I, too, could do that. Boy, was I wrong! I quickly discovered that wouldn't be the case because I could barely do a cartwheel, let alone any type of leap. Still, I wasn't ready to give it up and move on, allowing myself to be ridiculed by defeat. Not by anyone else, but rather by myself, because being a quitter was never a word anyone would use to describe Trisha Bailey. It was true then, just as it is today. I knew I had to get better. And I would have to do it soon. I practiced certain moves at home, stretched my body no matter where I was, and even ran as much as possible to get my breathing right.

I was fifteen years old, entering my sophomore year, and my mother still didn't want my sister and me going outside like most teenagers in the area. She was always treating me like a child. Then again, in her eyes, I was that same innocent girl from Jamaica. I don't blame her, though. The neighborhood wasn't always the safest place to wander around, especially for a girl like me. If the sketchy people walking up and down the avenue didn't make the hair on your arms stand at attention, then the cars zooming through the street like NASCAR certainly would. I remember days when I walked from school and had to pass by a strange man masturbating in his car. It was creepy. So, whenever I had to go home, I ran so I wouldn't see him. So yeah, that's the kind of neighborhood I grew up in.

The avoidance of what was happening to me at home and the internal cry for help introduced a rift between my mother and me. I grew tired of not being able to do anything. I never had privileges because, for some reason, I was always on punishment. When my stepfather would do all sorts of stupid things, I would repeat to myself like an affirmation, "You will never break me." One time, he took all my clothes, none of which he had purchased, and put them in a garbage bag then placed it on the curb in the morning just before the trash trucks came by. Despite that, I was able to retrieve most of the clothes he had discarded before the garbage men could grab them.

It seemed like there was always something happening, and my mom would never react. She'd just continue catering to him. More than anything, he was just mad that he couldn't molest me anymore because I found a way to avoid him. Not only that, but I was also learning to stand up for myself when it came to him, returning to the fighter I was. Therefore, he found other ways to make my life miserable by forcing problems between Mom and me. As evil as he was, he was meticulous. He figured if he could get my mother to put me on punishment, then I would have no choice but to be at home after school.

My mother never questioned him, so I knew there wasn't anything I could do to help my case. No matter what he said or did, she went along with it. That left me with no choice of my own. So, I snuck out of the house all the time, becoming a rebellious teenager. Once, the neighbor saw me sneak out and told my mom. My mother beat me so bad I saw blinking and flashing lights of all colors. That only further pulled me away from her.

Later in life, as an adult, I came to understand what my mother must've endured being married to my stepfather—especially after my experience with my share of men. As a woman under the influence of the one you love, it can be challenging to see past their deceitful habits and manipulation. For my mother, this was no exception. Soon, it became a coping mechanism for her to simply deal with it. I knew my mother wanted the best for me, but it still caused us to clash. She and I would fight about everything because she didn't want me to do anything! I couldn't use the phone. I couldn't watch TV. I wasn't allowed to have money. Every day was the same thing. Come home. Do homework. Clean up. Day in and day out.

Sometimes I would run away from home and head to a friend's house whenever I needed to get away. Most of them were teammates of mine I barely knew. See, running away was the most courageous choice because of the circumstances. Every time I decided to grab my stuff and run off to the unknown, I somehow trusted my instinct which had appeared out of nowhere. In all my life, I've never gone against my intuition. Not then, and certainly not now. However, I must admit, I was afraid to return home, but I'd always come back, hoping things would be different. Or better.

The moment I walked through the door, everything in the house was calm, with nothing out of place. Soon, my mother and sometimes my sister would welcome me back with open arms. As strange as it may sound, those were the best times I shared with my mother, because although I knew she loved me, it was the only time I felt wanted or needed.

On the days I decided to stay around and face my obstacles, I'd lock myself away in my bedroom, lie on the floor, and write random thoughts in my journal. Occasionally, I would doodle in my art book, drawing images of animals and plants. My life as a delicate teenager quickly became mundane with dark thoughts often plaguing my mind. I had thoughts of harming myself, running away, or even worse, inflicting pain on someone else. Indeed, I had damaging thoughts that no girl my age–or any age–should have. The images and voices swarmed in my head like a pack of butterflies—no, more like monkeys jumping around, ultimately pushing me into the darkest corner of my mind. That's when I knew I had to leave the house, even if it meant driving my mother and me further apart.

I stepped on the track one day after school to warm up for gymnastics as usual. A few sprints up and down the track to relax my muscles and then a long-distance run to help control breathing. I knew I wasn't the best at gymnastics, but I understood the only way I would improve was to start by doing all the small stuff like running and stretching more. That much I knew. That's how I approached anything. Always just start! And begin with the little things that will eventually help you attain your desired success.

Several athletes practiced on or around the track and field, so it wasn't always easy to tell who was on the track team. However, there was something about a few of the kids that stood out from the rest because of their stance, posture, and the way they glided across the track. While some looked like they were running to warm up, others looked to be running for a goal—a purpose. I saw the intensity in their eyes each time they came whooshing by.

One of the girls I saw flying across that track approached me on this occasion. Judith Stair was her name—a popular sprinter on the track team and well-known around Hartford.

"Hey! What are you out here for?" she asked.

"Gymnastics."

"Okay. I always see you running out here, so I wanted to ask. You should join the track team. You're pretty good."

I smiled and internally laughed. Not because I was interested or nervous, but because she saw something I hadn't yet recognized in myself. That was the first time I considered joining the track team, and it was because of Judith Stair, a girl I'd never met, who helped me see what I was truly capable of. That's the unique thing about life. We may not always recognize our talents, gifts, or purpose until God speaks through other people, allowing them to give you the message you need to hear, whether it be a family member, friend, or stranger. Besides, I knew I sucked at gymnastics, so I figured I would have to find something else to get into. Until that day, I had no idea that my running ability was dynamic enough to be part of a team.

Back in Jamaica, most people knew me as the girl who ran all over the town. That's in addition to being known as the fighter. Anywhere

I went, more than not, I ran. I couldn't help myself. Running gave me a sense of freedom and control I couldn't get anywhere else. If I was headed to school? I ran. Making a store run for my aunt? I ran. Visiting my grandma's house up the hill? I ran. I even did it once with a gash in my foot and a busted shin. I was climbing a mango tree to get the perfect juicy fruit, and as I made my way to the top, I spotted an iguana. We were always told that if an iguana bites you, the doctor must cut it out of your body. When I put my hand on the iguana, I jumped off the tree, hit my foot on a rock, and it ripped my shin. I got up and ran home fast! Probably faster than I had ever done before. So, you see, nothing could stop me from running.

Across the world, Jamaica has been known for its exceptional female track runners. Merlene Ottey. Deon Hemmings. Veronica Campbell-Brown. Juliet Cuthbert-Flynn. Shelly-Ann Fraser-Pryce. They are just a few of the many who blessed the world with their talent and speed. As a kid, I heard some of their names, but growing up in St. Elizabeth, I didn't get to compete because that was mainly for high school students. However, once I stepped on the track, my whole life became a part of it, ultimately saving me from the dreadful path I was headed down.

I'll be honest: As excited as I was to be introduced to track by Judith, I didn't think much of it because with volleyball, tennis, and gymnastics, how would I ever have time?

Suddenly, from across the way, I saw a girl gliding between the white lines like an angel on a mission. She was simply amazing. I could almost see the energy pouring from her body, casting a glow around her as if she had been suddenly born at that moment. Her name was Maxine Clarke, one of the nation's best runners. My eyes widened and my mouth hung open; my breathing stopped for a few seconds, and my mind went blank. I lost all sense of time, staring at her in a way no one else was. Or perhaps, in a way no one else could. A tingling sensation rushed through my body, like millions of ants crawling inside me, and slowly disappeared into the pit of my stomach. At that moment, I wanted to be on the track and be just like her. I was not only going to run track, but I was going to be the best.

Being a runner didn't always come with the glory of winning. At times, it was both my punishment and joy. Every time I ran, I learned more about myself and more about what nature had in store for me. It helped turn me from a shy, troubled girl who felt like a nobody, to a strong, confident, and outgoing person who mattered. It granted me a type of favor with people I never knew anything about. The great respect I earned on that track and field quickly seeped into my personal life. That feeling of worth saved me in ways I could never repay. *On your mark! Get set! Go!* Those set of words steered the way I live my life on and off the tracks, helping me survive through my process of becoming a woman.

I was just a sophomore when I joined Weaver High's track team, looking up to all the upperclassmen—specifically Maxine Clark. She had won just about every meet she competed in. Not only did Maxine win regionally, but also across the state. She crushed it! Her times were even good enough to qualify for national records.

A few days into practice, Coach Butterfield decided to pair me with Maxine. For most freshmen and sophomores, it might have been nerve-wracking and intimidating to train with Maxine, but for me, I was eager and grinning with excitement. I welcomed the idea of training alongside Maxine, because by doing so, I knew learning from her could help me defeat her one day. Everything she had worked for served as a standard of excellence that I needed to reach. Honestly, beating Maxine in a race became my first goal since I knew I would be the fastest girl in the country if I could do so.

Since Coach Butterfield had us running and training together, I ultimately started out competing in the 400 and 800-meter events just like Maxine. This meant I had to train harder, learning everything I could, from how she trained to the way she perfected her form every time she ran. Yes, we were on the same team, but the great thing about training with Maxine was that I could run against her in practice and in future track meets as well. Therefore, I became a servant of perfection, a master of my fate, and undoubtedly the enemy of my fear. That meant I would do all I could to win because that's what champions do. Although I was all about the people around me and helping others in my everyday life, it was a battle on the track. I didn't compete just to win. I competed to become better than I was before. Win or lose. Coach Butterfield must've seen that determination because he stayed on me, grooming me to be the next Maxine Clarke.

Although I started running as a way to escape the violation of my body and my innocence lost at home, I fell in love with every aspect of it. The ability to compete. The camaraderie I was building with my teammates. All eyes were on me as I took off from the white line, following the sound of the whistle or gun blasting in the air. Even the opportunity to train in building my muscles excited me.

With anything I did in life, I had a strategic plan for success, and then there were the small things like running to school. Part of my regimen to strengthen my legs was to run everywhere I had to go. If I was going to beat the best, I had to get my body and mind to *be* the best. Ten inches of snow outside in the sub-zero weather? I ran. I did it as I headed to school, the store, or anywhere else. Every second of my life was an opportunity to become perfect. If I couldn't be perfect, I would get as close to it as possible. Running everywhere wasn't foreign to me since that's what I did in Jamaica. This time, I had a purpose and shoes on my feet.

On your mark!

When I stepped on that track for the first time, I realized that I was surrounded by athletes wrestling with individual pressures to perform—to be the best. Eight runners, some of whom were my teammates, with just one goal. Win! I never had to look to my left or right to see that intense energy of desire to win passing by like an ocean's breeze. Between the white marker, staring straight ahead at the finish line, were girls beside me with the hope and promise of a new life reflected on their faces, all of whom were chasing their own version of a dream, yet experiencing some form of pain or trauma. I saw it in their eyes. It was easy because I had seen those same eyes many times in the mirror. I then realized I wasn't alone.

Like myself, they also raced toward the finish line to run *from* something else. For me, it was being raped at home. Others may have been looking to escape the poverty they were forced to live in. Even if it was for less than sixty seconds. The fear of being molested by a loved one. The grief they carried over someone they lost. Anger. Depression. It was all left off the track and field as we awaited the start of the run. The idea that running was the only way for any of us to become someone is what we were chasing.

Despite anything we may have been dealing with, we couldn't all be winners. It wasn't just a matter of who trained the hardest but rather whose reason to run was the strongest. The same could be said about the life we live today. The only difference between you and the successful person running that same race is not the lack of strength or knowledge. Instead, it's the lack of wanting. Better yet, it's the lack of making it a need! Nothing in this world could overtake perseverance and determination. Not even talent. I knew that then just like I know that today.

Runners! Take your mark!

My first run in high school was the 800-meter race. Seven other girls lined up alongside me, and all the preparation I had done for weeks went out the window, leaving me with a jittery feeling. I had no idea what to expect, and I didn't know how I would feel if I didn't measure up to the others. That first run was exhilarating, intense, and euphoric, but also stressful and almost unbearable. In every race I ran, there was never a question of stopping. Only when I crossed the finish line.

Although I wasn't good at pacing myself, I knew how to keep going no matter what—even when my body told me there was no more in the tank. Still, I came in second, right behind Maxine Clarke. Indeed, I was proud, yet I was far from satisfied. The season was ending, and I hadn't yet beat Maxine in any of the runs. She was a senior, and I was just a sophomore. I had to beat her before the season ended, or else I would not have accomplished my goal.

Get set!

Then came the day! 800 meters. That moment, getting ready to compete was a lot to take in. As the crowd watched, we all took our stances, toes to the line. Most were cheering on Maxine Clarke. She was stationed in Lane 3 while I was two slots over in Lane 5. Up to that moment, I was always coming in second place behind Maxine—whether it was an outdoor or indoor track meet, it didn't matter. I could not beat her. She even broke her record in one of the races, ultimately setting a new national record.

However, something about that bright spring day felt different. We were just a couple of meets away from the end of the season. The moment I stepped on the track, the negative thoughts in my head disappeared, as if a switch had been flipped on. The competitive spirit inside me reminded me of why I chose to run anyway. My purpose for winning! Like several of the other races, I had to run against Maxine. The same person that I had spent countless hours modeling my training after, yet still coming behind her during our events. Now, as confusing as this may sound, I didn't necessarily look up to Maxine. Instead, it was simply the record time that she put in place that I was chasing.

The sound of the crowd slowly faded into silence. Chills ran up and down my body as I became pleased with the unknown. My heart pounded like it was about to come to a stop. My lungs tightened as my mind began swirling with thoughts that caused me to doubt all the work I had put in. Somehow, the confidence I built during practice did not carry over to the actual race. Regardless, I didn't know who the best runners were when I stepped on the track. The only thing I knew was that I had to push myself beyond the line of excellence.

Go!

POW! The gun went off. I took off like a horse with no blinders, my breathing constricted, yet I ran as if my life depended on it. With each stride, I could feel the weight of my body colliding against the track. Then, an electric rush pierced through me as I transitioned from silence to a crowd screaming and yelling. At six hundred meters, I hit the infamous "wall," where my body's stored glycogen was depleted. My legs began to burn, and I gasped for air, but I kept running, even though it felt like I was barely moving. But I was, and boy, was I going fast!

Before I knew it, I was crossing the white line. It was over. All that preparation and hard work I put in to run that race was over in just 2:17:13. To my surprise, it was the leading time, and how I came to beat Maxine Clarke for the first time. From there, my track career would take off and no one could stop me!

* * *

During my sophomore year of high school, I began flourishing in life, even beyond the track. I gained the confidence to survive and stride on through my journey. I got my first job and mastered the habits of time management and handling money. Standing up to my stepfather wasn't as hard as before, and although it was sometimes a losing fight, I always fought back.

I recall a time when he attempted to assert his dominance. He rarely tried to discipline me, but there were some occasions. On this particular day, he approached me as I headed to my room with a bowl of ice cream. Thankfully, my mother was home. He would often bother me when she was around because he couldn't physically harm me.

"Don't take that ice cream in that room!" he said.

"Why not?'

As much as I despised my stepfather, my mother forced me to listen to him, or I'd be punished. Still, I didn't feel like doing whatever he asked of me at that moment because I was in the middle of eating. Besides, I knew he was only harassing me because he couldn't have his way with me as easily as before.

"Don't go in your room with the ice cream," he demanded.

I was never the person to disrespect any adult, but I couldn't show him the same respect I showed others. I despised him, and when he tried talking to me like a father would, I hated him even more. I would have rather taken the command from a crackhead lying in the back of an alley than listen to him. My mother would beat me if she felt I had done anything disrespectful to him. That was her husband. What else was I to expect?

Therefore, I walked away instead of hearing whatever bullshit he had to say. But he wouldn't have that. Immediately, he got mad and grabbed my left arm, and slung me to the wall. I yelled at him, and as he approached me, I smashed the glass bowl across his face. I didn't stay around long enough to notice if I knocked him out or if blood leaked from his head. I quickly ran out of the house, down Pershing Street, as if I were on the track—fast and focused. However, this time, I was running to an unknown destination. From that moment on, every time I ran, I would ensure I did it with a sense of purpose that encompassed more than just winning.

By the time I was a junior, I was competing at a high level across the state, New England, and eventually, nationals. Coach Butterfield had strategically placed me in Maxine Clarke's shoes with her going off to college. Not only was I running in high school, but I also ran the Junior Olympics, breaking all the qualifying records. To get to the Junior Olympics, we would raise money. No money, no running! As simple as that. Well, nothing was going to stop me. Therefore, I went from being just a runner to building a business. Believe it or not, obtaining donations from strangers was a business, the first business I practically ran. I had to manage my time strategically and know when to be at practice versus out in the neighborhoods knocking on doors. Developing my pitch was also crucial. I had it structured to the point I was pulling in donations from nearly every door I knocked on.

"Hello, my name is Trisha Bailey, and I need your support to get to the Junior Olympics, where I can continue to do what I love. Running! It's also tax deductible," I'd tell them with my prettiest smile.

I raised all the money I needed to run in the Junior Olympics alone. I knew I wouldn't get any money from my mother, because she was too busy taking care of other financial responsibilities, like my sister and brother. My future in track wasn't necessarily an item on the budget for my mother and her husband. Still, I would not be deterred or denied because of that, so I made a way. Those moments revealed that I must always be willing to grind for things that align with who I am and what I want. Also, it showed me how to get money!

By junior year of high school, Maxine had graduated and gone to college, leaving me to stand at the forefront of the track program. And that light was shining bright on me. So much so, my Junior Olympics teammates convinced me to give up all my other after-school involvements to focus primarily on track. That wasn't a difficult decision, especially when I saw my face in the local newspapers as the fastest girl in New England. So, with all my success in track, I became one of the most popular girls in high school, and I can't say for sure if it was a good or bad thing. I just knew I had to get used to it. Everyone knew me as the fast Jamaican girl seen in the newspaper. The track was my life! Even when I got an after-school job at Lee's Famous Recipe, I did not let it interfere with my practice or track meets.

Junior year was looking up, even with Coach Butterfield leaving. I asked him to stay, but he decided he wanted to leave after Maxine graduated. It sucked to lose him. But it sucked even more when Weaver High hired Butterfield's replacement, Coach Razenberry—A plump, creepy older guy who barely qualified to be a position coach, let alone a head coach. He was nothing like Butterfield. He'd show up to practice just minutes before it was over, always with some lame excuse and food in his hand. His idea of training was, *"Y'all go run around. Do a few laps."* Undoubtedly, he was nothing like my other coaches, especially Coach Lord. He was my junior Olympics coach, and God, did I admire that man. Not only did he train me to be the great runner I was, but he also saw a daughter in me. Someone he could love, protect, and help reach her full potential. The complete opposite of Coach Razenberry. Hell, the only time Razenberry said anything to the girls was when he was flirting.

Like so many perverted men, he preyed on us, saying some of the most inappropriate things a grown man could say to a teenage girl. *"Those shorts ain't short enough." "I see all that back there." "You know them lil boys don't know what to do with all that."* One time, he offered to drop me off. I saw that repulsive look on his face that reminded me of my stepfather. The twinkle in his eyes made me believe he was up to something. Besides, I had been through enough by that time to tell the difference between danger and safety.

"No thanks. I can walk." I replied.

He was a piece of shit. There was no telling how many girls he flirted with or had sex with beyond their consent. I loathed the idea that I was now having to deal with a pervert at home and creep on the track, but no matter what, I was determined to get through life, avoiding both of them at all costs.

Therefore, in order to succeed, I had to take it upon myself to train and stay motivated. Each day, I dedicated myself to the track, following the workouts that Coach Butterfield taught me and incorporating techniques I observed with Maxine. This included proper stretching, form exercises, and even focusing on my breathing. Despite my efforts to encourage the other girls to join me and adopt a structured practice routine, they never seemed interested. While they were occupied with fooling around and disregarding training, I was on a path to becoming one of the best runners in the state and eventually, the nation.

Senior year was amazing for me. Not only was I dominating the track, but now, I was getting national attention. Colleges across the country called with offers to run at their school. I could not believe that I was getting recruited to run in college. Me? A little girl from Jamaica? Going off to an American college to run? It was surreal to entertain what they were willing to put on the table just to get me to come to their school. The University of Georgia. Stanford. Louisiana State University. Morgan State University. Yale. The University of Connecticut. My phone rang nonstop with so many calls from schools.

Morgan State University was my top choice! I enjoyed my official visit to the school and knew I would get as far away from my mother and her husband as possible by going there. However, my mother wouldn't have that. She took away my ability to choose by forcing me to attend the University of Connecticut instead. I still remember being on the phone with a recruiter from a specific university and talking about my future at that school. In the middle of our conversation, my mother, who I had no idea was listening in from the phone upstairs, blurted out, "No, that's okay. She's not coming there. She's going to UCONN. Do you hear me, Trisha? You're going to Connecticut."

It was embarrassing, and I was fuming. However, despite how I was feeling or what little control I felt I had over my life, it was probably for the best. I wanted to go to Morgan State because I saw some attractive men clothed in purple and gold, stepping, and showing off their bodies during my recruitment visit. I thought I had died and gone to heaven, and because of that, that's where I wanted to be. What can I say? Men were my weakness, but fortunately for me, my mother wasn't having any of that.

That was Gloria Tomlinson for you, always inserting herself into all my affairs. I remember once where she even went as far as firing me from my high school job at Lee's Famous Recipe. My mother called up my manager and explained that I no longer worked there. It was partly because she found out I was using my job as an excuse to stay out later.

One day when I showed up for work, my boss laughed and said, *"Your mom called and fired you."* Ladies and gentlemen, I give you Gloria Tomlinson.

* * *

National signing day was a day of triumph for me. That's the day student-athletes across the country got to announce which college they'd be attending to play sports. I signed my name on the dotted line to run track at the University of Connecticut. The satisfaction I felt at that moment was a rush of positive emotions coming at me all at once—happiness, pride, relief, and even a sense of invincibility. It all made me feel as though I could conquer anything I set my mind to. Finally, my hard work had paid off, and I was going to pursue my passion for running at the collegiate level. But as they say, the path to success is never easy. And for me, the road ahead was riddled with obstacles.

As an athlete, I was eligible for a scholarship from the university to participate in track. That was only half the battle though. To be admitted for education, I had to meet the university's minimum grades and test requirements as well, which proved to be a challenge for me.

Now, this next part of my journey is something that many don't know about me. It's not one of my proudest moments, but it's a significant aspect of who I am. While it may not seem like a big deal to some, it haunted me at times and deeply affected my psyche. Unlike other students, I didn't always grasp the concepts of various subjects in high school so effortlessly. Don't get me wrong, I enjoyed going to class and learning, but there were days when I struggled to understand what the teacher was explaining—even in college.

Therefore, my concentration had to be more heightened than the average student's. Between my learning curve and all the distractions in and out of my home, there was no other way I'd be able to keep up. It was to the point I almost missed the chance to attend college due to my low SAT scores. This is the part that I never admitted to anyone because I was ashamed of it. The numbers printed on my results were a painful reminder of my shortcomings. I had always been an overachiever, striving for perfection in everything I did. But when it came to that damn SAT, no matter how hard I tried, I just couldn't seem to reach the minimum score required to attend UCONN, or any other college for that matter.

It was like trying to climb a mountain with no end in sight. Soon, failing became an overwhelming burden that I struggled to bear. Still, each time I stumbled, I picked myself up, dusted off my knees, and tried again. Yet, the weight of doubt became heavier. I nearly surrendered to depression, spending countless nights feeling helpless and isolated as tears and headaches became my comfort. My dreams of going to college, of becoming someone, seemed to slip further and further away with each passing day. I felt like a failure, like I didn't deserve to be anything more than what I was.

After all the studying and praying I had done to reach the minimum scores, I still fell short. It could see my dream of attending college slipping away, like a fading sunset sinking below the horizon. I nearly gave up. But as I grew increasingly disheartened, the University of Connecticut stepped in and offered me a lifeline by extending grace to a young girl from Woodlands, Jamaica, who had nothing but hopes and aspirations. Despite my subpar scores, they welcomed me into their institution and placed me in a program tailored to support my academic growth and ensure success at UCONN. For that, I will forever be grateful to the people of UCONN who turned my dream into a reality.

During my first weeks as a freshman in college, I was determined to do everything right to ensure I was on the level of my peers. I tried to associate with all the right people, trained hard, and spent countless hours studying for all my classes. One particular occasion stood out when I studied for hours on end for my first exam. When the day of the exam arrived, I entered the classroom bursting with confidence. Now, as I focused on the questions, the answers seemed to come to me effortlessly. I was not only confident in the work I had put in, but I was also certain that I had aced the exam.

The following week, when Professor Lichtenstein returned our exams, my heart sank as my eyes widened upon seeing a big red "D" staring back at me from the top of the paper. It felt like a punch to the gut, and I couldn't believe what I was seeing. A "D" minus? Are you kidding me? I walked out of that classroom dazed and confused, feeling like I was in a bad dream. My surroundings seemed surreal, and I questioned if I was even in the right place.

As some of my classmates streamed past me, with their heads held high, boasting of their excellent results, I sensed I didn't belong. Their faces were a blunt contrast to mine—beaming with smiles and pride, while I was consumed by self-doubt, feeling like an impostor who had snuck into the university. In that moment, I convinced myself that I was not cut out for college, and the gravity of that realization weighed heavily on my mind more than anyone ever knew. It was to the point where I wanted to leave on my own, to spare myself the embarrassment of being kicked out of school for terrible grades.

To make matters worse, the voice of my high school guidance counselor, Mrs. Whittaker, haunted me like an unwelcome melody. "Based on what you have here, you may not be college material," she had told me.

I walked out of her office feeling empty, unsure of what to believe. However, as I stood outside my college classroom, staring at the red "D-" on my paper, her words hit me hard. I mean, who was I to question someone whose only job was to shape and guide the futures of high school students? Especially seeing I was just a frail immigrant from Jamaica. So, I began to think that perhaps Mrs. Whittaker was right. Maybe I didn't belong in college. The feeling was overwhelming and persistent, like a weight on my shoulders that I couldn't shake off.

"Shit! I failed the exam!" one of my classmates suddenly stated.

Another classmate replied, "Me too."

Their exclamations were followed by another who actually laughed as he said it. As my classmates shared their struggles, a wave of relief washed over me like a warm embrace. Hearing their admissions made me feel less alone in my challenges with the material. Although Mrs. Whittaker's words still echoed in my mind, I would refuse to let them define me. My determination to work harder than anyone else was not about proving her wrong, but rather a reflection of my work ethic. This attitude gave me hope to push through my difficulties and emerge on the other side stronger.

My first year at UCONN, I was forced to take a backseat to track and therefore had to redshirt due to my college acceptance scores. That meant I had to sit out a whole year from competition and couldn't practice with the team, per NCAA regulations. I felt like I was being confined to a cage, watching my teammates run and train together while I had to figure it out on my own. But with the time I had, I pushed myself harder than ever before. I woke up before dawn, put on my running shoes, and took to the empty streets.

Some days, the cold air stung my lungs as I pounded the pavement, feeling each step as if it were carving a path toward my ultimate goal. Though I was alone in my training, I felt that sense of freedom that I had felt before. And with each passing day, my determination grew stronger. I knew that one day, I would be back on that track, with the wind in my hair and the sun on my face, doing what I loved most—running free.

CHAPTER 7

MY FIRST LOVE

"Until I met Kingsley, I never imagined I could have a friendship with a man without the occasional flirt or pressure to have sex."

For most of my life, I wondered if my past nightmare would allow me to trust a man enough to love him. That infectious thought filled my head like a thick fog over the hills. It ultimately impacted who I chose to date. I was drawn to men with specific characteristics and traits that reminded me of the sick bastard that turned my life into a nightmare. And I hated it! The fact that I couldn't realize it sooner made me angrier.

The truth is, subconsciously, I was fucked up in the head when it came to selecting the right partner. Yes, I knew I wanted a man that was nothing like my mother's husband, but somehow, I still ended up with assholes who were a lot like him. The majority of them displayed some form of narcissism. They were men with manipulative and deceitful behavior, lacking the patience to love and express genuine care. Men who wanted to be with me simply because they saw what they could take from me rather than what I could do for them. Men who could control me. Men who defined love through emotional, physical, or verbal abuse. Cold-hearted men with nothing to pour into me.

It was some sort of sick, twisted version of self-preservation. Without a doubt, I was too blind to realize what was happening then, and had it not been for the demise of my second marriage, I probably would have never known. Then again, I should have. I had dated enough of them to finally pull the wool from over my eyes, leading me to face the filthy truth. Internally, I was sick, disgusted, and downright miserable. I despised it with every part of my soul. I was repeatedly blindsided by what I considered to be love. Yet, still, that never stopped the woman I saw in the mirror from her quest to find true love.

I was transforming into a completely different woman when I arrived at the University of Connecticut—one with enough confidence and purpose to make it on her own. If I entered any room, I would make them see I belonged there. They would feel my presence on any track or field I competed on. I eagerly dove right into the internal growth occurring in my life. Yet, romantically, I was convinced that my love life would never be as colorful as I wanted it to be. So much shit had transpired for me to believe it ever would. So instead, mentally, I was caught in a world filled with dark, gloomy clouds burdening me with rainy days.

Millions of shards of glass covered the ground like dirt. However, rather than avoid wandering through this dark and perilous place, I had desperately made the best of it, hoping for the sun to appear one day. Or, possibly, I'd somehow stumble upon a bed of flowers and lay there until someone came by to carry me off into the sunset. God, I wanted to be in love so badly, or at the very least, be freed from the bondage of damaged thoughts. As much as I flirted with some of the guys around campus, wishing to find it, I never expected it to happen.

I was just a freshman walking through campus, looking for the time of my life. This was the first time I had been alone without anyone telling me what to do, what to wear, or anything else. No one could stop me from living my life as I wanted. On campus, there weren't too many people who sounded like me, let alone looked like me, so it was easy to spot those who did because they stood out. Man or woman.

Most of the Black students at UCONN hung around certain areas, gathering around their interests. Those who loved drama and acting spent their time in the theater department. The Black students looking to make a difference in the world or even those trying to find their place as students at a predominately white institution spent time at the African American culture center. As for the athletes, we mostly did everything together, hanging around the training facilities or dorms. Rarely did we mix with those who did not participate in sports. Not because we were better than anyone, but because most of our time was dedicated to our respective sport—sometimes along with different athletes. As a result, those who played sports for the school mostly dated other athletes.

That's how I met Mike Walker, a wide receiver on the football team. He was also my first college love interest. I was only weeks into my freedom as a seventeen-year-old when I met him while strolling through campus. Most girls liked Mike, so I supposed I was the lucky one. I didn't blame them, though, because the moment I saw him, I was also struck with emotions that ignited my thoughts of being with him. A tall, dark, and bald-headed specimen who forced time itself to stop is who Mike Walker was. My eyebrow raised in curiosity, my mouth became dry from hanging open for too long, and my brain shut down momentarily. If it were anyone else, I probably would have turned away, but with him, it felt… right. I wanted him to notice me staring at him because he had me drawn to him in some strange way that I could not explain.

Mike and I spent a lot of time together, but in my mind, it was never more than just two people of the opposite sex kicking it, having fun. In fact, I considered him a friend. Perhaps my naive ways were taking over because though we were intimately involved, I still had no clue that he had feelings for me in that way. I had not learned to connect sex with emotion bonds by then. Then again, deep down, I knew nothing would come of our fling, because I was still traveling through that dark, perilous world. We were both in different places mentally, and we were in college. The place where everyone went looking to find themselves while exploring others. Besides, our engagement was never meant to be shared with the rest of campus. It was almost as if I were his little secret. We'd spend the night together occasionally but then quickly part ways by morning. We barely dated, and yet we were full of ups and downs.

Then there was Marcel Robinson, who started as a gentleman but quickly became a thorn in my ass. He'd walk me to my dorm, study with me after class, and accompany me to late-night parties. He was always there to cheer me on at practice during the day, and then we'd spend the night talking about everything. Yet, nothing about our interaction screamed anything more than friends. Then again, I was a freshman still trying to assess my environment and relationships.

Not to mention Aaron, who I was still madly obsessed with. He decided to attend Clemson, so I would only communicate with him over the phone at night. That relationship quickly faded like the smoke from a midnight candle, leaving my eyes wandering off to new friends.

One night, while hanging out with a friend of mine, Clint, I came to uncover the truth about Marcel's feelings for me. As Clint and I talked and watched television in his room, Anthony, Marcel's roommate, entered and saw us sitting on his bed. That was nothing new for Clint and me, because as with Mike and Marcel, I also had a good friendship with Clint. He was innocent and refreshing to speak to—almost like the big brother I never had. Clint also played on the football team along with Mike and Marcel. I later found this to be a problem for some guys. That jealousy and egotistical demon haunted many of them, and Marcel was no exception. By the time I arrived at my dorm, my phone started ringing. As I answered the call, I soon realized the depth of one man's scorn.

"Oh, what's up Marcel?" I answered.

"I need my t-shirt. Bring it to me," Marcel said, stern and cold.

Still, nothing about the phone call made me think he was mad at me. I mean, why would he be? It's not like I had done anything to him. I didn't know Anthony would return and tell Marcel about my close relationship with Clint. Anyhow, it wasn't like I was hiding anything.

"Okay. I'll bring it after practice," I replied.

"No. Bring my shit back now!"

Suddenly, his entire demeanor shifted, followed by him screaming at me. This was so unlike Marcel. He continued to yell. "Bring my shirt back right now! Right fucking now!"

I wasn't the same woman who had arrived in America from Jamaica, and certainly not the same person I was when I left my mother's house. I wouldn't accept any man screaming at me. I dealt with enough of that back home. I hung up the phone and stormed over, furious, hoping to confront him. I wanted him to know he'd never talk to me, or any woman for that matter, like that ever again. But something clicked in my mind, and I immediately stopped and returned to my dorm. It wasn't worth it. In hindsight, I probably should have.

The next day, as promised, I brought him back his shirt after practice. Three knocks on the door were all it took for him to open it. Immediately, he snatched the shirt from my hand. Before I could say anything, he cursed at me, repeating a falsified story of Clint and me. Through his burning eyes and fuming voice, I saw the hurt boy inside the man who stood before me, short and furious. And for a moment, I sympathized with him. Nonetheless, my sympathy quickly vanished, and the moment of arguing with him had passed.

"You are not my man! So, I don't know why we're having this conversation," I snapped.

Just like that, I walked off, avoiding any further argument. Halfway down the hall, I heard him say the unthinkable.

"Fuck you, bitch!"

His voice echoed in my ears and pierced my soul like shiny daggers. What felt like ten minutes was just a millisecond. Thoughts and memories flashed through my head like a broken reel. My breathing became deliberately slow, and where there was once contentment… there was now emptiness. Anger had come coursing through my veins like some drug. Everything was blurred as the faint sounds outside went mute. Lord knows I hated being called a bitch! I turned and sprinted toward him with my fists balled tightly and eyes burning red. Noticing the rage in my eyes, he slammed the door shut before I could get to him. So, the only thing I could do was cuss at him as I banged on his door.

Hours later, I sat in my dorm room, still fuming when I heard four hard knocks. Surprisingly, when I answered the door, two campus police officers stood there with a look of concern.

"Hi. Can I help you?"

"Trisha Bailey?"

"Yes. That's me."

"We need you to come with us."

Just like that. They arrested me and took me off to the police station. That was the first time I had been in trouble with the law. I tried to beg and plead with the cops, telling them my side of the story. The truth! However, they wouldn't have any of it, as Marcel had already told them I had violently assaulted him. Even worse, he had a "witness." Anthony, his roommate at the time, was nowhere to be seen. It was as if they had concocted a scheme to get me in trouble, threatening my track scholarship. The University of Connecticut had already taken a chance on me because of my issues with my test scores, but now this? I was sure that my life was over, and it was all because of a fucking lie. Everyone asked him to drop the charges, but he was fixed on making me pay for something I had not done. The athletic director, the coach, and even his mother asked him to drop the charges, but he refused. Then I made the campus newspaper under the headlines…

TRACK ATHLETE ARRESTED FOR ASSAULT ON UCONN FOOTBALL PLAYER

I just knew my life was over, and everything I spent working and training for would be all for nothing. Thankfully, the judge dismissed the case, and I maintained my scholarship to remain on the track team.

After that occurrence with Marcel, I stayed far away from him—or any guy, for that matter. I was enraged, hurt, and felt the need to not make friends with anyone on campus. Sometimes, I even mistrusted myself, but I was sure I would never let someone jeopardize my future like Marcel had.

I would see him around campus from time to time, but we never spoke to one another. Despite my desperation to know why he did that to me, I never once approached him, hoping to get answers, until one day Marcel and I accidentally showed up at an elevator. It was the first time I had been around him enough to look into his eyes and finally ask him.

"Why did you do that to me? Why'd you press charges on me for something that never happened?"

With a blank stare and empty expression, he sucked his teeth and replied, "You deserved it." Then he walked off. That situation allowed me to take a step back and focus on who I could or could not let into my life—people who were aligned with the sort of kindness and morals I possessed. I was just seventeen years old, learning this valuable lesson, and as I did, that's how I came to meet Kingsley and fall in love.

Now, as small as the Black community at the University of Connecticut was, we all found ourselves at the African American culture center from time to time—a building on campus geared toward promoting Black awareness. It was also a place where most of the parties were held. As a freshman, I loved to party. I mean, what college girl didn't? It was the first time in my life I was free and on my own to do whatever the fuck I wanted to. At one of the parties is where I saw Kingsley. We locked eyes across the room through a crowd of warm bodies. It wasn't anything flirtatious. It was more of a subtle look that came with no intentions. That cordial smile with the tilt of the head is what we offered one another. The same look you'd give a stranger as they passed you at the grocery store for the second time. I didn't even know his name.

Kingsley wasn't like the other guys at the party; he was much calmer, focused, and more intelligent. He was true to himself, genuine, and marched to the beat of his own drum. Almost as if he had done college long enough to not be impressed by anything. Kingsley was a graduate student at UCONN finishing up his doctorate. He was handsome from the depth of his eyes to the soothing sound of his voice, with a sculptured athletic build. Only he wasn't an athlete.

One afternoon, I was strolling through the dining hall when I saw Kingsley grabbing some food. Immediately, we noticed each other, but like the first time, it wasn't anything more than a simple head nod and smile. However, I'll admit, it was enough to elicit a second look this time, but when I did, he was nowhere to be found.

"Hey, you," he said, appearing out of nowhere.

"Hi." I turned to face him, smiling coyly.

"We keep seeing each other, but we never talk. Where you from?"

Like myself, Kingsley was a Jamaican immigrant. I knew it the moment he spoke, because his accent, much thicker than mine, certainly stood out. Yet, his sudden appearance left me torn. On the one hand, it was impressive of him to approach me like a gentleman. On the other, I couldn't help but think he'd be like all the others I had encountered.

"You Jamaican?" My question carried a hint of excitement.

"Ya! I'm Jamaican."

"Okay. Me too. I'm from St. Elizabeth."

We stood in that dining room hall for nearly fifteen minutes, talking about our Jamaican background and all the other things we had in common. Admittedly, I was slightly interested in Kingsley, seeing as there was something special about speaking to a fellow Jamaican. It was hard to meet someone who knew more about the island than just the colors of the flag. Especially someone like Kingsley Stewart, who understood my lingo and connected to my experience growing up on the island.

Now, as sweet and kind as Kingsley was, he could sometimes turn very cold at the drop of a dime. Not the type of detached persona that brought about fear, but rather the non-threatening vindictiveness that made him cut people out of his life without thinking of restoring the relationship. It made sense because Kingsley was the type to give people trust instead of allowing them to earn it. Therefore, there was no way to rebuild that trust once it was gone. I learned the hard way when Kingsley stopped speaking to me over a situation we never discussed. I would see him on campus, and he'd ignore me like yesterday's trash.

No hellos or goodbyes. No "how are you?" Nothing! No matter how much I tried to deny that I was hurt, my heart could not seem to trick my mind. His absence left a void in me, affecting me in ways I wasn't prepared to handle. I surrendered to sleepless nights and struggled to function, throwing off my daily routines. Even my classes seemed to get more difficult without Kingsley. The worst part is that I believed I could get over him by entertaining other men. That was a mistake, because doing so only made me miss him more. Regardless, as much as I loved him, my ego simply would not allow me to run back begging. It got so bad that I even reached out to my high school sweetheart, Aaron, whom I had not talked to in months. Communication between me and Aaron quickly dwindled down to nothing, especially after I got banned from using the school phone. That was yet another crisis I had to overcome early in college, and it just happened to do with a man.

I would sneak into the coach's office, call up Aaron, and damn near spend the whole night talking on the phone. Little did I know, the school discovered an outstanding bill and investigated who could have done it. That didn't take much because all they had to do was call the number, and when they did, Aaron answered the phone…

"Hello, who do you know here at UCONN?" they asked him.

"Only Trisha Bailey," he replied.

Just like that, they brought me in and handed me a $1600 long-distance bill that I had to pay. Me? Pay a $1600 phone bill? Not only was I shocked, but I was terrified of what would happen next. Would I lose my scholarship over this, too? *Ugh!* If it's one thing I hated, it was getting in trouble, and because I rarely did, I didn't know how to react without the thought of shutting down. However, like always, I had to find a way. So, naturally, I decided I'd take care of the bill—even if I had to take on two jobs, all while running track. Yeah, my first few months in college were indeed no crystal stair.

I wasn't sure why I was reaching out to Aaron anyway. I was pretty sure he had moved on by then. Still, I emailed him, hoping to gain some comfort in return. SEND!

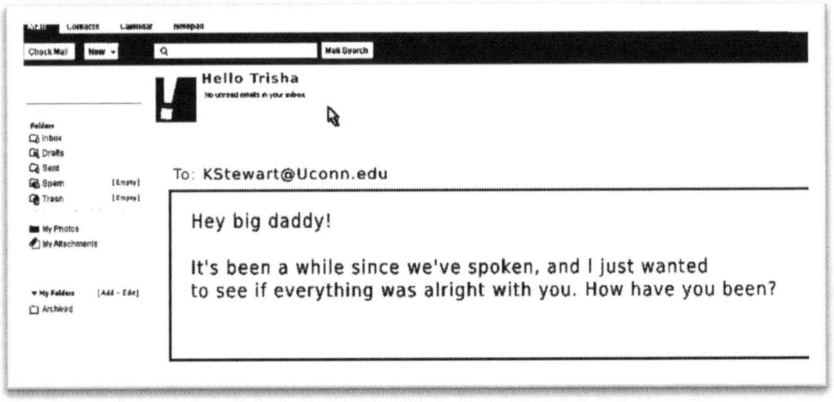

I must've been thinking about Kingsley when I decided to write the e-mail, because I accidentally sent it to him instead of Aaron. I didn't know I had done that until Kingsley sent a response. That allowed us to reconnect, and when that happened, our communication got a lot stronger, and his interest became much clearer. Swiftly, my physical attraction transitioned to mental stimulation. The more Kingsley and I spoke, the more intrigued I became. My body warmed with tingles every time he looked into my eyes. A sense of euphoria freed me from my worries, concerns, or anything else that didn't bring pleasure. This was the first time I was drawn to someone for more than their looks.

He understood me and connected with me beyond the physical. Part of it was because that's who Kingsley Stewart was, and the other half was because he was much older than any of the others I had been around. I was a tender eighteen-year-old girl starting college while he was a mature twenty-eight-year-old man preparing to take on the world. Once I knew that, it all made sense. Still, I looked at him as someone I could hang out with and be friends with due to our shared Jamaican background. Once again, the naive state of mind had taken over. As much as I was amazed by this man, I didn't stop to think for just one moment that he was interested in me beyond friendship.

Kingsley and I became closer as the moon and sun continued to switch shifts. He was my go-to for everything. Bad day at practice? Call up Kingsley. Couldn't understand an assignment or needed help with writing a paper? Meet up with Kingsley. He knew writing was the one area I struggled with the most in college, but it seemed to come effortlessly for him. I would write a paper, and then he'd review it and rewrite it. By the time I graduated, my writing woes were long behind me because of Kingsley. Even when I had issues with friends, he was there to be the companion I needed, especially as I endured the mess with Marcel. Kingsley was there to comfort me and offer encouraging words to help along the way.

"Don't stress it. You're going to be just fine. Do what you must, and God will take care of it."

Kingsley was right. Karma came banging on Marcel's front door three months after that situation. Well, maybe not karma, but more like a dozen police officers. Marcel had been charged with possessing marijuana with intent to sell, operating a drug factory, possessing marijuana near a school, and several other drug charges and criminal activities. He lost his scholarship, was kicked out of school, and was sentenced to jail. I couldn't have thought of a better payback than what he had done to himself.

TWO UCONN ATHLETES FACE DRUGS CHARGES

The dust cleared from my near college-ending ordeal, and Kingsley stood there like a soldier ready to take on the next mission. Our slow-burning friendship somehow transpired into something beautiful and natural. It was as if I had fallen in love with my best friend. Until I met Kingsley, I never imagined I could have a friendship with a man without the occasional flirting or need to have sex. He did not pressure me to do anything other than be my authentic self. And I did it effortlessly.

Kingsley and I went from eating lunch at the dining hall, where we would laugh and exchange childhood memories, to watching movies in our dorms through the late-night hours. We grew from quiet moments at the library to our first dramatic kiss. And when he took the city bus to the mall in Mansfield during the snowstorm to buy a relaxer for my hair, I knew he had feelings for me.

Emotions I had never experienced swirled in my body and mind, progressively strengthening as we dwelled in each other's space. Before I knew it, my heart skipped a beat whenever Kingsley looked at me because he saw me. Like, he really saw me. Not the physical side of me, but rather the once broken girl who was beginning to understand herself as a woman. He didn't just hear what I had to say when I spoke. Instead, he intently listened as I rambled on about any and everything. Simply put, Kingsley made the most mundane moments feel extraordinary.

I turned eighteen the summer of my sophomore year in college, and things swiftly changed. My focus on all my goals was much more intense. That type of focus channeled a sense of determination that helped me learn more about myself. I even got my driver's license and finally learned to drive. Kingsley taught me so much about myself and life, helping me develop a different sort of drive, and the way he pushed me was precisely what I needed. From then on, anything I did had to have a purpose, and anyone I surrounded myself with had to impact my life in some way. I became a true woman! That was also the summer Kingsley made love to me for the first time, allowing me to fall further in love with him. He was delicate yet passionate, taking the time to explore my body entirely. As much as he wanted to before, my age didn't allow him to take it there. Even though I was in college and mature enough to handle sex because it wouldn't have been my first time, I was still an innocent seventeen-year-old girl in his eyes. Now, at eighteen, that was a different story.

Not long after our first night of making love, Kingsley and I decided to move in together. We weren't married, but everything about us felt like we were. Or maybe that's just something I told myself to justify all my thoughts and actions. He never had to tell me, but I sensed his admiration and respect for my mother and grandmother, which made him fall deeper in love. They made him feel valued, as if he belonged to a family that he was missing.

Kingsley came from a small family, and his mother had already passed away by the time he and I started dating. Therefore, my mother unknowingly empowered him with the maternal influence he needed in his life. It wasn't just my mother, either. My grandmother gave him a mother's love, allowing him to care for me genuinely. I saw his eyes light up whenever he was around them, reflecting a piece of his mother in them. Mentally, I was jumping around on white clouds because Kingsley was my happily-ever-after.

The summer of my eighteenth birthday, Kingsley and I made it official by getting married. I remember the day when he proposed. I came home from a track meet on Valentine's Day, and he showed up at the bus with a ton of balloons and flowers. I could not stop smiling as I came off the bus. I shouldn't have been surprised that he proposed since we'd talked about it, but I was genuinely shocked. Out in the open, in front of everyone? It wasn't about the ring or the roses, though they were beautiful. It was about seeing him step outside his everyday self, down on one knee, to profess his love.

Here's the thing—Kingsley was at the University of Connecticut on a student visa. This meant he'd have to return to Jamaica once he was done with his doctorate. I didn't know about this until I came across a letter from the office of U.S. Immigration and Customs sitting on his nightstand. Gone? Leave? It didn't register to me that the man I had fallen in love with, my complete support system, would just pack his stuff and head back to Jamaica.

"You're leaving?"

"Yeah. I might have to," he replied.

"No! You can't leave. I don't want you to leave."

If we got married, he could get his green card to stay in the States. There was no way I would allow the man I loved to leave just like that. So, like always, I had to figure out how to help him while also getting what I wanted. Marriage became the only answer that made sense. Our passion for one another and his love for my family gave the relationship a stable foundation. Also, our common interests and similar cultural backgrounds made us a perfect fit. I was only eighteen, but I knew this was the right decision. We had discussed the idea of getting married and having kids, and as much as we both were on board, ultimately, I left it to Kingsley to decide what to do next. Thus, when he showed up to the bus with balloons and flowers and down on one knee, I knew my answer would be yes!

Our wedding day was exactly what I envisioned it to be. Like most weddings, our special day was filled with joy and anticipation as we joined our hearts and lives together. Over one hundred and fifty people gathered inside the church, ready to witness our love. I wasn't nervous or scared. Instead, I felt proud, glowing with joy as I stepped out of the car, my hair perfectly styled, and my makeup flawlessly applied. Then there was the dress, and oh my God, was it stunning. It was a breathtaking masterpiece of delicate lace adorned with twinkling sequins that seemed to flow behind me like a cloud as I walked down the aisle. My bouquet was a vibrant mix of white and pink roses, accented with greenery. The day was simply unbelievable.

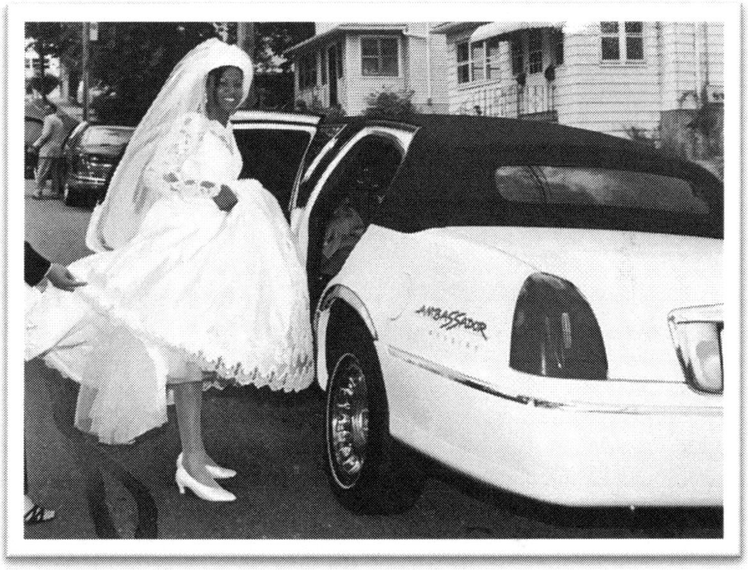

It's the day of my wedding to Kingsley Stewart

My family came together to fund our wedding, as Kingsley and I had no money to spare. We were just college students living off scholarships and loans, barely making ends meet, and I was still just eighteen. The church was decorated with delicate white flowers, ribbons, and other ornaments that brought a sense of elegance to the space. As I made my way down the aisle, lined with fragrant rose petals, Kingsley stood patiently at the altar, his eyes locked onto mine with unwavering adoration.

Despite the joy of the occasion, there was one part of the wedding that I dreaded. My mother's husband, the monster, was to walk me down the aisle. I had no desire for him to have any part in my special day, but I was somehow manipulated into letting it happen. However, I refused to let him or anything else spoil the magic of the moment. I was a married woman, and as much as I did not know what marriage entailed, I was elated.

After the wedding, we had to swiftly return to real life. I was back on track and field, running full-time to pay for college and working part-time at the bank as a teller to pay for our living necessities. Kingsley was still going through the doctoral program, so there wasn't much room to grow financially then. After producing a radio show on campus, he was also starting to blossom as a radio personality. Later in life, Kingsley, also known as Raggashanti, would become one of the West Indies' famous voices. Everyone knew him for the crass topic he discussed, heavy political debates, and his hosting appearances at some of the most significant Caribbean events. In some ways, he was Jamaica's version of Steve Harvey. However, in 1995, he was just Kingsley Stewart—my husband.

Kingsley and I lived in a one-bedroom off-campus apartment behind the track and field where I ran. Very convenient, but certainly not the best. The apartment wasn't much bigger than my dorm room. Sometimes, if I sat there in silence looking around, the off-white concrete block interior walls bordering us gave me the impression I was living in a cell. Around that time, I realized the difference between a house and a home, because the space seemed to be nothing more than four walls and a ceiling without him. Yet, as soon as Kingsley returned, it felt like home again. A place I could relax and call my sanctuary. We were just the perfect match to ignite each other's lives. If you had asked me back then if I thought he and I would ever split, my answer would have easily been, "Not in a million years." But like most stories, there was no happily ever after. Still, it was a story that helped me throughout my life.

He was a great man and everything I'd imagined a husband to be. Then again, I was only eighteen, and there was a chance my expectations for marriage weren't real. Up to that point, the only relationship I had to model my marriage off of was that of my aunt in Jamaica and her husband. They shared the type of love I had been wishing and praying for since I knew I could love a man. However, I'll admit, sometimes I believed what I witnessed from my mother's marriage somehow overshadowed the love I learned.

Consequently, I was going through the process of being a wife all alone. Although my family practically raised me to be a wife, it still didn't come naturally to me. How could I spare some of my love and time for myself while also giving everything I had to a man? I had so many questions, yet not enough answers.

All my life, I witnessed the women that I looked up to take care of their men just as their mothers, aunts, and grandmothers taught them to do. It was part of our culture and the backbone of the women in my family. Take care of your man. Uplift his spirits whenever he needs it. Support whatever passion or desires he may have. Always make sure he's fed and doing well. That's what I knew. However, I'll be lying if I said it was not complicated, because mentally, I was in a world much different than the woman who raised me. By age fifteen, I was on the path to greatness. It would require a high level of ambition and purpose to impact the lives of many. And trying to figure it out would require a level of grace for myself and from the man I called my husband, that did not always come easy.

Truthfully, the one piece of advice I was given was, *"Make sure you wear lingerie or something nice to bed every night."* That's what my aunt Joyce told me. So, that's what I knew. Be kind. Feed your husband. Be his everything! That's it! I didn't learn how to be kind when there was no love between us during dark times. Or what to feed him when he's either gone or there's no money to feed him. Be his everything? Ha! Now that's a whole other book on its own.

By the time I turned twenty, I was getting ready to graduate college and begin my life as an adult in some sense. For the first time, I could not depend on running to push me any further in life. Although running in the Olympics was a dream of mine, the cards were never in my favor. Therefore, I had to meet the world head-on without the crutch of running. My next move would have to be toward a bigger goal. Although Kingsley and I were on the same page, it didn't always feel that way. In our second year of marriage, not much about our living and financial situation changed. We still didn't have much, and the car we shared was still the crap it was when we got it. It was so bad that I was certain it would break down on me every time I drove it.

With my luck, it would happen during a left turn onto a major highway. He tried to work on it every so often, but every time he did, he'd either stop midway or didn't know what the hell he was doing. Either way, it got worse. The radio was missing because he wanted to replace the sound system, but he never did. The driver-side door panel was gone because Kingsley thought he could repair the window that way. The car could barely go over a specific speed limit without causing issues. It was just a complete mess. I started to do a lot of reflecting on my life upon graduation, while also looking ahead. Practically my entire time at UCONN, I was a married working woman. I didn't experience the college life that some of my friends and others did, and admittedly, I often wondered what I was missing out on.

Now, don't get it twisted, I enjoyed being married. After all, nothing was more romantic than sharing my life with someone I considered the love of my life. However, that didn't neglect real-life feelings disturbing me as well. As a wife, I was expected to keep no secrets from my husband. That much I knew. Yet, the deeper into our marriage Kingsley and I went, the harder it was to open up and share everything, which left me wondering with thoughts that no married woman should have.

Through an interesting turn of events, I became a stockbroker soon after I left UCONN, and my thoughts about life began to shift—some for good, and some not so good. I'll never claim to be perfect. That much I knew.

It's funny, because once I graduated, I spent countless hours applying for jobs I was either qualified or overqualified for but received no callbacks. It was frustrating and nerve-wracking. Then, the one call I received came for a position from Salomon Smith Barney, one of the largest stockbroker firms in the country. Initially, I wasn't going to apply because I thought there was no way they'd hire me if all the other companies had not called me back. And had it not been for Kingsley forcing me to apply for the position, I would have never done so. So, I did. I challenged myself to go for the job, and by doing so, they hired me after just one interview.

Kingsley was still working on his doctorate and working at the university. We moved out of Storrs and into a three-bedroom apartment in Hartford. Kingsley was taking the pursuit of his radio personality career more seriously while I was diving deeper into my career with Salomon Smith Barney. The job quickly became an addiction, and I badly wanted to be the best. The people I was surrounded by at the office had an intense determination to succeed—more drive and focus than I had ever seen from anyone else. Until then, outside the track and field, Kingsley was the only ambitious person I knew.

Furthermore, while working at Salomon Smith Barney, I was introduced to new life experiences and people. Athletes, celebrities, millionaires, and billionaires. People whose aim was not just to have a single big house, family, and a car, but instead, they wanted to be wealthy! They desired to own all the nice cars and have several lovely homes across the country. I was not interested in jumping in bed with or committing to any one of them. But there was a sudden realization that there was more to life.

Before I knew it, I found myself running in the fast lane while Kingsley remained in the safe zone, far behind. That difference slowly caused a rift between him and me. Then, I came to the realization that

I was too young to be a wife. Hell, I had not even become the woman I needed to be. And although Kingsley was the ideal husband that every woman dreamed of finding, I felt it still wasn't enough for me, particularly at that point in my life.

One morning, I woke up and realized I never had a passionate love for Kingsley. Instead, it was more of respect and admiration. The way I loved and cared for my uncle when I was young in Jamaica. Then, I stood in front of a mirror, staring at the woman before me, asking her the question I had longed to ask: "Why are you married?"

Kingsley must have felt the same way, because when I told him I no longer wanted to be with him, he didn't ask any questions and barely responded. Rather than fight for our relationship, he shrugged and said, "Okay." Four years of marriage, and just like that, it was over.

The following day, Kingsley packed up his belongings and left. We continued living our lives, pretending that we had never met each other. Despite this, I stayed married to Kingsley until he could obtain his green card, determined to help him achieve the American dream. Unfortunately, Kingsley's pride prevented him from accepting my assistance. As a result, he became cold, distant, and started to regard me with scorn.

"Fuck you! I don't want your pity or your crocodile tears! I'll do it on my own," he said.

He was wounded, and I couldn't blame him because I was hurting as well. At times, I felt like I deserved anything he said about me. By divorcing Kingsley, I took more than just my love away from him; I deprived him of a family. A family that he had desperately wanted to have. We were separated for about six months when he finally filed for divorce. Nothing probably made sense to Kingsley because of the heartache I caused him, and as much as I wanted to give him more answers, I had none. However, the truth is, I knew I had to walk away so that he could one day find the one who heard the calling of his soul, the one who truly loved him.

In the spring of 2006, my grandmother passed away. Not only was I hurt, but it also left an empty void in my heart. During that time, I was unable to make sense of anything. I was broken beyond measure, and had it not been for the comfort of Kingsley, I don't know if I would have ever recovered.

Kingsley loved my grandmother so much that it affected him just as much when she passed away as it did me. By the time he returned to my life, his radio personality career had taken off, making him one of Jamaica's well-known figures. My family asked him to do the eulogy for my grandmother's funeral, which brought him back into my life nearly eight years later. We had not spoken since our divorce. I mean, no exchange of any words at all. And there he was, giving the parting words at my grandmother's funeral. Following that day, he and I started rekindling the love that we once had. I wasn't sure if it was due to my brokenness or that I was in a dark, vulnerable space, but something brought us back together. Either way, I wanted him, and he wanted me.

Kingsley left his career behind and relocated to Florida to be with me. At that time, I already had a four-year-old daughter from a previous relationship. Having Natalia deepened my understanding of love, compassion, and selflessness. She profoundly influenced my outlook on life, determination, and various aspects of my identity. It prompted me to reevaluate my goals, reassess my values, and make choices that aligned with the needs of both myself and my daughter. Just as I was motivated to provide the best possible life for Natalia, I wanted to do the same for Kingsley.

Once again, he came into my life when I needed his light to shine the most. We were doing this again, and even spoke about remarrying and doing it correctly. It was like starting all over, and we quickly found our rhythm as if we had never split. Or so I thought. It didn't take long before I saw the romantic love for me begin to fade from Kingsley's eyes. On top of that, he struggled with the transition to Florida, mostly because he was no longer a celebrity. No more of that high, knowing that some stranger on the street might randomly scream your name. In Jamaica, he was Raggashanti. But in America, he was simply Kingsley Stewart. That realization wasn't easy for him. At the same time, I was coming to grips with my grandmother's death, and the vulnerability that was once there was no longer a thing. I became unbroken, and it was apparent that as much as I loved Kingsley, he would never be the one for me.

We were no longer sexually or mentally compatible. We barely communicated. To make matters worse, we had no common interest to glue ourselves together. I could handle it all, except for the lack of intimacy. That was an uphill battle that I was not looking to take on. At the same time, I didn't want to be the horrible person to tell him to leave for a second time, but I needed to do something, or else I felt like I would explore sex outside of my relationship. I was not prepared to do that because that's not who I was. One man, one love, is all I ever wanted. Although I was a sexual person, and he was not, I simply could not hurt him by doing such a thing.

I went on for days trying to find a way to tell him how I truly felt, but each time I did, I'd think to myself, *I can't leave this man again, can I?* If I broke his heart, this would be the absolute worst. Didn't matter, because before I could tell him that I wanted it to be over, Kingsley entered the house one day, stood there with a face of utter nonchalance, and said, "I'm leaving." I was neither shocked nor dispirited. I didn't say anything this time since I felt the same, which was a huge relief.

Before we got divorced, I shared my feelings about no longer wanting to be with Kingsley with Aunt Joyce. She was the most progressive woman I knew at the time. Having been raised with her father's wealth, she stood out amongst the other women in my family, especially with her speech and mannerisms.

"Leaving a good man is not the manners a young woman should display," she said.

Aunt Joyce gave me the spiritual and relational wisdom of working through marriage during tough times. That's the day my aunt shared that she sent her husband on vacation whenever they had spats and conflicts, but she never left the marriage. She sure picked a good time to tell me.

Despite Kingsley giving up his entire career and moving to the United States to be with me, I was ultimately glad when he decided to leave. It was best for our happiness and friendship. In the spring of 2007, that marked the end of my relationship with Kingsley. Without him, I would have never known what a man's kindness and love looked like. Even though Aunt Verona and Breddah displayed what true love looked like, Kingsley allowed me to put it into practice and learn so much. But unfortunately, that did not prevent me from continuing down the path of bad decisions when it came to finding love.

CHAPTER 8

FINDING ME

"More than anything, I knew that the more I saved, the more I could accomplish. The more I accomplished, the more I could give back to my family and community."

Everything we do as adults can be attributed to our childhood, and I am no exception. My kind and loving spirit is a direct result of those who surrounded me during those formative years. My grandmother, Rose Jones, played a pivotal role in shaping the person I am today. Her spirit lives on, and I am forever grateful for her influence over me. That's why when anyone asks me how I'm so humble, obedient, kind, and loving, I tell them it's because of people like my grandmother.

My memories of my grandmother are so colorful and vivid that I can see her clearly whenever I close my eyes. Imagine a petite lady with a huge heart. Her silver hair fell in soft waves over her shoulders, and her squinty almond-shaped eyes gleamed joyfully, especially when she laughed. Every wrinkle on her face told a story, making her beauty all the more remarkable.

She was a woman of few words; her actions spoke for her. I remember the days I would watch her bustling around the yard as she cooked Sunday dinner with just a few leftover items from the week. Sometimes, it didn't look like much, but somehow it was, and no matter what, she always had enough to feed the children in the town, some of whom I later discovered were not even related to me. Didn't matter who came knocking on her door; my grandmother would serve each of them her tasty cooking. It was her way of spreading love and kindness to the world, and it's a legacy that lives on in me. And despite anything she was going through, she always did everything with a sense of happiness and purpose, as if there was no greater feeling she could acquire.

While everyone gathered around to enjoy the food she prepared, my grandmother stood to the side, watching us eat. She rarely ate with us and never worried about eating as much as she cared about ensuring we had enough. Sometimes, I would see her off to the side, standing alone, and I'd walk over and offer her some of my food. But she would always just smile and say, "*No, Trisha. You eat. I'll get some later.*"

There were days when it was saddening to know she didn't eat with us because hardly any food was left. It was to the point where she had to drink the water that she used to cook to satisfy her hunger, drinking it as if it were soup. Yet no matter what she was dealing with, she never complained. She was content to know that her sacrifice was a small price to pay for the happiness of those she loved. Her ethereal presence commanded attention as she gracefully moved through any room, like an angel descending from heavens. Her radiant smile, adorned with a touch of serenity. That is who my grandmother was.

As I navigate through the complexities of adulthood, I find myself channeling the same moral compass that my grandmother instilled in me. From the smallest daily decisions to the weightier matters of life, her wisdom echoes in my mind, guiding me toward the path of compassion and grace. For example, there was a time when I rented my first house to a family that was headed by a minister, an ex-military man and his wife—Joseph and Sandra Milton. They seemed like the most loving and loyal family that I ever met. Well, I was wrong. They were the complete opposite. Conniving, lying, and deceitful individuals with fucked up morals. The day they moved in, they paid me the first month's rent and security deposit, signed the lease, and after that, stopped paying completely.

Due to my kindness, young age, and the fact that they believed I had money, they figured they didn't have to pay, deciding it was better to take advantage of a young, single mother. No matter how much I pleaded and begged them to pay the rent as we agreed, they just wouldn't. This went on for about six months. I kept asking them why they were taking advantage of me, but they told me to stop calling *THEIR* house, and then they would hang up on me. I stopped calling. Although I wanted to do some bad things because I hated being taken advantage of, my grandmother's spirit was right there to guide me to handle it the right way, the only way. Therefore, I got a lawyer who was able to get them evicted.

My grandmother's teachings have seeped into the fabric of my being, shaping me into the person I am today. It's not just my grandmother who left an unforgettable imprint in my DNA. My aunt, too, filled me with endless love and kindness that few could match. Her presence was almost supernatural, like an angel walking among us, leaving behind a trail of goodness and light. These two remarkable women are the secret ingredients that make up the essence of who stands before you.

As a little girl, I would often dream in colors. They were vivid, yet always simple and untainted by materialistic desires. So, I wasn't the girl who played with dolls, nor did I yearn to live in a grand mansion with the fanciest cars in my driveway. The thought of wearing extravagant clothes and adorned with precious jewelry never once crossed my mind, either. I never envisioned any of that stuff. Nowadays, people will tell me how they've always wanted to be wealthy just so they could buy random things—things I have yet to even consider. One guy told me that at the age of six, he dreamed of running a Fortune 500 company that exceeded billions of dollars. Six?! That was certainly not the case for me. In my mind, money was an abstract concept that was reserved for grownups, and even then, I had no real understanding of it.

My aspirations were focused solely on being a good person, just like my grandmother and aunt. The thought of owning a successful business with a net worth of over a million, let alone a billion dollars, never crossed my mind. I didn't know the true value of money and success until I arrived in America. It wasn't until years later, when I began to earn money on my own, that I understood the key to unlocking all of life's treasures was through currency. A veil had been lifted from my eyes, and I saw for the first time what money could buy and do for me and others. Regardless of that, for every dollar I received, I tried to save it. That's what I taught myself to do as a girl and what I would do as a woman to achieve success.

I remember playing in the yard with my cousins in Jamaica when my aunt would shout, "Trisha! Go to the store for me." She often sent me to Ms. Coolie's shop to buy a bottle of wine, which was her way of unwinding in the yard. With just five dollars in my pocket, I would eagerly head to the store, my heart racing with anticipation. The market was always a busy hub of color and noise. I would maneuver my skinny body through the crowd, passing the array of fruits, jerk chicken, and sweet treats, to reach the counter and pay for the wine bottle.

"Trisha, you have everything?" she'd ask.

"Yes. Thank you, Ms. Coolie."

I would hand her five dollars, and she would count out two dollars and thirty cents and place it in my hand, which I carefully tucked in my pocket. When I would return home to Aunt Verona, I'd give her the money, and without fail, she would give me a dollar and fifteen cents as a small reward for my hard work. I never cared to buy anything, so I just held on to it as if it were a keepsake. The truth was that the things that brought me the most joy in Jamaica, like spending time with loved ones, enjoying my grandmother's meals, and sharing laughter, didn't require any money, so there was nothing I could ever use the money for. Despite that, it wasn't about the amount of money but rather the sense of accomplishment it gave me. I knew my aunt didn't expect me to use the money in any particular way, but I felt a responsibility to make it count, to spend it wisely, and make it last just like she did.

Saving money became like the roots of a tree, grounding me in the face of life's challenges. Early on, I learned that having more of anything— whether water in a bucket, seeds in a field, or distance to run—could be a helpful advantage. Like a farmer tending to his crops, I carefully nurtured my savings, adding to it bit by bit until it grew into something substantial. More than anything, I knew that the more I saved, the more I could accomplish. The more I accomplished, the more I could give back to my family and community and ultimately invest in their dreams and future as well.

After moving to America, I continued practicing the art of saving like it was a game or a skill necessary for survival. At the beginning of each school week, my mother would give my sister and me ten dollars for lunch. That ten dollars was to be used throughout the week. While most kids eagerly lined up to purchase their food, I would either receive a voucher for free lunch or wait until I got home to eat. I never went to the corner store for snacks, either. Not only because I wasn't allowed to, but I also preferred to keep my money for as long as possible.

By the end of the week, my sister had no money left, but that wasn't the case for me. I always had five dollars left in my pocket, a small fortune that felt like a secret treasure. Over time, I became even more skilled at saving, looking for every opportunity to stash away any earnings. But no matter how well I hid my money, my mother always seemed to find it and take it without warning, claiming she was putting it in a bank for me.

So, I kept on saving, filling my bucket with every spare coin and dollar, planting every seed of opportunity. And as I watched my savings grow, I knew that I was building a foundation for a better life—one that was rooted in hard work, determination, and the belief that anything was possible.

Life has taught me many invaluable lessons through a ridiculous amount of trial and error. Luckily for me, I was raised to be fearless, so embracing challenges has always been part of my character. It's been that way since I could remember. In high school, I excelled in sports like volleyball and tennis with no prior experience and all alone. Gymnastics, in particular, posed a challenge. However, while I knew I wasn't the best, I never let that discourage me from striving to give my best, practicing vigorously, and learning from my failures. I knew that success was within reach with each effort I gave.

Oftentimes, people would ask me where I learned how to be such a successful entrepreneur. "Who was your mentor?" is the first question they would ask, or what books did I read? Truthfully, that question is relatively easy to answer yet tricky to explain. Here's why—my mother, a Jamaican immigrant, had an untiring focus on survival. She was only used to working hard to provide for our family, ensuring we always had the basic necessities—food on the table and a roof over our heads. Therefore, growing up as an immigrant child, I struggled to find my place in the world, a world that was entirely different from the one my mother had established for herself. Through no fault of her own, she didn't have the resources or mentorship to offer because her primary focus was to make ends meet by any means necessary. It became clear that the responsibility to forge my path toward success would rest on my shoulders.

So, from the moment I started working as a teenager, and even when I started training as a runner, I learned everything I could by watching everyone around me, or at least asking questions to gain enough knowledge to move on to the next. I used everything I experienced as a skillset. When I was going door-to-door, begging for donations to go to Junior Olympics, I was sharpening my sales skills. Those days spent training and running while others were slacking off built the endurance for the long hours and clearing hurdles that popped up along the journey.

College life was an entirely new challenge, one where I felt out of place. I stood out, different from most of the other students, and wondered if I was even on the same level as them. However, I refused to let feelings of inadequacy hold me back. Instead, I pushed myself harder, working tirelessly to overcome my doubts, knowing that success was within my grasp with enough hard work and focus.

My journey to success was paved with sacrifices that challenged me physically, mentally, emotionally, and definitely socially. For a long time, I had no friends. It was just me and my kids going through the grind. I had to push myself to the limit and display unparalleled determination and resilience. But all the sacrifice, hard work, and sleepless nights paid off in the end, allowing me to take immense pride in the successes that I have achieved. While many may see the accomplishments I have garnered today, they remain oblivious to the trials and tribulations I overcame to get here.

Through an interesting turn of events, I became a stockbroker. Like a ship lost at sea, I wandered aimlessly after graduating from the University of Connecticut, unsure what direction to take. My mother's words tossed aside the dream I had clung to for so long of becoming a superintendent, leaving me stuck in the middle of nowhere. She believed I lacked the patience to be a teacher. Everything I had done up to that point was preparing me to be a teacher, including my major—Early Childhood Education. I had it mapped out. I would teach for several years and then go into the superintendent role; my mother changed those plans.

Although we didn't have the best relationship at times, she always seemed to have the best advice. It was her special gift. So, with the newspaper in my hands, I set out in search of any job that could give me purpose, determined to work anywhere except the food industry. It was my husband at the time, Kingsley, who suggested I apply at Salomon Smith & Barney, one of the most prestigious stock brokerage firms in the country. Despite my doubts, I summoned the courage to interview, determined to be myself and sell my potential.

As I walked into that room, my nerves and excitement collided like waves crashing on the shore. The interviewers' eyes scrutinized me as I spoke, and I poured my heart and soul into every answer, hoping to impress them. It was a moment of truth, a test of my worth, and I was determined to succeed. Honestly, I sold the shit out of myself. So much so, that they hired me on the spot. It was as if fate had intervened, just as it had for my mother when she arrived in America and was hired on the spot as a bank teller after leaving behind her job as a housekeeper at a New York mansion. For my mother and me, an opportunity had come knocking when we least expected it, and it was up to us to seize it. The future was uncertain, but I knew I had found a new purpose, direction, and career that would challenge me in ways I could never have imagined.

At Salomon Smith & Barney, I started off working in administration as a planner, handling meetings and training at their national trainer center. It was a job I took at the time because I needed money. I wasn't even sure where it would lead me, but after watching the seasoned brokers train, I became fascinated by the stockbroking world. As they chatted about market trends and investment strategies, I absorbed every word, dreaming of one day joining their ranks. I made roughly $23,000 annually, watching some of these men and women make millions.

After gathering enough information about the business, I started to think about my next step in life and convinced myself that being a stockbroker would be that next step. So, with high hopes, I decided to apply for the stockbroker position. In doing so, I totally broke protocol since I was unaware that intra-company hiring required different steps. Instead of speaking to someone in the office about my interest and applying internally, I submitted my application to corporate as if I were a random jobseeker.

Funny enough, the person I needed to talk to the entire time was in the office where I worked. His name was Mark Willis. Mark was the director of the national training center. He and I didn't communicate as much, but his reputation spoke volumes. I often saw him roaming the building after hours, as I was always the last to leave. According to Mark, I was a dedicated worker who always exceeded yesterday's effort. From daunting tasks at work to something as simple as finishing a writing up reports to fixing up the office space. No matter what I was working on, I wouldn't stop until I was completely done. That was one of the few lessons I learned from running. I never did anything to compete with others. It was always to please my own efforts. While running, I competed with myself as others floated around. The same concept translated into my work and the building of my company.

Nowadays, as an entrepreneur, I remind others that the same dedication and work ethic that they bring to their 9-to-5 can be applied to their businesses. Just like a business owner who must wear many hats, an employee must also be able to adapt to new situations, make critical decisions, and work with others to achieve a common goal. Otherwise, you should not start a business.

I took pride in my work and gave it my all every day since I never knew who might be watching. At Salomon Smith & Barney, I learned that my hard work and dedication did not go unnoticed when I was called into the office. My heart pounded because I assumed I was being fired.

"Trisha, I didn't know you wanted to be a broker." Mark approached me. "Had I known, I would have been grooming you this whole time. Why didn't you tell me?" he inquired.

A sigh of relief came over me. I admitted that the idea had only occurred to me after seeing the potential financial gains of the other brokers. I wanted that! Living a life totally in contrast to where I came from before? Heck yes, I wanted to be a broker. It was the first time I could envision myself coming from the poorest of Jamaica to the slums of Hartford to now living in a beautiful home with nice cars parked in the driveway. He looked at me skeptically, asking how I planned to succeed in such a cutthroat industry. I stumbled through my answer, trying to sound confident despite the doubt gnawing at me. I told him I had connections as a University of Connecticut alum, which would help garner the results I needed to succeed. To my surprise, Mark didn't dismiss me. Instead, he seemed confident in my plan, which gave me the push I needed to become a stockbroker.

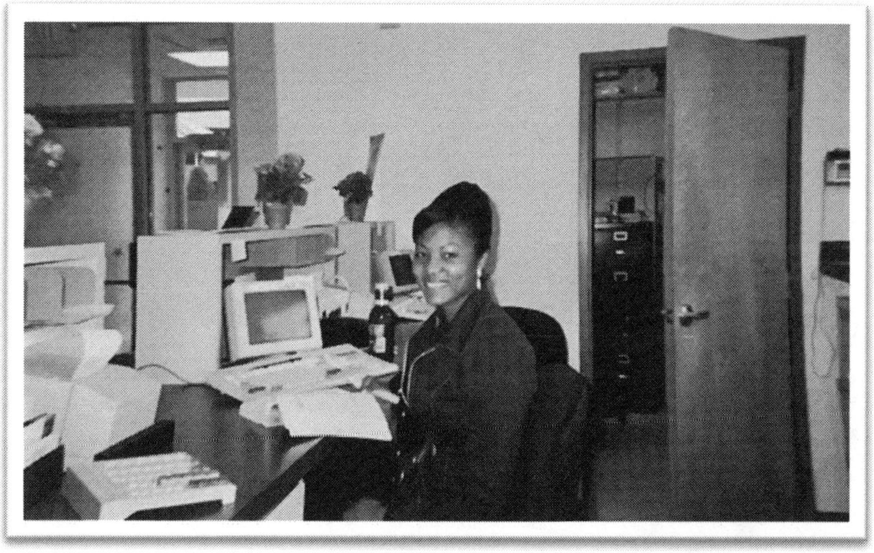

Just another day at work

After we negotiated my salary, Mark and others began teaching me the ropes of the business. But it wasn't easy. I'd have to teach myself the things I couldn't grasp from them in a simpler form. They'd trained me tirelessly in stockbroking, drowning me in a sea of information. We would spend hours reviewing graphs and charts, analyzing the market, and strategizing the best moves. What started as three months of training turned into six as we delved deeper into the intricacies of the business. Before I knew it, I was finally deemed ready to take on the role of a stockbroker.

Pride swelled in my chest as I sat behind my desk, surrounded by the fancy gadgets and tools of the trade. The opportunity to further prove myself came, and I faced it head-on. I had to travel to Boston to present a business plan, armed with everything I had learned on my own while watching the other guys in the training program. It was nerve-wracking, but I knew I had to give it my all. After all, I had a lot to prove. I was the only Black woman in all of New England working for Salomon Smith & Barney, and at twenty-two, the youngest of nearly 57,000 brokers.

My journey to success was challenging, especially considering I was still healing from the wounds of a divorce. Still, it felt special and refreshing to know I was headed in the right direction. I had come a long way. For goodness' sake, I was the daughter of a woman who once spent her evenings cleaning houses to make ends meet. Knowing I could go from a girl running barefoot in the mountainous terrains of Jamaica to a woman making millions brought a sense of pride. Despite my drive for excellence, there were times when my hunger for success took over my vision for love. I had caused hurt to Kingsley at the expense of my true happiness. That I am guilty of, and although I was still trying to forgive myself, I knew I had to keep pushing forward, one step at a time.

As a broker, I learned to navigate the choppy waters of rejection effortlessly. The constant stream of "no's" didn't faze me. Besides, I knew I had two choices: sink or swim, and because I had already been at the bottom, heading to the top was the only direction for me.

I had grown accustomed to creating my own "yes" and finding ways to turn every setback into a stepping stone toward my goals. The first few years tested my will and determination, but I knew the rewards were worth it because I saw it with my own eyes. Like a sailor riding the course through uncharted waters, I pressed on with confidence, knowing that the horizon had limitless potential for those willing to brave the storm.

The average stockbroker could expect to generate between 1% and 1.5% in revenue on their managed assets. After the brokerage firm takes its cut, the broker may only see 30% to 40% of that revenue in their pocket. As a new broker, I would have to work tirelessly to accumulate at least $10,000,000 in new client assets to earn a meager income of $30,000 to $40,000 in the first year. However, I was making triple that in my first year. Many of my clients were professional athletes, thanks to my referrals from Tom Seaborn, a good friend and partner early on in my career.

Athletes often like to network and talk business at parties and events, allowing me to have fun and handle business simultaneously. That was how I closed some deals and serviced some clients. However, it was important that I not cross any professional boundaries.

I was young and making money, but at some point, it wasn't enough. Every night when I went home, I was alone. Yes, financially, I was fulfilled, but emotionally, I was empty for many days. Always out on the road for long periods of time became exhausting, and the desire to be a mother continued to tug at me. I went from not knowing the value of a dollar to managing portfolios in the millions if not billions.

And despite all that, I knew I needed to get out of the business if I was ever going to have the love and family I so desperately wanted.

Fate has a way of opening doors when you least expect it, and that's precisely what happened to me on the night I met a friend for dinner. At that time, I was on the fence about leaving my career as a stockbroker behind. As we sat down at Max Downtown, my friend's husband joined us, and our conversation soon turned to business and professional matters. He spoke highly of his career in pharmaceutical sales, and I was immediately intrigued. I had heard of pharmaceutical sales before, but I knew little about the intricacies or the earning potential. However, as he shared more about his work, my interest grew. In just an hour, my life took a turn, and I found a new path that would change everything.

The one thing he said that really piqued my interest was that all the clients were given to them. What? Are you kidding me? All the clients were given to the reps?! That alone sold me. So, that meant the company would provide the sales reps with potential clients, and all the reps had to do was close the deal. As a stockbroker, I had to go out and find my potential clients, and God, was it a constant grind. Most of this was done through heavy networking, socializing in different venues, kissing up, late-night partying, and endless lunches. There was no end to what you would do to get ahold of someone's assets.

Nevertheless, being a stockbroker offered me certain skills, like the ability to grind harder, understand people's level of interest versus a bullshitter, and of course, how to sell my ass off. Negotiating and convincing was all I did, and since I mastered that, it was safe to say I would be successful as a pharmaceutical sales rep.

After that dinner, I began researching the pharmaceutical sales business, which led me to apply for an open position with a company known as Takeda Pharmaceutical. Just like after my interview with Salomon Smith & Barney, I was hired on the spot. Based on my experience as a stockbroker, they were able to see my value and offer me a really great salary to start with. Even better, they gave me a thriving territory with a growing client base.

I quickly discovered that the life of a pharmaceutical sales representative is a whirlwind of fast-paced demands and multiple responsibilities to manage daily. My schedule was consumed by constant travel, hopping from one location to another, engaging with physicians and medical professionals. During that time, I found myself shuttling back and forth between Connecticut and Florida, driven by my budding romance with Ricky. In all honesty, I was excelling in my career, making significant strides. However, the universe had different plans in store for me as I unexpectedly learned of my pregnancy with Natalia.

While this was always a cherished desire, the dynamics of my long-distance relationship, coupled with the challenges of work and travel, intensified. Gradually, I witnessed a darker side of Ricky, one tainted by jealousy and possessiveness. Recognizing my growing fear of his behavior, I realized that my safety and well-being were paramount, compelling me to create distance and prioritize my own peace.

However, despite the challenges, I remained convinced that we could work through our struggles and become a family. Natalia was ten months old when I made the difficult decision to uproot my entire life from Connecticut and move to Florida. I didn't want Natalia growing up anywhere near my stepfather, which helped make the decision easier. Now, I was in Florida, covering territories throughout central Florida and trying to give Natalia a chance at having a relationship with her father.

Each day, I was tasked with meeting with doctors, nurses, and other medical professionals to educate them on the benefits of the company's products. In order for me to get paid, I had to make sure they were knowledgeable about the drugs they were buying as well.

That's the thing about the pharmaceutical business. It can have you up from the financial rewards of one day, with the potential to earn high commissions based on sales performance. Then, on the next, it's leaving you stressed the fuck out, requiring long hours and frequent travel. There were times when I had to get creative to demonstrate my level of commitment and hard work. For instance, when I was in Florida and didn't have anyone to watch Natalia, I would fly to Connecticut, drop her off with my mom, then catch a flight to Canada for meetings and training. Afterward, I would fly back to Connecticut to pick up my baby and bring her back to Florida with me.

Soon, my work in the industry became tumultuous. The company frequently changed bosses, leaving me confused about who I was working with from one quarter to the next. To make matters worse, I was the only Black representative in the Southeast, surrounded by a sea of white colleagues. One of the company's policies required us to inventory the drugs we sold. Many reps kept their inventory in private storage, but I decided to keep mine at home for convenience. One evening, the current boss, a woman, came to my home to check my inventory. However, she seemed more interested in my house and how I could afford it than the task at hand.

"This is a nice house. How can you afford it?" she asked.

Her intrusive questions annoyed me, even after I explained that I was a former stockbroker who had saved a significant amount of money. Despite earning a base salary of only $30,000, I had made over half a million dollars as a stockbroker. I tried to live within my means, treating myself to luxuries only occasionally, and of course, saving all my commission checks.

My lifestyle and home seemed to somehow disturb this woman, because from that day on, she made it her business to make my life hell. It was as if her number one agenda was to get me fired. She would frequently write me up without reason or explanation. After much of the run-around and bullshit, I decided to apply for other jobs because I had lost patience for the foolishness. Besides, it was another time in my life when I knew I had to move on.

As fate would have it, my next opportunity came through an unexpected referral from a representative at a competing company. I still remember the feeling of anticipation as I walked into the interview. I had prepared for days, researching the company and rehearsing my answers to potential questions. To my surprise, the interviewer barely glanced at my resume before declaring, "You're hired." The joy I felt at that moment was tempered by the realization that this job required me to move yet again. It seemed that with every new opportunity came a new sacrifice, but I was determined to make it work. Once again, Natalia and I were moving. This time we were relocating from Riverview to Indian Harbor Beach, Florida, more than 145 miles away.

With my transition to a new company, success seemed to be a faithful companion, as I consistently climbed the ladder in the company. Each passing year brought forth a new promotion. One particularly notable promotion led me to work with doctors in the highly sought-after field of cardiopulmonary medicine. Yet, my good fortune did not halt there. The company recognized my exceptional performance and decided to invest in my growth by sending me to the University of Kentucky for specialized training in pulmonary disease. This invaluable opportunity afforded me the privilege of studying at Kentucky's renowned medical school and being trained by some of the country's top professors. As a result, I achieved a coveted certificate as a pulmonary specialist, marking a significant milestone in my flourishing career.

Furthermore, I was granted the opportunity to attend New York University, where I went through demanding training to obtain certification in the field of cardiovascular medicine. Through both certifications, I embarked on a journey to pursue my MBA as a full-time student, all while navigating the challenges of being a single mother. The result of these achievements allowed me to exhale deeply and fully embrace the moment. My heart was filled with both gratitude for the hurdles overcome and excitement for the path ahead. Despite the initial struggles and a sense of not quite fitting in during my early years at UCONN, I had accomplished something truly extraordinary. It was the result of my unwavering determination and remaining faithful to my passion, which ushered opportunities into my life at precisely the right time.

I was going into eight years in the industry, and during that time, I was simultaneously finishing my doctorate, all while being a mother to Natalia. Everything was going great until my last promotion that landed me in California as a cardiopulmonary specialist. That meant I would be working with doctors who specialized in cardiology and pulmonary disease. The company's standard was to conduct a grueling manager-led interview process, but due to my accolades and performance in the company, they chose to overlook the interview and hired me based on my background. I had been number one in sales every year and held the claim of Rookie of the Year and Sales Rep of the Year. Also, I had received every award they could give over the past five years. So once again, Natalia and I hit the road, headed to Corona, California to start a new life. However, I would not be prepared for all the shit that would soon follow.

I should have known there were going to be issues when I met the manager and the first thing he said was, *"Oh! I didn't know you were Black."* At the time, I didn't think much of it, as I was not used to racism, having grown up in Jamaica where classism was more prevalent. I assumed it was just an observation and didn't dwell on it. However, it quickly became clear that my skin color had become an issue for him. Despite my highly qualified and decorated professional background, including a pending doctorate, he began making my life miserable with unnecessary reports and trivial demands. He even handed me a letter giving me thirty days to move into my assigned territory, which was Orange County, California. He knew I couldn't afford it, and by forcing me to move to Orange County, that was his way trying to fuck me over.

Corona was fifteen miles outside of my assigned territory, but I had received clearance to live there before I moved out to California. However, upon my arrival, my manager had a change of heart and demanded that I move to Orange County, despite it being unnecessary and not hindering my work. Early on, he began to give me all sorts of fits about everything, making my job harder than it needed to be. It was a shock to witness his actions, and it was disheartening to realize that my skin color was the cause of his behavior.

To make matters worse, I was paired with a deceitful and backstabbing colleague who happened to be a white woman. During our presentations to doctors, she would pretend to be nice, but in private, she was cold and always treated me like I was some sort of peasant. The negative energy from work spilled into my home, causing me to constantly complain about their actions to everyone while taking away energy I could have spent playing with Natalia. In a nutshell, it was a living hell. Nonetheless, it was all for a reason I would discover later in life. Through that situation, I found the motivation I needed to venture into the world of true entrepreneurship and start my own business, eventually becoming one of the wealthiest women in America.

CHAPTER 9

RISE OF THE EMPIRE

"More than anything, I knew that the more I saved, the more I could accomplish. The more I accomplished, the more I could give back to my family and community."

As I stood there on the soil, overlooking the construction site of my soon-to-be beach house in Portland, Jamaica, I couldn't help but feel a sense of excitement and anticipation wash over me. The builders and workers around me were fussing about my heels clacking on the beams, saying it wasn't safe. It's too bad that they couldn't see that I was walking on clouds. At least that's what it felt like. The breeze carried the promise of tomorrow, and I felt goosebumps rise on my skin. The beach house wasn't even completed, but I could already see it.

Steps from the house would lead straight down to the beach, providing a secluded paradise for me and my family. Beyond our little oasis was a high-end luxury villa that lined up to a beachfront park. It was overwhelming to think about what God had done for me as I stood there in awe, speechless. Soon, the sounds faded away, and I found myself standing in my happy place. The realization that my kids and I would soon have the opportunity to enjoy this paradise whenever we desired felt surreal. However, it was the beckoning of the water that made me truly feel like I had finally achieved my dreams.

By the time I was sixteen, it had become crystal clear that I had no choice but to succeed by any means necessary. My surroundings had opened my eyes to a reality where living life any other way was not an option.

During my junior year of high school, I formed a close bond with two girls, both named Stephanie—Stephanie Roberts and Stephanie Little-John. Each of them possessed unique qualities. Little-John came from a privileged background, with her father being the pastor of a church. Many people saw her as an angel, someone who could do no wrong. Then there was Stephanie Roberts. I spent most of my time with her because she, like me, came from a home that others might consider less fortunate. However, she was the brightest and most intelligent girl I knew. Consistently excelling in advanced placement courses and always making the honor roll, she stood out from the rest. This contrasted with my own academic struggles that began back in junior high school. In fact, my performance was so poor that school officials had considered holding me back.

As a result, when I entered high school, I was placed in classes that didn't challenge me at all. I despised that situation. It only intensified when I witnessed Stephanie Roberts thriving in her advanced courses. This ignited a strong desire within me to do more, to want more for myself. Roberts encouraged me to switch to more challenging classes, and with her guidance and support, I confidently walked into the office of Mrs. Whittaker, a guidance counselor, and demanded to be placed in accelerated courses. Initially, she dismissed my request, claiming that I couldn't handle the curriculum. However, I refused to give up until I was placed in the more rigorous classes. Eventually, I succeeded in being enrolled in those courses, and with Stephanie's assistance, I began to flourish academically.

At the age of sixteen, Stephanie Roberts took me to the Department of Children and Families to pick up food stamps for her mother. I didn't question it because Stephanie had a knack for getting what she wanted. She was a resourceful individual and always found a way to navigate through any situation. In fact, she even claimed she could help me obtain food stamps, too. Although I was initially confused about how a high school junior could qualify for government assistance, I decided to go along with it, albeit with some hesitation. I thought to myself, *"Why not? What's the worst that can happen?"* Little did I know that this pivotal moment would serve as a turning point in my life, as I came to realize that nothing would stand in the way of my success.

The moment we entered the office, the weight of the situation hit me real hard. Despair and fatigue were etched on the faces of the women around us, and the cries of children echoed through the halls. I couldn't ignore the feeling that something was wrong. Then, a desperate mother approached the counter and begged for assistance, only to be met with coldness and indifference from the clerk. My heart broke to see the woman accept the clerk's behavior because what she needed was more important. At that moment, I realized I never wanted to be in her position. No one would ever make me feel helpless or inferior, as if I were a peasant. Instead, I wanted to be the one who helped women like her. I was determined to succeed and make a difference in the world.

* * *

By the time I turned thirty, I realized my purpose. That's only after going through a grueling experience. Like many others who have found their purpose, I wasn't sure how to manifest it into reality. The thing is, I understood that purpose wasn't something you just thought of as you climbed out of your bed or mustered up after a hot shower. Instead, it is something that happens when you intentionally act upon your gift, skill, niche, talent, or love. Fortunately, I discovered that at the right time and place.

Before discovering my purpose, I was in the midst of establishing my own business while simultaneously seeking an escape from another company where I was constantly undervalued. Despite my efforts, it seemed that I could not change their prejudiced views of me. Therefore, I had to find a way out. However, with my daughter Natalia by my side, I knew that any decision I made had to be based on her needs rather than mine. I did not want Natalia to move around any longer, and I refused to be in a position where I was continuously traveling across America, too busy to witness my daughter's growth. Countless nights were spent pondering my next move on the path to success.

"Why don't you just do your own shit? Why you working for someone else anyway? You have all these degrees, right? Create your own business and do your own shit," my boyfriend at the time, blurted out.

He had planted the idea of running my own company in my head like a ticking time bomb, waiting for it to explode. Evidently, he was sick and tired of me complaining about my job, and to be honest, so was I. Not doing anything about it only made it worse. So, when he challenged me on that random Thursday night, it was pretty much the first time the thought of running my own company crossed my mind. Do my own thing? Yeah, I could do that. He was right, because at the time, it truly was my only option, especially when I felt uncertain about my future in the company.

"Maybe. I do have all these recruiters calling me, and I know so many doctors. I could create a recruiting business for doctors," I replied.

The reality was, I knew everything about the structure of the recruiting business. All the resources that I had gathered through my years of working in the medical industry would certainly pave the way. Also, I had all the necessary connections to sustain my venture. And most importantly, I had the drive and determination to be successful. I was committed to giving my all in everything I did, approaching every task with full force and unwavering energy. Success was like an extreme sport to me, feeding my passion to pursue my heart's desires. I knew that in order to achieve success, I had to give it my all, or else, I would never really know if I could succeed.

Most of all, I knew I had God by my side. That alone was enough to push forward because I believed that no matter what I was doing, if I had faith in mind, there was no doubt I would be successful at it. No question.

With a burning desire to succeed and a thirst for knowledge, I scoured the internet for any information that could help me start a recruiting business. I bought a book and studied it cover to cover, taking notes and brainstorming names for the company. One of the first challenges I faced was finding the perfect name for my company that accurately reflected my brand and values. I finally settled on Bailey's Medical Recruiting LLC, seeing as how I knew I was going to someday pass the business on to my children. But Devin had a different idea.

"Choose a name that starts with an A," he said. "That way, you'll always be at the top of the listings."

And so, with the advice of Devin, I branded my company to fit my strength and named it Association of Medical Recruiters. On top of that, he also helped me register the business with the state and obtain any necessary licenses or permits. I had formed a list that detailed my goals and steps to guide me every step of the way. And I made sure to stick to it by any means necessary. Since then, I've been making a list at the start of every year to make sure I kept myself accountable.

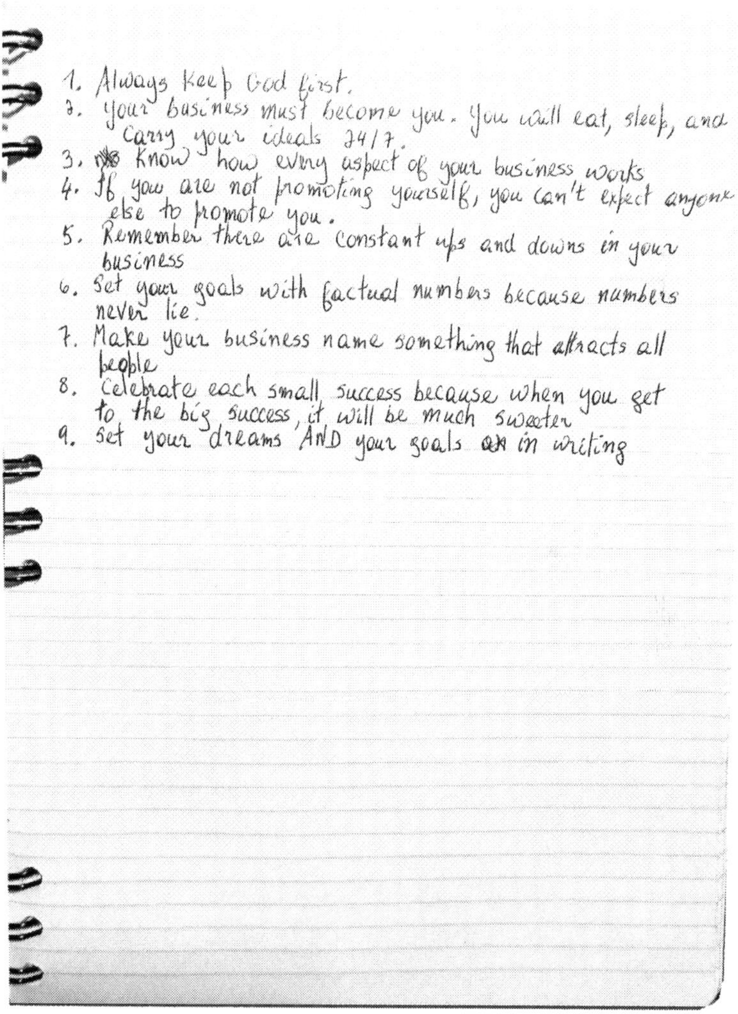

1. Always keep God first.
2. Your business must become you. You will eat, sleep, and carry your ideals 24/7.
3. Know how every aspect of your business works
4. If you are not promoting yourself, you can't expect anyone else to promote you.
5. Remember there are constant ups and downs in your business
6. Set your goals with factual numbers because numbers never lie.
7. Make your business name something that attracts all people
8. Celebrate each small success because when you get to the big success, it will be much sweeter
9. Set your dreams AND your goals in writing

A page from my journal

From there, I jumped headfirst into the world of recruiting. I quit my job and began building the business from the ground up while tirelessly working toward my doctorate. And boy, did it pay off. Within six months, I had generated over $15,000, and by the eighth month, I was up to nearly $280,000 in revenue. All by myself. Indeed, my business was thriving, and I knew I had made the right decision to take the leap and start my own company.

Even when I became pregnant with my son Gabriel, I continued to thrive. In fact, I pushed myself even harder, working long hours while juggling my responsibilities as a mother, student, and business owner. Despite feeling exhausted, I managed to achieve exceptional results. It seemed like everything I touched turned to gold, and I attributed it to God's favor. That year, I earned a staggering $800,000 with seemingly little effort. It was truly unbelievable. I was actually living the American dream that my mother and many of my family members had sought to achieve.

I built an efficient client base and attracted some of the top candidates through networking, advertising, and word of mouth. No one was better at developing relationships with potential clients and candidates than I was, and thanks to my deep understanding of the industry, I was easily able to match clients with candidates who had the right skills and qualifications. It was as though every doctor I spoke with was eager to take the job offered. That was a rarity; in the medical recruiting industry, it was usually the doctors who chose where they wanted to go. Without a doubt, it was clear that God was blessing me, providing me with the help I needed during that challenging time. Now, although I was doing well and functioning at a high level, through a string of events, God showed me that my purpose was greater than what I was doing. And it happened in the strangest way.

* * *

I found myself lying on a stretcher, with a fluorescent light above me passing by like the streetlights on a highway. I was unable to move my hands, feet, or eyes, but I could still feel everything around me. Some things moved in slow motion, while others were a complete blur. The smell of body fluids and cleaning products filled the room. It was cold–the kind of cold that pierced your bones if you weren't covered comfortably. I heard people's voices, but I couldn't see them. They were almost like blurs as they walked by. Even breathing seemed problematic, as the more I tried to do so, the less I could. It was one of the many times I would connect myself to God, feeling like I had died and gone to some unknown place. I was hoping it was heaven.

I was in a coma for eight days, and when I came out of it, I could not understand what had happened, leaving me to give up. Beyond that, I wanted to leave California and return to Florida to be with my loved ones—especially Natalia. The doctors clipped my vocal cords the day I left the hospital, therefore I couldn't communicate with anyone. Furthermore, my knees were shattered, so it was impossible to walk. Desperate to get away from California, Devin, whom I barely had a relationship with at that time, took me to the airport so that I could return to Florida as I desired. However, one thing I did not consider was that I would have to do everything alone.

During my trip, I had a layover in Atlanta. The airport staff pulled me off the airplane, rolled me down the tunnel, and placed me in the middle of the terminal, where a crowd passed me by like I was in the middle of Times Square. I had to figure it out alone. However, the problem was that I didn't know where I was headed. So, unable to talk or walk, I was left helpless, sitting in my squeaky wheelchair for nearly two hours, watching everyone go on like I didn't even exist. I tried desperately to get someone's attention, but no one would stop to help. The feeling of helplessness angered me to the core, and all I could do was cry. It was as if that were an indication of my entire life.

Finally, after trying to get myself over to my connecting flight, a woman appeared, almost as if she were an angel. With my little bit of energy, I mumbled to her what was going on, and from there, she helped me get to my gate to catch the flight to Florida. At that moment, as I was desperate, terrified, and alone, I realized that the disabled and elderly were nearly invisible to the world. That sudden realization would open my world up to possibilities I never imagined could happen.

When I finally reached Florida, I prayed and thanked God for the second chance I was given. Then I conceded to the fact that caring for people was my purpose. It became my passion and something my grandmother instilled in me. With my feet firmly back on the ground in Florida, I felt that familiar itch of restlessness. The one that whispers, "*What's next?*" in my ear, urging me to seek out new horizons. It's an itch that shouldn't be ignored, for it holds the promise of adventure and the thrill of uncertainty. And so, I scratched at it, curious to see what lay beyond.

Soon enough, an opportunity presented itself, arriving in the form of an unexpected knock on my door. It was one evening when my dear friend Donald, accompanied by his associate Diego, paid me a visit. Diego was from Alabama, and his occupation involved him supplying oxygen to doctors and patients, an interesting line of work that piqued my interest. Laughter filled the air before our conversation explored the realm of Diego's job. Before I knew it, my curiosity blossomed, fueled by a desire to explore this newfound vision. I learned that the sale of oxygen fell under the umbrella of medical equipment and that Diego had found a lucrative niche in the market. With only twenty patients, he could earn $20,000 a month, thanks to the orders he received from the doctors he served.

I was intrigued. The idea of branching out into the medical field had never occurred to me before, but it made perfect sense. I knew so much about it already. Also, all the connections I had were still in place. Diego had planted a seed in my mind, and it was one that I was determined to nurture. He offered to let me piggyback off his license to get started, or even operate under it entirely. It was a generous offer, but one that I wasn't willing to take lightly. I called him for weeks on end, determined to follow through on my newfound ambition. Yet, he never answered or returned my phone calls.

At the time, I still wasn't sure if Diego's claims were entirely true, or if he was simply trying to impress me, but I was motivated to find out. Even if he was only pulling in ten to twelve patient orders a month, I knew that there were more out there, waiting to be captured. And so, with a sense of determination burning in my heart, I took my first steps toward a new chapter in my life.

I downloaded the Medicare manual to get myself up to speed on everything related to the business. The book was thick and heavy, containing a vast array of information, including Medicare benefits policies, national coverage determinations, claims processing, program integrity, quality reporting incentives, and much more.

While reading, I came across so many acronyms that I nearly forgot the alphabet. DME, MPI, MSP, CMS, HCPCS, CPCs—oh my God! Mentally, I was exhausted, more than I had ever been. But no matter what, I knew I had to keep going. That's one of the things that running track taught me: never give up, because when you think you can't do any more, that's when you can actually do more. Like my college track days, my pursuit of operating a DME business required a lot of hard work and dedication. I had to be persistent and keep pushing even when it got tough. So, whenever I faced challenges, I kept that in mind, kept my head up, blinders on, and kept moving forward.

The intricate world of medical equipment sales was a code-infested maze, where a single mistake could mean the difference between profit and loss. It was a world in which I had no prior experience, yet I was determined to make a name for myself in the industry. Fate seemed to be on my side when I met a woman who worked in a similar field with Medicare. Desperate for guidance, I asked her to consult with me on the ins and outs of contracting and billing.

She and I worked together for a few sessions, and eventually, what once seemed foreign now made perfect sense.

Soon after, I applied for my license, and to my surprise, I learned that the only difference between HME (Home medical equipment) and DME (Durable medical equipment) was a matter of terminology. On April 11, 2011, Bailey's Medical was established and incorporated. Eight months from that date, on December 5, 2011, I received my license and began operating. With my license in hand, I was ready to embark on my journey to build an empire that would not only be lucrative but would also help millions of people.

By the time I turned thirty-five, I would become a millionaire. Yet, I didn't think anything of it because I knew I had more work to do. Besides, I was also a mother of two with one on the way. Oftentimes, people would rather see the money than hear about the success. They would listen to glories while ignoring the pain. The roadmap to crossing into millionaire status was nothing short of my passion, upbringing, and faith in God. Was it demanding work? Absolutely. I would be lying if I said it wasn't. Over time, I lost friends, shared moments with my family, and missed days with my kids that I could never get back or replace.

I became addicted to working, pouring every ounce of energy into the business, and when I was running low, I prayed for more. Luckily, I was never what you would consider scatter-brained, especially when it came to business or anything I set my mind to. If there's a word that means more than obsessed, that would be me. I eat and sleep with the thought of my business being successful until it manifests in its own way. Twenty-four hours a day, seven days a week, I was grinding. Literally! I've never been wrong in a business decision because I always believed in what I was doing. That's how confident I was in everything.

It's going to work. I'm doing it! That's what I would internally scream. Grasping the concepts of anything came quickly, and running numbers in my head, that came effortlessly. I could feel my younger self laughing at me, wondering where I was when she needed me in school. If you put something on the table, I would quickly calculate it, and if it's solid, then I'll say, "Okay, that's good. That's what we're going to go with." No second-guessing it. No being indecisive. Straight to the matter and no time wasted. Besides, numbers were the only thing I trusted.

Obtaining the license was just the first step—accreditation was the next hurdle. This process required me to have at least eight to ten patients before insurance companies would allow me to bill them. So, I had to find patients. Like any entrepreneur, I started with my friends and family. They bought items from me through prescriptions they requested from their doctors to become my patients. Not everyone believed in what I was doing, but I refused to let them discourage me. I always tell new business owners not to expect help or support from their inner circle or for them to be the ones who lift you up. Most of the time, they won't.

The money that I believed I could make was slowly starting to materialize. After obtaining accreditation, I received a Medicare number that also allowed me to work with private insurance companies. It took a year before I started marketing and recruiting for the business. The recruiting never stopped, and the marketing was a constant grind. A steady and increasing flow of new clients, contracts, services, and billing are key to any business' success, and that's what kept my company operational.

At that point, I had two businesses up and running, and the income looked even better. The crazy part was that I was doing it all alone with minimal overhead costs. I was out there marketing and pitching, printing and learning, answering phone calls, and compiling an email list to send out informational e-blasts. Everything! Even when I received an order, I was the one processing it, and then I would hop in my car to make the delivery. I was a big old team of one, with my babies, Natalia and Gabriel, by my side.

Nevertheless, one thing is for sure: running a business isn't always perfect, and I learned that quickly. Although the growth impressed and encouraged me, things were still slow. At some point, I was working more than I was receiving. And to make matters worse, the people of Vero Beach were hesitant about buying from me because I was a Black woman with an accent. For the longest time, I ignored the idea that the color of my skin could be a factor in my failure, but what I was experiencing started to make me question myself. Then again, even some Black doctors weren't receptive to sending me orders. That included those who were friends.

Then one day, on a visit to one of the facilities that placed orders with me, I couldn't help but feel overwhelmed. Yvette, the facility director, asked me if I was all right.

"Yvette, I think I'm going to need help. A white boy who could be the face of the company because it's hard out here by myself," I said, half-jokingly. Yvette chuckled, and to my surprise, she replied, "Maybe I could help you."

That's when I learned about Sean Wideberg, the Director of Rehabilitation's son, who had just graduated with a degree in marketing. At the time, Sean had been through a string of jobs before he ended up selling lawn services for a local company. At first glance, his resume wasn't impressive. If I'm being honest, it was god-awful, and I wasn't the least bit interested. But then, I remembered times when others had taken a chance on me in the past, so I decided I should do the same and at least interview him. Well, that interview was just as bad as the resume. Sean stumbled over every question and said inappropriate things in almost every other word. However, I saw something in him that wasn't on the resume—character! He was young, hungry, and focused. Sean was also sharp and charming. The kind of guy that everyone wouldn't mind grabbing a drink with. So, I figured I could teach him everything I knew and mold him into a natural salesperson.

On October 1, 2012, I hired Sean Wideberg, starting him off at $9 an hour, and together we built Bailey's Medical Equipment & Supply. Sean was, and still is, not afraid of hard work. He would return to the office from his sales duties, put the orders together, and deliver them without hesitation. In that first week of October, Sean went right to work, and by December, we were growing out of the space we were in.

"We should look into this building on the corner, and it's bigger," Sean suggested.

The current landlord was being a pest, and we were slammed with sales. So, we did it. We moved into a larger office. The industry was becoming increasingly competitive at the time, and we had to step up our game. I had already hired three people by this point. While they managed the medical equipment side of things, I worked on competitive bids for other areas. Even if we didn't win a bid, I learned from it.

The building was spacious and had an ideal location, but its condition was beyond neglected. It was plagued with roaches, rats, and all kinds of creepy crawlies. Despite the unsanitary environment, its prime location at the intersection of two bustling city streets made it an opportunity not to be missed. Without a second thought, I signed the lease and embarked on a mission to clean and renovate the space. We worked tirelessly, pushing ourselves to the brink of exhaustion but motivated by our determination to open those doors.

Once we finally moved into the five thousand square feet, we were immediately awarded a multi-million-dollar hospice contract. This gave us the incredible opportunity to work with hospice patients and gain invaluable experience with the practices and processes. Shortly thereafter, I received a letter from Medicare, informing me that I had won all of the competitive bids that I put in for. Now, we needed to open a store in Orlando.

I convinced Karla, our newest hire fresh from Washington D.C., to relocate and oversee the opening of the new store. Today, Sean sits on my executive board, where he serves as the COO of the company, making well over $9 an hour. Sean had believed in my vision when few others did not, and worked tirelessly to get the business rolling to where it is today. He was not only efficient and loyal, but also my confidant and best friend.

In my pursuit of building an empire, I remained dedicated to my goals and never lost sight of them. I believed in collaborating with my employees during the planning stage, assigning them specific tasks, and working alongside them to ensure they learned the skills necessary for their successes. By doing so, I was able to mold them into responsible individuals capable of managing the operation effectively.

Fast forward to 2023… I have a team that can run both the office and stores without my physical presence. I understand that in order to successfully develop and expand a business, it is imperative to have a team that can operate independently. In fact, I have taken extended leaves of absence, and Bailey's ran seamlessly without my direct involvement. This was possible because I had faith and trust in my team, and I invested time in training and cultivating them. I worked to identify and fix any issues that arose within my team.

My grandmother, Rose Jones, smiling.

Spending time with my grandmother.

Taking a swing during Sophomore year.

Trisha Bailey

School: Weaver-Hartford
Coaches: Wilbert Jones and Janice La-Penna

■ **800, Senior:** Repeat All-State selection. . . . Overcame sore back all season to win the State Open (2:19.58) and Class LL (2:21.13). . . . A member of Weaver's 4x400 Class LL relay champion (4:01.88). . . . "She has made this [10-2] team rise close to the top," Jones said. . . . Won 800 (2:18.07) at Hartford Public Invitational. . . . Ranked No. 7 of 225 students, Trisha plans to attend UConn.

The days of running at Weaver High.

Coming in 1st place in the 800m race.

Taking off on the 4X400m race.

Addressing UConn's class of 23'.

Speaking at UConn's Title IX Celebration.

Bailey's Student Athlete Success Center—
A building named Dr. Trisha Bailey.

First Bailey's Building - Vero Beach, FL
780 US 1 Suite 100
Vero Beach, FL 32962

Fourth Bailey's Building - St. Petersburg, FL
3065 34th St N Suite A
St. Petersburg, FL 33713

Twelfth Bailey's Building - Fort Worth, TX
6700 W Vickery Blvd,
Fort Worth, TX 76116

Thirteenth Bailey's Building - Hartford, CT
1137 Main Street
East Hartford, CT 06108

CHAPTER 10

LOVE HURTS

"More than anything, I needed someone to look at me in a way that brought chills down my spine, leaving my stomach fluttering with butterflies. The way all women secretly desired to be gazed upon. That's what I wanted."

A friend of mine once told me if I shared all the stories of the men in my life with a stranger, that person would think I was referring to just one man—just one man who put me through all the heartaches, tears, and pain. One man who gave me good times somewhere in between all the bad ones. One man who emotionally and physically abused me while telling me he loved me. Just one man! Sometimes, I wish that was the case.

Here's a not-so-secret secret about me—for most of my life, I've been crazy about love. A hopeless romantic woman, yearning for the love that feels like oxygen pouring into my soul. Or the sort of love that binds me to someone both physically and emotionally, reaching a level of deep mutual investment. Not only that, but the idea of being in love brought me joy just as much as actually being in love. If I was watching a movie, it had to have some romance. What can I say? I am a sucker for love. That's one thing everyone that knows me can attest to. And because of that, I did everything in my power to immerse myself in it, even if it meant compromising my own well-being, self-esteem, and at times, even my life.

When I was running around Jamaica's dirt roads as a little girl, playing around with my family and friends, the notion of love didn't cross my mind. However, when I arrived in America, acquiring those feelings came effortlessly with all the handsome boys around me. I never said anything to them, though. But by the time I was fifteen, I no longer wanted to just stare at them because they were simply good looking. No! It was more than that. Instead, I wanted to know more about them, as they also desired to know about me. Feeling their lips pressed against mine as we held hands was an image that repeatedly played in my mind. More than anything, I needed someone to look at me in a way that sent chills down my spine, leaving my stomach fluttering with butterflies. The way all women secretly desired to be gazed upon. Like when Sam saw Annie for the first time, standing by the telescope in *Sleepless in Seattle*. Yeah, that look!

I watched how my uncle treated my aunt, thinking this is what love looks like. They weren't overly expressive, but you could sense they truly cared about each other. Here and there, they would spend time laughing with one another. They always ate dinner together. And not once did I see them fight. My aunt and uncle displayed a love that made me subconsciously chase it in hopes of masking all my traumas. At times, I was even puzzled by the idea that I could ever be in love with anyone after what I had been through. Still, I had to find out.

Ironically, as successful as I have been with everything throughout my life, that is the one area of my life that's been dark as the pits of hell. Perhaps, even darker. I've managed to do well starting my own business, raising my children, and growing my finances—even navigating through this world as a woman on my own. With God by my side, I have had complete control over everything. Except for this fucking shit called love. Ugh!

Over the years, I learned that we can only be accountable for ourselves when it comes to being in a relationship. Hoping the other person treats us the same way is the least we can do. It's like driving a car. You check to ensure the tire pressure is good, the car is filled with gas, and that you have your seatbelt on, but none of that prepares you for what someone else will do to you on the road.

At times, I discovered this too late, and it became more apparent when I fell in love. That's because, like many others, I failed to see the person as they were, with no filter or expectations. Instead, I saw only what I wanted to do for them, loving them consistently and in all seasons.

I was just twenty-two years old and living the life most women would have dreamed of. Buying all sorts of expensive shoes, clothes, and jewelry. Eating at all the fancy restaurants. Traveling around the country to attend some of the most significant events you could imagine. Every night offered me something new that filled me with adrenaline and power. I was a young stockbroker, and business was booming. I had made so much money and connections that I was now managing the portfolios of several well-known athletes. It was going great.

* * *

On January 28, 2001, Super Bowl XXXV took place in Tampa, FL, featuring a matchup between the Baltimore Ravens and the New York Giants. The city of Tampa was flooded with millions of people immersed in the festivities, and I must admit, it was an overwhelming experience. However, I basked in it because, to me, it represented a vast pool of potential clients. I met so many individuals that weekend, both men and women. As someone who had never attended a Super Bowl game, I was determined to seize every opportunity. The night left me floating on a high that nearly mirrored the euphoric feeling I experienced while running. Unbeknownst to me, my focus shifted entirely to having a good time, causing me to momentarily disregard any business matter. It's how I came to first meet Ricky Bates.

I remember it vividly. The night progressed into late hours, and I found myself headed to a Super Bowl party. The club wasn't really my thing, but on that night, I honestly felt differently about it. I wanted to be out, surrounded by warm bodies and flashing fluorescent lights. Besides, it was a Super Bowl party!

When I arrived at the club, I heard music blaring from outside, and in the middle of the parking lot, I met the gaze of a man. A man who took me by surprise. At that moment, I was stuck like a rock in water. His eyes intently focused on me, just as my gaze was on him. It was as if he and I were in a stare-off contest that neither of us wanted to lose. I blushed. He smiled. It was fun and innocent, yet it felt natural. He had the physique that I yearned to feel in the palm of my hands. He approached me through the crowded parking lot. I still remember the scent of his refreshing smell fondling my senses. He grabbed my left hand and softly kissed it before he shook it. Our energy vibrated, my stomach turned, and my skin tingled.

I couldn't stop smiling, staring at him like he was the last man on Earth. Or better yet, as if he were already mine. Ricky wasn't overly talkative, but he wasn't painfully shy either. Truthfully, getting a read on him wasn't the easiest thing to do. At first, nothing about Ricky seemed threatening. He was a great listener who focused on me when I spoke. He always knew what to say, offering great feedback whenever we talked. Nothing like the man I'd come to later know.

By the time I met Ricky, he was starting his NFL career as a rookie for the Jacksonville Jaguars. Like all men who dreamed of playing in the NFL, finding his place on a team was all that he cared about. I couldn't blame him, though. I had been around and dated enough players to know that much about their focus. As a former athlete myself, I appreciated their drive, dedication, and passion for the game they love. Still, the idea of dating one of them didn't excite me as much as it did the other women. Those women saw a chance at fast money, a glamorous lifestyle, and the opportunity to meet celebrities. I, on the other hand, wanted someone to love me just as much as I loved them.

Besides, nothing about the other things excited me; quite frankly, their lifestyle left much to be desired. They were constantly under pressure from the weight of having to win, making it almost impossible for them not to put stress on themselves or their relationships. Then, there was the idea of dealing with the groupies who seemed to make their way into hotels, jumping from player to player. Oh! There's also the trust thing. Many of the players didn't trust anyone because they couldn't figure out who wanted them for them versus who wanted them for their money. As a result, they'd treat everyone with little to no respect. Lastly, it didn't seem that many of them had a life outside of football, and for Ricky, this was no exception. That is probably all the more reason why I should have never gotten that close to him.

Nevertheless, the initial spark continued to blossom into a full flame. My heart began to flutter with anticipation of this new romance, and I found myself opening up to a realm of possibilities. Before I knew it, I had fallen in love with Ricky, taking on a journey where we'd explore each other's interests, hopes, and dreams through countless experiences. Whether it was a candlelit dinner at a fancy restaurant, hushed whispers and giggles in a dark movie theater, or the adrenaline rush of going to a football game, the moments we spent together built a foundation of intimacy and trust.

Ricky's calls throughout the day and at night were like a lifeline, a spark of joy in my mundane routine. Talking on the phone with him was like being transported back to teenage years, when all that mattered was the connection between two people. His kindness and sweetness awakened a part of me that had been dead for too long, the part that craved love and affection. For a while, I had been chasing success and wealth, blinded by the illusion that they were my ultimate needs. But

Ricky showed me that love was what I had been missing, what I had been craving all along.

However, as is often the case in life, love possesses the power to reveal both the brightest and darkest side of us. For Ricky, the radiant light that had brought him into my world had gradually faded, and in its place, a foreboding darkness crept in. It was as if I were walking down a hallway so narrow that I could brush the walls with outstretched arms the further I ventured in. At the far end of that hallway, was a dingy lightbulb that flickered and casted an uncertain glow.

Ricky's calls became increasingly shorter, sporadic, and vague. He started asking me about my whereabouts and the people I was with more frequently. At the time, I didn't mind because I believed it was a sign of trust between us. But looking back, I realized that I had mistaken his controlling behavior for charming gestures, causing me to disregard the concerns raised by others. It wasn't long before my innocence was shattered, and I saw him for the person he truly was. The man who once adored and idolized me had transformed into an emotionless monster, and I became his victim.

When I was in a relationship with Ricky, he lived with his mother in Sarasota, Florida, while I was in Connecticut. We would visit each other every other weekend, although I was the one doing most of the traveling. Over time, I witnessed Ricky's struggle to secure a spot on a roster in the NFL. As he faced setbacks, I saw the innocence in his eyes gradually fade into an empty void. His once gentle smile vanished, replaced by a hardened expression with downturned eyebrows. His touch no longer brought comfort, but rather a sense of unease, and there was something unsettling about the way he would often gaze at me. The warm persona he had presented, which was meant to captivate, disappeared as quickly as summer rain. Soon, the time we spent together would turn into arguments, ending in him gripping my throat or striking my body like a punching bag.

I remember the time Ricky and I went to the supermarket to buy groceries. That was typical of us. We did just about everything together, and on that day, it all seemed normal. For goodness' sake, we didn't even have an argument. When it was time to check out, I joined a cashier line with three customers ahead of me. But I noticed a shorter line three lanes over. Without hesitation, I quickly grabbed my cart and hurried over to claim my spot before anyone else could beat me to it. Ricky followed behind me at a slower pace, seemingly unaffected. Or at least, that's what I initially thought. Somewhere between the lane change and the process of cashing out, something shifted. I can't pinpoint exactly what had transpired, but it became evident in the way he distanced himself and the energy he gave off.

The moment we got into the car and shut the door, I felt the tension suffocating me as if I were walking through a thick black smoke. Silence filled the car with almost no air to breathe. Ricky's burning eyes stared at me as I watched the white around his pupil overcome with red veins. His scowl wasn't deliberately cold, but it was a look I hadn't seen from him before. His breathing was slow as he bit his bottom lip with a closed mouth. Then, suddenly, he placed his right hand behind my head and repeatedly slammed my face against the dashboard.

"I saw you looking at that nigga! You think you slick. You went in the other line so he could see your ass!" he said to me.

I don't know what startled me the most at that moment. Was it the fact that Ricky had come up with such a delusional story? Or was it the fact that blood was dripping from my nose like a broken faucet? I was so shocked that I couldn't do anything but stare at him in disbelief, wondering where that came from. I knew that leaving him at that moment would have been the wise thing to do, and I desperately wanted to, but I didn't. And when I finally attempted to pull away from him completely, he planted a seed inside me that would later give birth to my beautiful daughter Natalia.

Despite the violence, I convinced myself that beneath the anger and aggression, he still loved me and wanted the best for our relationship. I believed that things would improve if I could somehow help him return to the NFL. Damn, was I wrong!

I was moving up in my field while Ricky was navigating his path in the world after it became apparent that the NFL was no longer a part of his plans. Ricky experienced both good and bad days as he searched for his purpose, but I stood by his side, offering unwavering support and motivation. Despite the occasional uncertainty, there were moments of greatness during our relationship, particularly for me as a soon-to-be mother.

I'll admit, when I discovered I was having a girl, I felt a mixture of excitement and nervousness. Disturbing memories of my abusive stepfather would often flood my mind, causing terrifying thoughts to surface. I couldn't help but wonder if my daughter would endure the same fate as I did. Would I be able to protect her throughout her entire life? Could I be the kind of mother who recognizes signs of neglect and abuse? Did I even possess the necessary skills to be a good mother? These questions plagued me, and yet, there were no answers to be found.

One thing, however, remained crystal clear: I would go to great lengths to make sure she was safe. Even in the womb, I became very protective of this precious angel. No one would violate her as I had been violated. Even if it meant keeping my mother at a distance, denying her the role of an ideal grandmother. It wasn't because I didn't have love for my mother, because I truly did. But I never wanted her to face the agonizing choice between sticking by the man she loves and the safety of my daughter.

February 3, 2002, Super Bowl XXXVI took place at the Superdome in New Orleans. Ricky informed me that he would be attending the game, but due to my condition as a pregnant woman, I decided not to go with him. Not that he invited me. Besides, it was a time when things were unclear for both of us, and I believed that giving the relationship some space was the best course of action, as my Aunt Joyce had advised. So, I stayed home with Ms. Jennifer, Ricky's mother, while Ricky went off to enjoy himself in New Orleans.

Ms. Jennifer held a special place in my heart, and our bond was akin to the mother-daughter relationship that I had longed for during my teenage years. Although she didn't know much about me, Ms. Jennifer was always warm and supportive, effortlessly making me feel understood. I cherished our conversations, as they fulfilled my spirit. She consistently offered words of encouragement, making me feel appreciated and essential as if I could do no wrong. Most importantly, Ms. Jennifer protected me, even when I didn't perceive the need for it, sometimes even against her own son—except the one time I needed her to do so.

While I was dating Ricky, I had a nagging suspicion that he was being unfaithful to me, which wasn't the first time I had felt this way. This time, though, I couldn't ignore the feeling churning in the pit of my stomach and I needed to know for sure. So, I resorted to an immature approach and decided to check his phone. It wasn't something I was proud of because it was entirely out of character for me. Ricky was quite the simple man, so his password was easy to guess, and within seconds, I had forwarded all his voicemails and messages to my phone.

As I listened to countless voicemails from various women, my heart sank deeper and deeper. A few of the messages were full of nothing. Then again, plenty were sexually inappropriate and unbearable for a woman in love to hear. Each message weakened me further, and I couldn't help but wonder when it would all end.

I was young and often confused, and I didn't always handle situations in the best way. I can admit that. Throughout my life, I had to defend myself even when there was no real threat. Sometimes, I would react quickly and only consider the consequences later. It wasn't always the right thing to do, and there were times I would regret it. But in that moment, with his phone in my hand, I felt as empty as a broken promise. I allowed my relationship with Ricky to define me in a strange way, turning me into someone afraid of being alone. I became the kind of woman who would do anything to salvage a relationship that wasn't worth saving. And so, I did it. I wrote down the numbers of all the women who left messages and went back to Connecticut to listen to them all. I had no idea what I would do, but I felt obligated to do it. One of the numbers stood out more than the others, so I dialed it first.

"Hello," she answered. Suddenly, everything went silent, and a faint ringing grew between my ears. Anxiety increasingly crept into my soul, suffocating my ability to breathe. It felt almost impossible to control my emotions.

I told the woman everything about myself, my pregnancy, and how I came to learn about her. I felt she needed to understand the nature of my relationship with Ricky. She was genuinely shocked. I asked if she ever met his mom. I had to know if she had a relationship with Ms. Jennifer. To my surprise, the woman told me she hadn't, and that was evident when Ms. Jennifer cursed the woman out for calling her phone.

After the Super Bowl, I didn't receive a call from Ricky. I found that to be strange. As I rested in bed, waiting for his phone call, my thoughts collided with my intuition like freight trains going two hundred miles per hour. In the pit of my stomach, I felt trouble rumbling like a pack of wild boars running around. I was sure the feeling had nothing to do with the baby growing inside me. Instead, it had everything to do with my connection to Ricky. Unsure if something terrible had happened, I called him once again. This time, he answered, and immediately, I heard the celebrations and music blaring in the background. That was expected, but what he said next left me with an eerie feeling.

"Babe, you got the hotel room yet?"

"What? What are you talking about?" I responded.

He took a moment to gather his thoughts, but that didn't do much because he fumbled over his words anyway. At that point, Ricky didn't have to tell me what he was up to because I knew precisely that my suspicions were correct. Immediately, I felt a tingle blossom in my chest, spreading throughout my entire body, causing me to lose track of time. Even the ability to blink surrendered to my rage.

"Are you cheating? Really?" I screamed over the phone just before I began to cry over a reality yet to come. And like before, he denied as much as he could, but what else would he say. That he wasn't with another woman? Not a chance. He was much too stubborn and manipulative to do that.

It wasn't just the fact that he had been with another woman that left me shattered into pieces like a broken vase. Honestly, what truly crushed me was the thought of raising my child all alone. The image of subjecting my little girl to emotional stress, even before she entered this world, made me mistake my anger for fear. I had witnessed my mother endure all kinds of bullshit from her husband, just so she wouldn't become a single mother. And I vowed to never find myself in that position. Despite feeling strong enough to face any challenge, the fear of losing my sense of security became more overwhelming than the pain of enduring abuse. It dominated my spirit and resided in my subconscious like a ticking time bomb, waiting for its moment to detonate.

Not only did I not want that life for Natalia, but I also vowed never to be that woman. I began wondering how I'd navigate the unknown avenues of single parenting. Would she judge me later in her adulthood for the choices I made for her as a child? I had no answers to my questions, but I knew whatever I did would permanently imprint my life and the lives of those I love.

I screamed and argued with Ricky over the phone for nearly five minutes, begging him to tell me the truth. Five minutes! Yet, it felt like a lifetime. That's the thing about being cheated on. It makes everything in life seem longer and slower than it does harder. Whoever coined the term cheating must have been afraid of calling someone a traitor. Or better yet, that person believed referring to the individual that cheated as a liar would be too emotionally honest. Lord knows my heart was broken. Not just by a guy I was in love with, but also by someone I believed to be a true friend.

A couple of days later, Ricky returned from New Orleans, and as usual, he reached out to touch my stomach, eager to feel the baby. I forced a smile and pretended to be filled with joy, but internally, I despised him touching me. If I could have slammed a brick against his forehead, I would have done so without a hint of regret. Instead, I chose to play the role of the happy, naive woman he expected me to be. On our way home, he told me all about his Super Bowl experience. I could barely pay attention because my mind was consumed with the need to make him confess.

I badly wanted him to know that I knew all about his lies and deceitful actions. So, I began revealing things that only he and the other woman would know—vivid secrets and shared memories. After a while, he finally realized that I was aware of his infidelity. I don't know what I expected to gain from confronting him, but all he could muster was a simple, "I'm sorry." That's it! What infuriated me the most was the fact that I had to sulk in his betrayal while he moved on as if he had just stepped off a Disney ride.

Ricky would make me feel wrong for accusing him of being with other women. He had done it so many times that I couldn't tell when he was lying or speaking the truth. Oddly enough, though, sometimes it worked. As much as I knew about the other women, he found a way to make me feel guilty and ashamed. I was conditioned to feel responsible for being a victim. His manipulative behavior was reminiscent of my stepfather's, allowing the truth and my intuition to take a backseat to his lies. Part of me believed that if I could somehow persuade myself that what he was saying was true, then maybe, just maybe, I could pretend like it had never happened.

"Just move on!" That was always my advice. To make matters worse, I somehow convinced myself that everything between Ricky and me was going just fine. Besides, there's no way Ricky would do that to me again. Especially not with his seed growing inside of me, right? Yeah right. Nothing was ever that easy with Ricky.

There have been days in my life when I suffered alone, both emotionally and physically, but I never allowed myself to remain trapped in that state. That makes it all the more puzzling that I lacked the confidence and self-esteem to walk away from Ricky. So often, I wanted to gather my shit and just leave, but a voice in my head made me believe that he and I could somehow make it work. This was especially true on the day after I stumbled upon Ricky's sex tapes sitting inside his nightstand. I was certain that nothing could compel me to return to him after witnessing that. However, that turned out not to be the case.

It was my birthday, and instead of going out to enjoy myself, I spent my time sitting on the floor, foolishly sifting through several videos of the man I loved fuck other women. Not just one woman, either, but countless. Some of these women were oblivious to being filmed. Among them were white women, Black women, skinny women, and even women whom I would never have expected Ricky to be involved with. I watched so many videos that they left me numb, unable to shed any more tears. After the tenth or twelfth woman, I gave up, but something told me to watch one more. Unsure of why I wanted to put myself through any more torture, I pressed play and then witnessed something that left me as lifeless as a rotten corpse. I would have rather him force a knife in my throat.

In this particular tape, I watched as Ricky lay the woman down on the bed he and I shared, intently trailing kisses across her body as if she were the last woman on Earth. Or better yet, as if he were her man. From there, he began to have sex with her like he had done with all the other women, but with this particular woman, he spoke to her. While fucking this woman, I mean literally inside this woman, Ricky invited her to our wedding. Our wedding? I could not believe what I was hearing. This was the same woman I had spoken to about Ricky over the phone. The one who told me she knew nothing about me and understood where I was coming from.

"Okay, yeah. I'll come to your wedding," the woman declared as his erection thrust in and out of her.

And just like that, the tears that welled up in my soul spilled over, streaming down my cheeks, while an ache throbbed against my heart like the booming strike of a Chinese gong. The ticking of the clock grew increasingly louder as my breaths came in short, rapid bursts. I felt an overwhelming sense of isolation from the world, as if I had lost every ounce of pride I once possessed. Feeling worthless and unlovable, I started to doubt myself in all areas of life. To make matters worse, I truly believed that this was karma getting back at me for the way I had left Kingsley, and because of that, I convinced myself that I deserved it. That's why I didn't confront Ricky about the tapes and just stayed with him. I was young and foolishly believed that it would be better to be with him than to be a single mother.

We were still doing our long-distance relationship when one day, as he and I were at his house, he proposed. It was unexpected and somewhat unwelcome. As if Ricky were casually thinking about what he wanted for dinner. He didn't do any sort of grand gesture like getting down on one knee or anything elaborate like I was used to seeing in movies. Certainly nothing like when Landon proposed to Jamie underneath a shooting star in *A Walk to Remember*. Or how Andrew took Melanie into the jewelry store, got down on one knee, and proposed in *Sweet Home Alabama*. Better yet, how Andre confessed his love to Sydney on live radio before he proposed to her in *Brown Sugar*.

Despite everything, I said yes. People couldn't comprehend my decision to marry him any more than I could, because honestly, it didn't make much sense. Yet, somewhere within the dark and gloomy days, there were also moments of passion and intensity that fueled my belief that saying yes would bring more good than bad. I yearned to experience the love I deserved, reminiscent of the love I had left behind with Kingsley. Moreover, with a child in our lives, I convinced myself that Ricky could no longer treat me the way he had before. It was a naive way of thinking, assuming that marriage and parenthood would completely alter my situation with him. Didn't help that he and Ms. Jennifer convinced me that this would be the best for Natalia and me. So, I went along with it. I got my company to transfer me to Florida, uprooting my entire life in Hartford to move to Sarasota.

And for a moment, things were looking up for me, and all my aspirations were beginning to materialize. I was excelling in my profession, so much so that they promoted me to the next level. My first home was nearing completion, situated nearly fifty miles north of Sarasota in Riverview, Florida. Ricky and I were nurturing our daughter, creating a haven where we would engage in countless conversations about our dreams for ourselves and Natalia. Those cherished moments filled me with a sense of normalcy and uplifted my spirits. Regrettably, this period of bliss was short-lived.

My baby Natalia was ten months old when I finally gathered the courage to say enough was enough. It was a Thursday morning, and I woke up to a fresh start, intending to complete all my work. Ricky spent most of his time at home since his dream to play in the NFL was now a distant memory. Therefore, he'd watch Natalia as I went to work. At that time, he loved fishing. That's all he did most days. So much so that Ricky later found a job catching fish then selling them to local seafood markets. He had so much love for his work, but it was never enough to satisfy him, especially when Ricky considered the money I brought in with my job. In the back of my mind, I knew that wasn't something he could deal with. Thus, the only way to show his dominance in our relationship, since he couldn't do it financially, was to overpower me with his abuse.

We argued constantly. His insulting and hurtful words had become my new norm. Calling me a "dirty bitch" and countless other names no longer held any weight. However, when his words failed to break me, he resorted to physical violence. I could feel the tension in his voice as he screamed, "You raggedy ass bitch! Fuck you!" It enraged me to hear him talk to me that way, but not enough for me to fight back as I usually would, because I simply didn't have the mental strength. He left me drained beyond measure.

"I'm jealous of you. All these good things keep happening to you and nothing's happening for me," he said to me one day.

When I think about it, I believe he even grew to be jealous of Natalia. Breastfeeding her was as painful and he would look at me and say, "That's what you get. You're the one that wanted a baby." I couldn't wrap my head around his insanity.

Then, on that Thursday morning, as I was heading out for work, he asked to borrow my car. I told him no, because it was a company car that no one was allowed to drive. Besides, I needed to go to work, too. The next thing I knew, he followed me outside the house and kicked my car repeatedly with his left foot while holding my baby in his right arm. He caused so much damage to the vehicle that I was sure I would be fired. Dents and scratches all over the driver's side. The side view mirrors dangled like an old lightbulb. It was a total mess.

"What the fuck are you doing? Stop! Please!" I screamed.

"Fuck you and your raggedy ass car. You dirty bitch!"

He continued kicking the car over and over again. There was a great deal of emotion behind each kick. My only concern was Natalia. I tried to take her from him, but he wouldn't hand over my child. My core system began to shut down, terrified of what he might do next. My worst thoughts and nightmares flooded my mind like a broken dam. My purpose in life was to protect my baby by any means necessary, and there I was, unable to do shit!

"Give me my child," I politely said. My voice was warm and emotionally apologetic.

"Fuck you!" he screamed.

Suddenly, he got tired of kicking the car and turned his rage on me. The first kick, forceful and brutal, knocked me to the ground. Then, he attacked me with no regard for my life. Over and over again, he kicked and punched me until I could no longer feel the pain.

Punch across my face.

Stomp over my body.

Kick in the stomach.

Punch here. Kick there!

As much as I wanted to fight back, I couldn't. It wasn't because Ricky was stronger or because I was afraid. No. It was because I believed it was the only way I could protect my baby. I knew that as long as he beat on me, he wouldn't do anything to her. Then, Natalia let out a loud squeal just before she started crying, and that gave me the strength to finally fight back. Just as I was about to do that, from the corner of my eye, I saw Ms. Jennifer run outside like an angel from the sky. I was thrilled to see her face, coming over to help de-escalate the situation. A sigh of relief took over me at that very moment.

"Boy, give me this child," Ms. Jennifer said as she took my daughter from his arms.

And then she turned her back to Ricky and me, cradling Natalia in her arms as Ricky beat me heartlessly in the middle of the street. Every so often, she'd turn to observe Ricky's kicking my ass as if it were her own personal entertainment. Even my baby looked on crying, dazed and confused, as Ricky grabbed my ankle and dragged my battered body along the sidewalk, tearing off my skin as we went. The blows seemed to go on forever, but I kept my focus on my child, determined to protect her at all costs. Admittedly, I was filled with rage, and if I could have, I would have hurt him right then and there. But at that moment, I was too weak to fight back. So, I waited until Ricky was finished, then gathered my belongings and my child, finally mustering the courage to leave for good.

I had to learn the hard way, but through that experience, I understood the importance of valuing myself and recognizing my own worth. If anything, Ricky allowed me to develop a newfound sense of strength and resilience that I could forever spread throughout my life. My stepfather made me realize my ability to overcome the challenges I faced, but Ricky helped me learn to rebuild trust in myself when I didn't think I deserved it. That was the last time I saw him, and I vowed that I would never allow anyone into my life who would cause harm to me or my child again—or so I thought.

CHAPTER 11

THE COMA, THE TRUTH

"I didn't want anyone to know that deep down inside, I was stuck in that filthy pit, crying, and screaming internally. I didn't want them to offer pity remarks or, even worse, look at me like some sort of rescued dog."

I've reached the part of the book, a point in my life, where I wouldn't consider it the prettiest. Pay close attention, because it's taken me quite some time to get to this point, physically and mentally. Of course, that's not to say there haven't been a few bumps in the road before now, but this particular stretch isn't one I'd care to revisit. I realize it can be challenging for people to wrap their heads around what I am about to say, given the success and recognition I've experienced. Still, here I am, baring my soul like I'm reclining on a cream-colored sofa across from someone sporting thick-rimmed glasses. Even some of my closest friends remain oblivious to this chapter of my life. However, I'm sharing my story not to display courage, but rather to open the doors on a widely stigmatized subject involving an illness that can strike any of us. Now, I'm ready to dive into the details.

I spent years burying this dark memory so deep in my mind that I had hoped to reach a point where it never happened. However, no matter how much I'd like to run away from my past, I couldn't seem to do so. Instead, I've accepted that it is part of who I am. It is engraved in my identity and a critical factor in how I've chosen to remain unbroken.

The memory of that day lingers in my mind, a fleeting moment that still feels like a surreal blur. At times, I think of it as just a figment of my imagination until I catch a glimpse of my face in the mirror and quickly see the scars that remind me of its reality. Yet, even in the midst of it all, I felt incredibly grateful to be counted among the fortunate, among those blessed with the opportunity to recover. I am the same person I always was, driven by my desire to make a difference in the world and to spread love wherever I go. But now, that drive is ingrained with a newfound purpose filled with intentions, a testament to the growth I have experienced since that fateful day.

As the bright sun rays danced through the window blinds and the silence surrounding me became deafening, I found myself consumed by a heavy burden that I could no longer bear. The weight of life's stressors had finally caught up to me, leaving me feeling lost and isolated. Looking back, I realize I should have approached the situation differently, but the signs of an impending mental breakdown were already looming overhead. During a significant life transition and constant challenges, sleeping became a challenge, my appetite dwindled, and I found myself shouldering the problems of others as if they were my own. In the end, I became a mere shadow of my former self, barely recognizable to even my own eyes.

Beep… Beep… Beep…

The cold air and darkness completely surrounded me, leaving me with only the faint sound of a heart monitor and distant murmurs echoing in the background. Random bursts of white light flickered in and out of my mind like a broken reel while I remained paralyzed and trapped beneath thin sheets that clung to my skin and toes.

As time passed, the beeping and chatter grew quieter until everything faded into an unfamiliar blackness. Suddenly, I stood in a wide-open field surrounded by vibrant sunflowers and delicate daisies. The sawgrass swayed gently in the breeze, painting the landscape with a kaleidoscope of hues that no artist could ever replicate. In this place, time was irrelevant as it came to a standstill. The silence was soon broken by the joyful chirping of birds and a gust of wind that effortlessly flowed through my hair. The sun shone so brightly that it was hard to keep my eyes open, but I felt no discomfort. There was no rejection or isolation in that peaceful place—only a deep sense of belonging and oneness with the land.

I could hear the crunch of grass beneath my feet with each step I took. It was exhilarating to feel so alive. I didn't question how or why I was there. Instead, I just welcomed the beauty of this place as if I had been to that place countless times before. Strangely, in the distance, I noticed a heat haze shimmering, and yet despite the bright sunshine, I couldn't shake the cold that clung to my bones like a winter day in Hartford. Wait a minute. Before I continue, let me take a step back for a moment.

* * *

In my twenties, I was convinced that going out was the only way to meet someone. It was the ultimate solution to finding love, or so I believed. As I entered my thirties, that quickly died down like a failed dream. Going out became more of a chore than a pleasure. The hours spent getting ready, driving to the venue, searching for parking, and waiting in line were a waste of time. Time that could have been better spent with my daughter or building my business.

As a stockbroker, however, partying was a vital part of my job. It was an opportunity to impress potential clients and make new connections. I mingled with millionaires seeking to reinvent themselves and professional athletes chasing the dream of a celebrity lifestyle. I even rubbed shoulders with music industry power players like Boogie

Sheist, a renowned music producer whose mere presence commanded respect.

When I first encountered Boogie Sheist, I couldn't help but feel intimidated by his stature. However, the more I got to know him, the more I saw a different side of him. He was soft, kind, humorous, and generous. I was in Las Vegas with my friend Kathy when I met Boogie. A friend who coached in the NBA had given us tickets to the All-Star game. So, not only would it be a good time, but it was the perfect opportunity to escape from all the bullshit I was going through—especially after everything I dealt with Ricky nearly three years earlier. So, that's what we did. We came prepared to have a good time and forget about any of the problems troubling us.

As I walked out of the after-party, my eyes met the gaze of a towering figure. His commanding presence drew me in, and the longer he looked at me, the more I became curious. At first glance, I didn't know who he was. I assumed he was a football player because everything about him seemed to fit the mold. His massive build, adorned with jewelry and tattoos, gave off an air of dominance that led me to believe that. He had a thick black beard and a bald head, and how he carried himself spoke volumes about his character. I couldn't help but be intrigued by him, and when he motioned me over with just one finger, I strolled with little resistance. His attractiveness didn't hurt, either.

"What are you doing after this? You wanna hang out with me and some friends?"

I didn't feel like this guy was a threat or would harm me. I'm not sure why, but I didn't.

"Umm… sure," I replied.

As I locked eyes with him, it was as if he stared into my soul, his gaze filling with a deep and primal desire that sent a shiver down my spine. At that moment, I realized the danger of the situation, but my mind was clouded with thoughts of excitement and anticipation. I had assumed that our night would be filled with the glitz and glamor of the Vegas nightlife—the flashing lights of a casino, the thumping bass of a strip club, or the wild energy of an after-party. But fate had other plans, and before I knew it, we were standing in the plush surroundings of his hotel room. He urged me to stay the night with him, but I hesitated, torn between my attraction to him and my fear of what could happen next. I was young and naive, but I had never expected our date to lead to his bed. I knew I was not ready for what he wanted, and I struggled to find a way out of the situation. Sitting there, I wondered if I was reading too much into his intentions. Perhaps we would just share a few drinks and some laughter. But deep down, I knew that the truth was much more complicated than that.

As we approached Boogie's hotel room, I couldn't help but notice the looming figure standing next to the door. He was a husky man with a mountain of muscle surging down his arm and into his robust forearm. He had shoulders that rivaled a linebacker and a neck that looked like it could crush a watermelon. His outfit was simple but gave off an air of intimidation—black jeans, a black blazer, and a plain black t-shirt. His face was clean-shaven, but his expression was anything but friendly.

This man had the posture of a secret agent with eyes that dared anyone to speak to him. Indeed, he was one that you'd never want to cross paths with. A man that had seen enough dead bodies to ever be affected by another one. As we got closer, I could see the intensity in his eyes. Devin Gates was his name, Boogie's bodyguard. Everyone called him Dee. I later learned that Devin was a notorious gang leader in Los Angeles and was known as an "Unc" to many. In the gang culture, that meant he was high up in the chain of command, and his ties reached far and wide.

Devin stood beside me as we made our way down to the taxi after I said goodbye to Boogie. Although Devin didn't utter a word, his presence spoke volumes. His eyes scanned our surroundings like a hawk, ensuring my safety with every step we took. He took the lead as we approached the car and opened the door, motioning for me to get in first. It was an act of chivalry that caught me off guard, because it was the first time I had seen a man go out of his way to ensure a woman's safety in that manner. At that moment, I realized that Devin wasn't just a bodyguard but a true protector, willing to go above and beyond to keep those under his watchful eye safe.

"Hope you make it home safe. I'm sure Boogie would like it. So would I," Devin said to me.

I promptly turned to him, catching a glimpse of his smile as he disappeared behind the closing doors. He remembered my name. And the way he said it didn't sound platonic or flirtatious. It sounded more… endearing.

The second night, I returned to see Boogie, and my jaw dropped when I saw him with none other than Kobe Bryant. Kobe Bryant?! Are you kidding me? We couldn't walk a few steps without people yelling out Boogie's name. How did I not recognize him the night before? I spent the whole night in the presence of Boogie Shiest, oblivious to his true identity. Despite his notorious reputation and larger-than-life persona, I found myself lost in his world, caught up in his allure. Despite that, the night quickly got tiring after watching Boogie live the celebrity lifestyle. If anything, with Boogie, I still felt like we were more like friends. No spark. No romance. A strictly platonic interaction between him and me. Surprisingly, though, it was Devin who caught my attention as the night went on. I felt more comfortable conversing with him since he appreciated the simple things in life and kept a low profile. We hit it off so well that even after returning home from Las Vegas, we continued our friendly chats. Boogie and I never spoke again, but it was okay because I didn't sense a potential future between us anyway.

Devin was a mystery, a tough nut to crack, but as our friendship deepened, I saw a different side of him. His stoic exterior melted away, revealing a tender, loving soul. He was like a child again, yearning for the warmth of a loving embrace. His beauty radiated from the depths of his soul, drawing me in like a moth to a flame. The more time we spent together, the more I became his confidante, his sounding board, and his safe haven. I was his most precious gift from God. The moments we shared were special, but they came at a price. Being his sanctuary would become dreadful and frightening, leading me to some of my darkest days.

Devin's calls came in daily, and most of the time, our conversations sounded like some masterclass in entrepreneurship. He'd entertain me with tales of his latest business ventures, from his high-end clubs to top-notch bodyguard services, and even his gourmet restaurants. The man was a hustler in every sense of the word, always on the lookout for the next opportunity to add to his ever-growing empire. What was most impressive was that he had accomplished all this without ever stepping foot in a college classroom. Yet, he possessed a keen business acumen that put even the most successful millionaires, CEOs, and business owners I knew to shame. Under his watch, I learned the ins and outs of marketing, business structuring, and real estate. With each conversation, I felt like I was taking one step closer to unlocking the secret of his success.

"Come out to LA and hang out with me. Let me show you around," he said one day.

He was a master persuader, so much so that he talked me into visiting California for a weekend. I playfully set some high standards, telling him I would only go if he flew me first-class and put me in a luxurious five-star hotel. Astonishingly, Devin didn't even blink at my challenge. In fact, he reserved everything precisely to my specifications. During our trip, we dove deeper into each other's minds while exploring the social scene in Los Angeles. Devin was an excellent tour guide, taking me to all the hotspots, including places that I didn't even know I needed to visit.

Devin and I were like jet setters, hopping between Florida and California, visiting each other whenever possible. When we were in LA, it was as if we had the keys to the city—red carpet treatment at every turn, living the life of a celebrity. I was quite shocked because Devin didn't seem to be that kind of guy on our first encounter. We were never seen waiting in line at any club or restaurant and always adorned ourselves with the most exquisite designer jewelry. And the cash he carried around was mind-boggling—not just a couple of hundred dollars, but stacks of thousands of dollars. I couldn't help but find it intriguing, but I chalked it up to his extravagant lifestyle. To be honest, I was utterly enamored with it all.

I remember lying in the hotel room with Devin one night when an insatiable craving for Courvoisier struck me at 3:00 a.m. The next thing I knew, two minutes later, there was a knock on the door. I couldn't believe my eyes when I saw someone holding a bottle of Courvoisier. It was as if Devin had a magical power to manifest my desires at will. His ability to make anything happen with the snap of his fingers was beyond impressive. Whether we were in Florida or California, he always seemed to have the perfect connection for anything I needed. It was a power that I couldn't help but find intoxicating.

Even one night, while I was out with my friends in Florida, Devin, who was in California, called me and inquired about my funds. I mentioned I had some cash but nothing substantial. Without hesitation, he asked if I needed more, and jokingly, I said sure because I assumed there was no way for him to get it to me in the middle of the night. "Someone will be there soon," he assured me. His confident and authoritative tone left me in awe and admiration, further enhancing my feelings toward him. And when someone actually showed up and handed me money, I couldn't help but respect his commanding presence and become more infatuated with him.

At first, Devin was the picture-perfect partner, a mix of sexual exploration, kindness, sweetness, gentleness, and financial independence. With him, I felt secure and worshiped, causing our time together to fly by. Soon, we both knew we were meant to be together. Devin even went and picked out a stunning six-carat diamond ring. I was elated, believing that the troubles I had with Kingsley and Ricky were far behind me. Devin's business acumen rubbed off on me, and he urged me to launch my own entrepreneurial venture when my career with the company was going downhill. Things were looking up, until they weren't. Before I knew it, I was staring at the bottom of an empty bottle, wondering how everything had fallen apart.

It didn't take long before my life took a sharp turn toward the West Coast. My job offered me a promotion to move to California, where I would become a cardiopulmonary specialist. With Natalia and Devin by my side, I was eager to start my life in a place known for its sunshine and glamour. He whisked me away to a sprawling and immaculate home in Corona, a neighborhood reserved for the middle class. Despite its brilliance, I noticed the home was pretty empty inside, except for a few essentials. It was a bit odd, but I brushed it off, excited to decorate the house with my belongings en route from Florida.

Slowly, the cracks in our seemingly perfect life began to show. The first breadcrumb came in the form of Devin's family. When Natalia and I entered the house with Devin, we were greeted by his mother, brother, sister, and nephew, all living under the same roof. I had no idea they were living there because the first time I went to the house, there was no one there. Seeing such a large family in one home was a bit overwhelming, but I tried not to let it bother me too much. However, internally, I was fuming.

"Babe, I don't want to live with your family. I thought I would be living with you. That's what I want," I expressed.

Devin and I didn't have as much conflict as I had with Ricky, but his family was a different story. They had their reservations about me from the moment they laid eyes on me and held a low opinion of me. Despite my sincere efforts to win their approval, their disdain remained unchanged. I exhausted myself trying to prove my worth, and no amount of money or time seemed to bring us any closer. It appeared that they were used to Devin showering them with expensive gifts and lavish attention, but when he decided to devote himself to me, the love of his life, they suddenly took issue with my presence in his life. Somehow, I allowed myself to endure the hardships of living in an unwelcoming environment alongside Devin for far too long.

I still recall the day we had a heated argument, and I declared, "I've had it with your family! I'm leaving for Florida. You can join me if you want, but I'm not sticking around here anymore." And without hesitation, I gathered Natalia, booked a hotel room in L.A. for the night, and departed for Florida the next day. Devin's attempts to reassure me that staying in the house would be fine fell on deaf ears. I had already learned the hard way from my experience with Ricky that living with a man and his mother was a recipe for disaster. I was determined not to repeat the same mistake. Despite his persistent efforts to persuade me, I stood my ground and refused to budge.

"Alright. I'll get us another spot. Just give me some time," he said.

He was true to his word, moving us into a new house, but something felt off about it. Despite being spacious and to my liking, it seemed like the memories of countless tragedies haunted the walls. Sort of reminded me of the first day I arrived in America and stepped into my mother's apartment. The lack of sunlight that made the place gloomy and unsettling, both physically and emotionally. It didn't help that Devin frequently left at odd hours of the day to handle business matters, sometimes not returning until late at night. With Natalia and me often alone in the eerie house, I found myself sinking into sadness. Devin often discouraged me from going out, insisting that Los Angeles wasn't safe.

"Just stay in the house. I'll bring you something. You don't know L.A. like that."

Devin's voice held a protective and caring tone, which reminded me of a nurturing father. It was never forceful or condemning but reassuring and loving. I could sense that he genuinely cared about my well-being and safety, which made me feel secure around him. Despite his busy schedule, he never failed to show his thoughtfulness and kindness, often going out of his way to make me breakfast and pack Natalia's lunch before taking her to school. He had a way of making us both feel loved and cherished, and the bond between him and Natalia was undeniable. I felt like I had finally found the happiness and stability that I had been searching for all along.

"Okay. But I don't like this house. I want to move," I confessed.

Devin always had a knack for fulfilling my every wish and command. He promised to find us a home that would truly make us feel alive, and he delivered on that promise. One day, he took me on a tour of the most breathtaking house in Anaheim Hills, California that felt like something out of a movie. It was magnificent with an amazing view overlooking all of Orange County. I knew this house must have cost a fortune, but I also knew Devin was determined to make it ours. The mere thought of living in that house was enough to keep me in California with the hope of a brighter future. I was like a child in a candy store, eager to move in immediately. And when Devin asked me to help finance the purchase, I didn't hesitate to give him the hard-earned savings I had accumulated from years of commission checks. In total, I handed him nearly $200,000 for the sake of turning our dreams into reality.

Nevertheless, each day, the weight of my unease grew heavier, like a boulder resting on my chest. Even with Devin's constant protection and care, a nagging voice within me persisted. It was as if my intuition was whispering in my ear, urging me to flee. But somehow, I couldn't bring myself to do it. Before I started therapy with Dr. Kelley, I overlooked the warning signs of trauma, even if they were coming at me like an eagle soaring through the sky. I thought I could find a way to make everything work out in my favor. However, the universe had other plans, and I soon learned that fighting against fate was a battle I couldn't win.

As days turned to weeks and weeks turned to months, I noticed a pattern of peculiar behavior from Devin, unlike anything I had seen before. He was staying out later and having random secretive phone calls throughout the day. Some nights, he'd invite friends over at the most irregular hours and ask me to cook for them with little to no notice. Everywhere I looked, there were wads of cash rolled in a fat knot or neatly stacked in a bag. If that wasn't sketchy enough, it was as though he had eyes everywhere, observing my every move. He knew intimate details about me before I even told him. To top it all off, there were little to no talks of moving into our new house.

At first, I questioned the legitimacy of my suspicions, but the feeling persisted like a sweltering fever. Despite his odd behavior, I wasn't ready to pack my bags and bolt just yet. I figured he was just getting more comfortable, working harder, and with all the other stuff, I believed it was just the little things that men do. But then, Devin's behavior took a turn for the worse.

He began to make disturbing statements that sent chills down my spine. "If someone comes to the door, don't answer it. Call me first," he warned me. "Always make sure the door is locked."

I couldn't shake the feeling that danger lurked around every corner. Every creak of the floorboards and rustle of the leaves outside made me nervous. It didn't help that he slept with a gun under his pillow and always left the house dressed in full security gear when he had to go to his club, leaving Natalia and me alone. Some nights I was unbothered, but on other nights, I felt puzzled and sometimes petrified, like I was a prisoner in my own home.

One day, an uneasy feeling consumed me, and I knew I had to confront Devin about what was bothering me. I trailed behind him like a shadow, demanding answers about his behavior that made me feel like he was a stranger in our relationship. But he was too caught up in his search for whatever it was that he badly needed even to acknowledge my presence, almost as if he was trying to keep something hidden.

"Devin, I can't keep pretending everything is fine between us. I need to know what's really going on," I declared, my voice shaky with frustration and uncertainty.

Devin remained silent. However, my heart sank as he emerged from the closet, clutching a massive block of cocaine wrapped tightly in plastic. I froze as a chill ran through my body. With my eyes bugged wide open, I stared at the brick in horror, trying to process the reality of the situation. It was clear that I was living with a drug dealer, but to what extent, I had no idea. I knew I couldn't stay in that situation any longer. Therefore, I grabbed Natalia and made a beeline out the door, heading back to Florida once again. Devin begged and pleaded with me to stay, but my mind was made up. Even as I drove away, I couldn't shake the feeling that I had left a part of myself behind. Despite the danger and uncertainty of his world, I still loved him and wanted to give us another chance. And so, at some point, I made the difficult decision to return to California, alone, hoping that we could make it work this time.

CHAPTER 12

LESSON LEARNED

As my eyes remained fixed on the bottle, watching it slowly vanish into thin air. Each second brought me closer to a light-headed trance, and soon, stars danced around the room, bringing me to an unfamiliar place.

My life was quickly spinning out of control, through an endless maze without any clear path out. Every turn seemed to lead to another dead end, in a gloomy place without taste, smell, or a hint of hope. My emotions were a chaotic storm, crashing down on me with no warning. Happiness felt like a burden, weighing me down like a bag of rocks, while fear consumed me even in the moments I was supposed to be carefree.

Beyond my control, Devin and I grew apart as our fights escalated to dangerous levels. I constantly bugged him about the house I had given my entire savings for, and each time I did, he responded with the same bullshit excuses and lies. Until one day, he exploded, and what he did to me was not expected. Yes, I knew my mouth could be too much to deal with, but when his fists pummeled me mercilessly, and he tossed me around the room like a rag doll, I knew then I was in trouble. This was the first time his rage resulted in my blood and pain. I called the police immediately and had him arrested. It was a heartbreaking but necessary decision, and I knew then that we were no longer meant to be together, regardless of the love I had for him.

Despite the chaos and turmoil of my life, I had to put on a facade that everything was okay. That way, everyone would suspect I was the same old Trisha Bailey they'd come to know. Yet, beneath the surface, I felt like I was drowning in misery. Every smile and every laugh felt empty. It was as if a dark cloud had settled over my soul, casting a shadow over everything I did, reminding me that things were not as they seemed.

My life had fallen into a monotonous routine, lacking any sense of balance. I poured all of myself, my time, and my money into the needs of others, always putting their priorities above my own. The days I had spent shopping were either for my daughter or Devin. I was becoming the cornerstone of support for everyone in my life, yet I was constantly pouring out without taking the time to replenish myself. To add to that, the stresses of starting a business had only worsened my exhaustion and frustration. When that happened, it didn't take too long for me to feel myself quickly approaching the brink of a burnout. Point blank, I was over it all.

I remember the days when Natalia would scramble around with nothing but joy, her laughter filling the room as she played all alone. It was a beautiful sight to behold, but it was one that I couldn't connect with. I stood there, a mere bystander, hidden in the shadows, as my mind and emotions lay dormant, almost as if I was a puppet, manipulated by an unseen force that dictated every single one of my movements.

"Mommy! Mommy!" she would yell, leaping into my arms with contagious enthusiasm.

And just like that, the sound of my daughter's voice would pull me back to reality. Unbeknownst to me, I couldn't bear to tell anyone how I felt because I didn't want their pity or any sort of judgment from anyone. Nor did I want to hear the same tired advice I had heard before. *"It'll be alright. Just pray about it."* Or *"Don't worry about it. You're just going through a funk."* And my favorite one, *"You need to speak to someone."* So, I questioned what good would it do to talk to anyone if they couldn't offer any real solution anyway?

* * *

Then it happened. The moment that changed my life forever occurred in the comfort of my own home. It was the day I hit rock bottom and my world was plunged into an abyss of darkness. For too long, I tried to ignore Devin's lies and secrets, including his involvement in drug dealing, despite his promises to quit. His late-night disappearances, sketchy behavior, and family problems had all taken a toll on me. On top of that, he had been dragging his feet on the house we had planned to move into for months, leaving me feeling stranded between California and Florida, uncertain about my next steps. The voice in my head grew louder until I finally submitted to it and decided to leave.

Fourth of July weekend, in 2008, I returned to California to tie up loose ends from my job after starting my own business. I had to return all the products to the company along with the company car, credit card, computer, and everything else. That's the only reason why I returned to California. When I arrived at the house to retrieve all my things, Devin was home. This was no surprise as he was expecting me there. At first, he seemed apologetic, stating how he screwed everything up—even wanting to get married and have the child we always desired.

For a moment, I believed him, but then, things swiftly got out of hand. Our cordial conversation quickly escalated into a shouting match, hurling venomous insults at each other. All the shit he had been holding onto came pouring out. The more he spoke, the more he exposed himself through all the lies and deceit. I could not bear to hear his voice, let alone see his face. Overwhelming anger consumed me as a faint buzzing and ringing drowned out the noise. I was beyond myself, so much so that my body weakened, and my hands began shaking without my control. Indeed, I was defeated.

Overcome by life's stressors, I felt like I was drifting away to an isolated place. In this place, the silence around me seemed to get louder as I sat at the kitchen table, crying and lost in thought. Then, I clung to a bottle, hoping it would offer an escape from all my problems. It all happened so fast, making everything moving through time seem like a blur. It was like watching myself from outside my body, begging me to stop. But I couldn't. Before I knew it, my fingers were typing away at my laptop, pouring out my feelings and desires as if I might never return to this world again.

All the colors around me seemed to fade into nothingness, and the air was stale. I was numb, lost in a haze of hopelessness. But then I heard my daughter's voice echoing in my head, *"Mommy, I need you. Please don't die."* It was the same thing she had murmured to me the last time she saw me fully dressed, crouched in a fetal position while crying in the shower. I couldn't bear to put her through that pain again. It's too bad she was not in the house with me, because this part of the book might not have been a chapter in my life.

Nevertheless, I couldn't take my eyes off the bottle. As that happened, bright stars danced around the room, taking me to that unfamiliar place. Suddenly, the bottle slipped from my grasp, and I watched it disappear into thin air as if it had never existed. Panic seized my body, leaving my heart pounding as the room began to spin. I had surrendered to a light-headed trance, with the stars on the ceiling mocking me, taunting me with their brightness.

I tried to stand up, but my legs felt like jelly, buckling beneath me. Then, BAM! I hit the ground with a loud thud, the empty bottle crashing beside me. My body was too weak to hold me up, and I just lay there, helpless, and vulnerable. I don't remember much after that, but I do recall the room spinning even more as if I were on a gravitron ride, spiraling faster and faster until the bright stars dimmed into a pitch-black void.

When the bright light finally appeared from the darkness, the world around me looked different. The colors were more vibrant, and the sounds more pronounced. I found myself standing in the open field of sunflowers and daisies gently swaying through the breeze. The rustling sounds of the trees combined with the gentle chirping of birds was all I could hear. This was the most peaceful and serene place I'd ever witnessed. The outside world was a distant memory, and in there, smiling came effortlessly and naturally. The field was a haven of serenity, casting a spell on me with its tranquil beauty. For a moment, I couldn't feel whether I was in a dream or a different reality. But it hardly mattered. What mattered was the sheer thrill of being there, amidst the rolling grass and the golden sunlight. The birds' joyful chirping increased and filled the air with music, and their melodies soothed my senses. The wind's caress was gentle, like a soft embrace, making me feel weightless and carefree.

As I stood there, awed by the beauty, a sense of belonging washed over me. It was as if my soul had finally found its true home, a place where I was meant to be. But just as I began to lose myself in the moment, everything around me swiftly changed. I was now standing on the shores of an ocean, watching the waves crashing against my legs. In the water, I could see my reflection, and what I saw was the little girl who loved to run all over Woodland, laughing and smiling. She wore the prettiest sunflower dress I had ever seen, making her that much more innocent. A joyous sight indeed, and I couldn't help but smile as I gazed upon it, reminding me of simpler times—a life filled with unbridled joy and wonder.

For a moment, I was that little girl, standing there, cheerful, and unaffected by the world's weight, until everything instantly shifted to me standing in acres of a cornfield. The cornfield's plants were tall, with the bright light of a horizon being the only thing I could see beyond them. Very similar to Kevin Costner in *Field of Dreams*. The scent of dirt and crops took me back to that sacred place of mine in Jamaica when I was a little girl, helping my uncle out on the farm. I could not stop beaming from the pleasure as it all happened before my eyes, and as I took a deep breath, my body was overcome with tingles in a very strange way.

Then, something peculiar in the distance caught my attention. The heat haze shimmered like a mirage, beckoning me forward. Despite the bright sun's warmth, a chill ran down my spine, settling deep in my bones. It was as if the field knew something I didn't, warning me of the danger ahead. Despite the fear that bubbled inside, I couldn't stop walking toward the haze. I took each step cautiously, my heart pounding in my chest as I moved closer and closer. The next thing I knew, I was waking up eight days later in a hospital with tubes in me like a fucking robot.

As my eyes slowly flickered open, an intense pain pierced through my skull like a fiery inferno. My face felt bloated and distorted to the point that I could not recognize myself. I had a severely deep gash on my left side that throbbed with agony. My shoulder was raw and tender, pulsating with each breath I took, while my knee felt like it had been shattered into a million pieces. It was as if I had been in a brutal battle, fighting for my life, but sadly enough, I couldn't recall any of it. The events leading up to my injuries remain a hazy and bizarre mystery.

When I emerged from my coma, my body was consumed by excruciating pain. It was so unbearable that I desperately wanted to slip back into the soothing abyss of unconsciousness where the light gleamed as bright as the sun. Realizing that I was lying in a hospital bed, I tried to speak, but the world around me was a blur, and my voice came out struggling in a rasping whisper. "I want to go," I murmured to Devin, who was standing by my side, tears streaming down his face as he held onto my hand. Seeing him filled with so much emotion and distress made me realize that something terrible must have happened to me. It was enough to scare me even more than I had been before.

As I slowly regained consciousness, I tried to make sense of what had occurred, and through the confusion, I managed to gasp out the question, "What happened?"

Devin looked at me as if I had a monkey standing on my chest. At a loss for words, his expression conveyed a sense of shock and disbelief. "I don't know," he muttered.

The hazy memories of that day left my mind swirling with endless thoughts and a gnawing feeling, suggesting that Devin held the key to the truth. Yet, for some odd reason, he refused to tell me. This all happened in 2008. I still don't know what actually occurred. Despite my attempt to take my own life, the injuries that scarred my body seemed inconsistent with the method I had chosen. It wasn't like I had flung myself off a building, that much was clear to me. Then, in a startling revelation, Devin disclosed that he had left our home earlier, leaving me alone with my troubles. This was news to me because I distinctly remembered being in a seriously heated fight with him before I blacked out.

Devin said he was worried about me when he realized I wasn't responding to his calls, so he sent his nephew, Sam, to check on me. According to Sam, he found me lying on the floor, unresponsive and bleeding everywhere. Sam wasted no time calling 911, and following that, he called Devin, who raced to the hospital to stand by my side. The only problem with that story is that because Devin was always so protective and safety-conscious, he had built the house like a fortress. Even if someone managed to get past the vicious dog, they would still have difficulty getting in because of the bolted locks on the doors and windows. Devin never trusted anyone enough to give out an extra key, and no one could come over if he wasn't there. It has always been a mystery to me. How did Sam break into the house on that day and just happen to be there at the right time?

"How long have I been here?" I murmured.

His words sent shivers down my spine when he uttered, "You've been in a coma for eight days."

I could not believe it, and as the fog of unconsciousness cleared, I stood at the beginning of my torment.

"Where's my mom? I need my mom. Did you tell her what happened?" I cried.

Devin told me that he had called my mother, the person I should have been able to turn to for comfort and support, but she had decided not to come. My heart was broken, even though my mind understood why she couldn't be with me. It was the week when my entire family had gone to Jamaica to commemorate the anniversary of my grandmother's death. Nevertheless, I still longed for her presence by my side.

For a while, tension hung heavily between my mother and me after that situation. It was a heavy presence we both effortlessly ignored. Perhaps it may sound selfish on my part, but I simply couldn't fathom leaving my child alone in her time of desperate need. The unspoken words about what had transpired and the reasons behind her decision to go to Jamaica instead of being by my side were topics we both danced around, especially after I discovered that my dear friend Marjorie had tried to convince my mother to change her plans and come to California instead. It was a cruel twist of fate, and whatever I had to face that day, I would have to face it alone.

I spent years burying this dark memory so deep in my mind that I hoped to reach a point where it never happened. But as I reflected on it, I came to realize what had truly happened years earlier. Life's challenges hadn't become too overwhelming, and Devin's dishonesty, anger, or disappearing acts were not the main causes of my collapse.

Upon deep consideration, I discovered that those were among the least of my troubles. However, I was too hurt and blind to see what had caused me to fall to the point where I would try to end it all.

Here's the truth. Before that fateful day, something about my grandmother's death haunted my thoughts like an infectious disease. It wasn't her passing itself that tormented me. Instead, it was the weight of the last words she heard me say: "Why don't you take her with you?"

In a moment of frustration, those words slipped from my lips in response to my mother asking me to accompany my grandmother to the specialist. Regrettably, my grandmother became caught in the crossfire of my emotions toward my mother, and it was profoundly unfair to her. I was already shouldering the responsibilities of caring for my little brother, raising my daughter, working, building my business, and attending school full-time. All I had wanted was a little help from my mother. However, none of those circumstances should have justified my words. I should have been there for my grandmother, who tragically passed away the following day. In the years that followed, the consequences of those last words haunted me relentlessly and were unbearably heavy. Especially since she was a woman I cherished deeply. It left me feeling empty, driving me to seek comfort in others just to fill the void of a lost love. The men I encountered, including Devin, temporarily provided that peace, but the guilt always returned, gnawing at me like ants on a piece of candy.

It wasn't until therapy that I truly comprehended the profound impact of my grandmother's death. The woman who embodied the essence of an angel, a celestial being whose radiant light touched the lives of all who encountered her, was no longer here with me. Therefore, on that fateful morning when I attempted to take my own life, it wasn't to escape from the world I had grown familiar with. Instead, it was a desperate attempt to reunite with my grandmother, to seek forgiveness for my perceived wrongdoing, and to find the peace that had eluded me for far too long.

Strange things happen at the weakest point in your life, and you can't explain it. Trying to understand it could be a miserable failure. Therefore, we find ourselves asking the person in the mirror what he or she is willing to give up in order to receive something else. So many of us want to believe that we can only find pleasure in a life with no pain, success without failure, or an abundance of acceptance and no rejection. But at that weakest point is where you find that it is impossible.

When I woke from my coma, the only thing I wanted was to hold my daughter. I needed to have my arms wrapped around her and smell the top of her head so badly that it overshadowed my physical pain. It was a heart-wrenching feeling that resided deep within me, impossible to shake. The thought of having a baby growing inside me filled me with joy and ultimately became more important than anything else in my life. But the reality was harsher than I could have imagined. Devin was the only man I trusted enough to consider having a child with, but our relationship was going nowhere fast. Although I didn't love him enough to be with him, my desire for a child was stronger than anything else. It was as if God had sent an angel to me during my coma and gave me a vision of a child. I could feel just how much my world would change. Sadly, after leaving the hospital, I knew my relationship with Devin would never be the same.

* * *

Devin always wanted a child, especially a boy, and I knew he would go to great lengths to make it happen. His previous girlfriend got pregnant, but it turned out the child wasn't his, which devastated him. Another woman he dated chose to abort their baby without his knowledge, leaving him with a profound sense of loss. As for me, I had never felt the urge to have a child with Devin. We tried to conceive many times, but nothing seemed to work. He felt defeated and believed it wasn't meant to be, but after several conversations about starting a family, I knew I had to come clean. The desire to have a child had consumed me and I couldn't keep the truth from him any longer. I took a deep breath and revealed something I had kept hidden for far too long.

"I'm sorry, but we couldn't get pregnant because I had an IUD the whole time," I confessed.

It was deceitful to use a method of birth control without telling him, and I felt ashamed, but I had no regrets. I didn't know what I would do if Devin chose not to be a part of our child's life. I couldn't bear the thought of going through what I had gone through with Natalia's father. Besides, I never intended to have any more children. So, I had to face Devin's anger before telling him I had changed my mind, but I did it because I wanted my baby so badly. Even if it meant taking the risk of being a single mom.

Months passed, and Devin and I continued to speak every day. He would update me on the highs and lows of his professional and personal life while I shared my deepest feelings and thoughts. Sometimes we'd laugh together while also sharing profound emotional moments. Speaking to him was strange because I didn't know where our relationship stood, but for some reason, I was okay with that. Despite my lingering apprehension toward him, Devin was my comfort in the most toxic way possible. At a time when I felt alone and lost, speaking to him made me feel differently. I couldn't explain it, nor did I want to. Looking back, I can see how detached from reality I was, using him as a way to cope with the missing void in my life. That's the thing about trauma. It has a way of significantly impacting our mental health and well-being, ultimately affecting how we think, feel, and behave. Associating with Devin made me realize this more than ever.

Over and over, I answered his calls and engaged in small talk out of kindness and comfort, yet he barely made an effort to see me in person. Then, one day, he surprised me by telling me that he was getting ready to purchase our dream house and wanted me to be with him when he did. I closed my eyes, took a deep breath, and faintly smiled. That's what I had been waiting to hear from him for a long time, but strangely, I didn't feel the happiness I thought I would. Instead, a nagging feeling rose up inside me, begging me not to go.

In the fall of 2009, I went to Washington D.C. for my final doctoral residency. Devin came to visit me, apologizing and telling me he wanted everything to be right between us. He even convinced me that he was the one for me and that the life we both wanted was waiting for us in California. It was like an out-of-body experience, watching myself continuing to fall for a man I knew I had no business being with.

"Where's my ring?" I asked.

Devin was evasive and refused to give me a straight answer about the whereabouts of my ring, constantly deflecting and avoiding the topic. He would say he didn't remember where he placed it. On other occasions, he would claim that one of his family members had it. All sorts of explanations, yet none of them felt like the truth. Then again, it was probably just another sign I was overlooking because when I didn't think things could get any worse, they did just that. Still, I wanted the ring he promised.

After returning to Florida from D.C., I was ready to take on the world and make strides in my career. While at the gym, my nose suddenly started to bleed. Since I had never experienced a nosebleed before and had recently gone through a traumatic experience in California, I thought it best to go to the hospital. After picking up Natalia from school, I explained my symptoms, including some unusual stomach cramps to the doctor. It turned out to be nothing, but on my way home, I stopped to buy a pregnancy test as it was the only explanation left for how I was feeling. When I got home, I brought Natalia into the bathroom with me, and we took the test together. To my excitement, the test came back positive, and I was pregnant! Natalia and I danced and rejoiced over the news, as I had been hoping for a child more than anything in the world. I immediately called Devin to share the news, but he did not answer. Despite repeatedly calling him, he never answered.

Upon discovering that I was expecting a baby boy, I knew I had to name him Gabriel. The name reminded me of the angel I had seen in my subconscious, and I believed that just like the angel, my son would be my savior from all the pain and suffering I had endured. For the first time in a while, I saw a glimmer of hope that things could return to normal. Even though Devin wasn't responding, the fact that Gabriel was growing inside me made me the happiest I had been in a long time. He was truly a bright spot in my life.

I was weeks into my pregnancy when suddenly I could no longer get in touch with Devin. I mean, no calls. No texts. Nothing! It was as if he never existed. But then, I discovered he had changed his number without telling me. Even his family members weren't answering any of my calls. I tried emailing Devin but despite reading the messages, I received no replies. I was emotionally and physically exhausted, unable to work as many hours as I usually would. Natalia was often late for school, and the teachers had to give her techniques to wake me up in the morning. The weight of it all was crushing, and I could feel myself sinking deeper into despair with each passing day. Most of the time, I walked around fuming with anger, having to go through the pregnancy all alone. Again! If anything, I was more upset with myself than I was with Devin because I knew better, but I refused to do better. How could I let this happen to me? I trusted a man I was not supposed to, and it backfired on me. But before I could leave, I needed to get my money. That became my sole mission, my only tie to Devin, and I was determined not to walk away without it.

"I want my money back! Now!" I ordered.

I was determined to get what I was owed, demanding that he return every penny I had given him from my savings. But the more I asked, the more he grew indifferent to my words. Eventually, he stopped caring altogether and did whatever he pleased, ignoring my requests.

One morning, I found myself staring out the window, watching the sun rise over the city, when the realization hit me: I was alone. But I couldn't let that stop me, not with Natalia and a baby on the way who depended on me. So, I faced the truth head-on, determined to move forward with my life. I made sure Natalia was enrolled in one of the best schools in the area, and soon enough, she was excelling in her studies. My business was doing well, and I learned to manage my time efficiently by focusing on what was truly necessary. I didn't have many friends, and my contact with family was limited, but I knew I needed help. A friend of mine suggested his cousin Ralph, who lived in the area, could come over on weekends to help with tasks around the house—from hanging paintings to assembling baby furniture. He even brought his daughters along to play with Natalia. Before long, Ralph became a source of comfort and good company. While our relationship remained strictly platonic, he gave me hope that one day I might find a man who could truly be my friend.

The phone rang while I was in the kitchen cooking one night, and the caller ID showed an unknown number. Reluctantly, I answered, hoping it was Devin.

"Hello?" I answered.

"What's up?"

It was him. He responded as if we had just spoken minutes ago. I don't know what I was expecting, but I thought by hearing his voice, it would bring me comfort. Instead, it only brought back a wave of emotion that left me in a funk, especially when he asked if I had put a root on him. What? I was appalled by the fact that he would think that I'd do such a thing.

Devin's phone calls would come in sporadically, and each time he called it was from another number. One day, my phone rang again with an unknown number appearing on the screen. I winced at the sound because I knew it was Devin calling. I was thirty-one weeks pregnant, waiting in a room surrounded by a cold four-sided white wall with a large window looking out to nothing. I could hear the distant sounds of crying babies and beeping machines. "I'm at the hospital because I'm having contractions," I told him.

I was on the verge of a breakdown, reminiscent of the day when I sat in front of the bottle, feeling like life had gotten the best of me. If it hadn't been for my friend Holly, I might have given up. Holly was an angel who became an integral part of my life. Our kids were classmates, and through their friendship, Holly and I formed our own bond. At the time, Holly was nine months pregnant, and she quickly became someone I could rely on during my own pregnancy. Like Ralph, she helped with the little things and looked after Natalia while I had to work. Being around Holly was a breath of fresh air, and I'm sure my life would have taken a more difficult path without her. She reminded me of all the strong women in my life, like my aunts, grandmother, mother, and track coaches, who supported me along the way. When I went into labor with Gabriel, Holly took Natalia home with her as I drove myself to the hospital in excruciating pain. She was there for me every step of the way.

When I told Devin I was in the hospital, his response was flat, almost indifferent. "Okay," was all he said. I hesitated at first but then asked the question that had been burning in my mind. "Are you going to try to help me at the end of this pregnancy or what?"

"Yes," he murmured. But the way he said it, I could hear the lie slip between his lips. Then, out of nowhere, he asked me an odd question. "What car insurance company do you have?"

My mind reeled with confusion. What did car insurance have to do with anything? But I answered anyway, thinking maybe, there was something that he was doing for our child and me. "Geico."

Just like that, the call was over, leaving me feeling confused and helpless. It wasn't until later that I discovered that Devin had called the insurance company and added his truck to my policy. I was stuck with his bill and still couldn't reach him. Weeks passed, with several run-ins with his family as I tried to contact him to get my money. I even remember his mother telling me that the baby I was carrying wasn't his. I despised the fact that she would utter such blasphemous remarks. After several attempts to get in touch with Devin, his brother cussed me out and threatened to put a restraining order on me if I ever called him again.

Then, one day, I went into labor and returned to the hospital. This time, it was the real deal. The room was cold, sterile, and the bright lights made my head pound. To my surprise, Devin's brother showed up to the hospital while I was in labor wanting to witness the birth of my son Gabriel. I was furious and beyond annoyed, yet I was in too much pain to care about his presence. However, as the pain grew more intense, I felt his eyes boring into me as if he were trying to assert some control over my body and my baby.

"Ms. Bailey, would you like him to be in the room with you?" the nurse inquired. Despite the lack of energy that I possessed, I managed to respond with a loud, "Hell no!"

The next thing I knew, while in labor, Devin called me. His voice was crackling over the phone with nasty and spiteful words. He lashed out at me, hurling insults and curses like daggers aimed at my heart. All because I refused to let his brother into the delivery room. It was as if he had forgotten I was carrying his child. Alone! I was the one enduring the pain and uncertainty of childbirth. In all our conversations, he never wanted to show up. He only wanted to speak over the phone, and I found it extremely strange. Following the birth of Gabriel, it would all come to light. I've always said the universe has a way of being on my side, and with Devin, there was no exception.

For my 32nd birthday, all I wanted was to be home with my family in Florida. California had become a place I despised, and I couldn't bear the thought of celebrating my birthday there. So, that's exactly what I did. I took Natalia and three-week-old Gabriel and flew back to Florida. Once I arrived, a part of me longed to stay there and never return to California. However, different plans were in store for me.

On August 8, 2010, I returned to the West Coast with my two children. I wanted to move back to Florida because that's where I found comfort from friends and family, but I had to return to California so that Natalia could attend school. Despite my constant emails to Devin, updating him on our son Gabriel's life, he never responded. I was still waiting for a phone call or text. Nothing! Even while dealing with Gabe's doctor visits, I wrote to Devin as if he were a soldier off to war who could return home at any moment. Perhaps that's how I found a way to feel like I was giving Gabriel a chance to have his father in his life.

When I arrived home, I decided to check my emails and came across a message from Devin's best friend, Randall. He urgently requested my phone number, and without hesitation, I shared it with him via email. Within moments, my phone rang, and it was Randall on the other end. As we began our conversation, he dropped a bombshell on me. He revealed that Devin was in jail, charged with attempted murder and accessory to kidnapping. The news hit me with force, leaving me speechless and struggling to process the information. I couldn't believe it. How could this be happening? I had never known anyone to be arrested or in jail before. In the middle of my shock, Randall insisted that Devin was innocent, claiming that anything I would hear about Devin is a lie. Devin was not dealing drugs. He was not the muscle man behind one of the most notorious Russian mafia families. According to Randall, it was all a lie.

I sat there, contemplating what to do in the wake of Devin's arrest, and my mind wandered to thoughts of Gabriel. I thought of how much he deserved a chance to have a relationship with his father, to feel the warmth of his embrace, to hear his voice, to know his love. The thought of Gabriel being denied that chance filled me with a sense of anxiety and guilt. It was as if I could see him in front of me, a small and vulnerable figure, reaching out for the father he never knew he had. The image of his little hand grasping at the air tugged at my heartstrings, pulling me in a direction I never thought I'd go.

The news came as a shock, and soon after, Devin's family started reaching out to me, seeking help and support for his legal expenses. It felt incredibly ironic given our turbulent history. Despite all the name-calling and the fact that they had stolen over $200,000 from me, they had the audacity to come running to me for assistance. I was dumbfounded. Hell, I couldn't forget the time when I returned to California while five months pregnant, and they treated me like a piece of shit simply because I wanted my belongings back. They recklessly packed all my things into a U-Haul truck and left me, a pregnant woman, to move everything by myself behind a shopping center as they watched me. If it hadn't been for the kind help of two strangers, I wouldn't have been able to manage it at all.

The pain, both physical and emotional, that Devin and his family had caused me was overwhelming. I couldn't understand why they treated me so poorly. But despite their actions, I couldn't ignore the fact that Gabriel shared their blood. The love I had for my child outweighed everything else, and I knew I had to endure their presence for his sake. Besides, my grandmother's voice continued to echo in my head, leading me to follow the moral compass she instilled in me.

To make matters worse, through their seeking help, I discovered that Devin was dating another woman who was six months pregnant and living with his family. I felt like I had hit rock bottom. However, despite all the new revelations, I could hear my grandmother's spirit echoing in my head, telling me to do what was right and forgive. I didn't want to. Instead, I wanted him to rot in prison as his family suffered from him not being there to support them. Nevertheless, I couldn't let my experiences with Devin and his family dictate the kind of woman I was at my core.

I had to be a forgiving woman with a heart of gold, grounded in morals that elevated my spirit. I punished myself for years, feeling love would never blossom if I didn't learn to forgive completely. Therefore, forgiving Devin was more for me than it was for him and his family. It gave me the freedom to love again and to heal my heart, mind, and soul. It allowed me to begin moving on with only positivity and break free from conformity.

So, despite the ugliest of ugly times, I decided to stand by Devin's side, fight for him, and do everything in my power to clear his name. It wasn't an easy decision, and I knew that many would question my sanity. Hell, I questioned myself on many occasions, too. But in my heart, I knew that it was the right thing to do. He was still the father of my child. Natalia and I didn't have a relationship with dads. I didn't want the same for Gabriel. I could see Gabriel's smiling face, his eyes lighting up with joy, as he learned that his father was not the monster the world had painted him to be. I envisioned a day where I could see Gabriel running toward Devin, throwing his arms around his father, and holding him tight as his little heart beats with happiness.

And at that moment, with those thoughts in mind, all the pain, hurt, and betrayal went out the door. So, if there was something I could do to help keep him out of jail I would do it. And hopefully it would give him a chance at a life with the son he always wanted. Besides, despite it all, I still deeply loved him, so I would do whatever it took.

Before I stepped in to help, I was unaware of the true nature of his crime, but I still paid over $50,000 for his legal fees. On the first day of Devin's trial, I sat in the front row, eager to see Devin's face and find out the truth. It was only the second time I had seen him since I got pregnant with Gabriel, and he looked more rugged than I remembered. At some point, our eyes met, and I noticed a stillness in his gaze that suggested a defeated spirit. But then, he did something strange and switched his gaze to a pregnant Black woman right next to me. That was her, the woman he had left me for, sitting so close to me that I could smell her fresh, floral, and sweet scent.

For the next several days, I went to court, waiting to discover all the details of the man I had come to know. The more I learned, the worse I felt about myself. How could I have been so blind and stupid not to see the things they were accusing him of? During the trial, I learned about Devin's drug activities and shady dealings from what seemed like a distant past, but now it was all too real. He was involved with the Armenians and the Russians, both of whom were mafia families.

Their deal had gone bad, and they decided to kidnap a man named Arman Kevorkian. Arman was accused of engaging in fraudulent mortgage scams—the same scam Devin was part of. Turns out that Mr. Kevorkian had allegedly stolen a considerable amount of money, and the mafia guys couldn't close on the properties they were juggling.

As they were kidnapping him, things got out of hand. The man's bodyguard started shooting, and it quickly turned into a shootout. That's when everything became a whole fiasco. Devin and the others took the kidnapped man to Devin's restaurant, contacted the man's family, and asked for a one-million-dollar ransom. From the restaurant, they took the man to Devin's house. Meanwhile, the man's family saw an ATM withdrawal and called the police. Somehow, the police figured out where the kidnapped man was being held and kicked in Devin's door. My heart was pounding, and my eyes were wide open, listening to the truth unfold as if I were watching a Christopher Nolan movie.

I found myself in court every day for the trial, along with the woman who had also been involved with Devin. After the first trial, the woman began talking to me, and that's when she told me everything I needed to know. All the questions I wanted answered were coming straight from her mouth. The woman believed that Devin was going to prison and refused to have any ties to him, so at six months pregnant, she decided to have an abortion. For days, my heart remained heavy for the woman because her shallow mind allowed her to make a decision so drastic as killing a baby. It's not that she cared about Devin going to prison. She was more concerned that he wouldn't be able to give her the money or lifestyle she had been accustomed to.

On the last day of the trial, I stole a glance at her, and my eyes traced the line of her arm until I spotted my engagement ring glistening on her finger. The sight plunged a dagger into my heart, tearing open old wounds. At that moment, I knew it was over. I had forgiven them, but I could no longer bear to be tied to him—even if it meant sacrificing my son's relationship with his father.

Turns out, Devin was initially fortunate to have a mistrial. However, his luck didn't last long as he was scheduled for a second trial. By that time, I had gathered my belongings and children and fled to Florida. I wanted nothing to do with him or California anymore. Despite my desire for closure, I found myself going back to see him in court. And on that day, the judge's gavel struck, delivering the verdict of guilty!

And just like that, it was all over. He received a twenty-seven-year sentence in federal prison. A strange and overwhelming mix of emotions engulfed me, leading to nights filled with tears. It wasn't just my own pain I cried for, but also for Gabriel. I felt like I had failed him. He would grow up without his father, and since I had vowed to never let Gabriel step foot in a prison, he wouldn't see Devin until his release. At that moment, I questioned myself, wondering why I had even bothered being there. From that day forward, I never looked back.

I thought about how much money I'd lost being with Devin. It was all gone, lost in the middle of a mafia deal gone wrong. I shuddered to think about all the potential dangers I would have faced if he had not left me. Even the FBI had forcefully entered my life, interrogating me about my dealings with Devin, and threatening me with possible consequences. However, after their thorough investigation, they discovered I was not involved with Devin's affairs. Fortunately, he chose to cut me off and left me to fend for myself at the right time; otherwise, my story would have been vastly different, perhaps one told from prison.

The entire experience was surreal, and it will forever be etched in my memory. It showed me that even when you think things are going badly for you, God has a way of protecting you, even if it isn't in your ideal situation, as long as you remain kind and true to yourself. That lesson became clearer when I discovered that Devin had placed his restaurant in my name. I had no intention of running a burger joint, so I sold it, and interestingly, all the money that had been taken from me had returned to me.

Deuteronomy 30:3 - God will restore your fortunes, and have compassion upon you, and he will gather you again from all the peoples…

CHAPTER 13

SAME MISTAKES

"With my heart guarded, I was determined to keep my head down and stay on track without anyone distracting me. However, fate had other plans."

They say with age comes wisdom, and I am a living testament to that truth. As I gracefully get older, I find myself gravitating toward the simpler pleasures in life. I no longer chase after the latest trends or seek the validation of others. Instead, I find myself cherishing the small moments of bliss, like the soothing sound of raindrops pattering against my window or the comforting warmth of the sun on my skin. With each passing day, I feel more connected to the world around me, as though I'm a vital part of something much greater than myself. Unfortunately, I had to reach my forties before I could truly understand the reasons behind my failed relationships through moments of self-reflection.

It's no secret that the trauma inflicted by my stepfather led to significant challenges for me, but its impact extended even further in my life. I came to realize that, at times, I was seeking a loving partner only to fulfill the role of a good father for my children. It felt as though this became my sole purpose in life. Instead of finding someone who truly valued me to allow our love to pour into my children, I found myself trapped in an unfavorable and unhealthy situation that was detrimental to us all. What's worse, I was drawn to men based solely on the superficial stuff like looks, physique, or even their hairstyle. Hell, sometimes I got distracted by the way someone looked at me and mistook it for love. It's a common slip-up that many of us, especially women, make when selecting partners. We prioritize appearances over vital traits like trust, communication, empathy, and shared values. It was crucial for me to confront this truth and find someone who was a genuine match for both me and my family. It just sucked that I sadly learned this lesson far too late.

By now, I believed I would have a big family with lots of kids. Maybe even ten of them. At least, that was the goal because I love children. Unfortunately, life had other plans for me. It didn't help that I could never be with a man long enough to share my time, love, or body. I had no issue finding a man but keeping him was another matter. Perhaps they were good men I happened to meet at the wrong time. Or maybe I tell myself that to rationalize all the shit I had been through trying to find love.

The first time I believed I had fallen in love; I was fifteen years old. I was competing in a Junior Olympics meet in Louisiana when I found myself glaring at a dark-skinned specimen with broad shoulders. He had a neatly groomed low haircut, a perfect white smile, and a flawless complexion that radiated a natural glow. Instantly, I felt the blood rushing through my body, raising my temperature and making it hard to control my focus. When it came to anything dealing with boys, I was slightly a late bloomer compared to my peers. So, whatever it was that I felt at the moment was new to me, yet certainly welcomed.

Despite it all, I experienced what I presumed to be love when I met my first male friend, first crush, and first boyfriend all wrapped up in a boy named Tyrell Hunter. He was sixteen years old and lived out of New Haven—one of the fastest sprinters to come out of the New England area. We also went to different schools, so I saw less of him than I would like. Tyrell competed in the 110 hurdles and 200-meter races, and God, did I ever love watching him run. Not only because I was fascinated by him, but because of the passion and determination he ran with every time he stepped on the track. He had the "it" factor that everyone wanted, including me.

So, there I was, between the white lines, in my peaceful zone, awaiting the pop of the gunshot. The air was cool and calm, but inside I was burning with eagerness, awaiting the sound of the gun. Nothing could break my focus. Nothing ever did—until I saw him across the way warming up with his teammates, all while staring at me. You know, the look you give when you're staring at something you badly want through a window? That kind of look. He undoubtedly caught my attention, from the depths of his eyes to the charming way he smiled when he laughed. I still remember his dark skin and African roots chiseled into his face, looking into my eyes as I warmed up. How he looked at me filled me with emotions I hadn't felt before.

Consequently, the only time I saw him was when I went to junior Olympic track meets. Until that time came around, we would spend hours on the phone, laughing about everything while talking about nothing. It was the love I had wanted— even at a young age. My mother loathed the fact that I spent so much time on the phone, causing more of a rift between us. Most of my arguments stemmed from being on the phone for so long. There were days I spent more time talking to him than I did sleeping. He was my first kiss. He was my first love. He was the first person I gave my body to consensually.

I remember a particular instance when Tyrell and I got a little carried away at a track meet, right before my race. I was going through a phase of heightened sexuality, and I couldn't quite tell if it was due to the trauma my stepfather inflicted on me, or just my own natural urges, but my attraction toward boys was intense. I knew it wasn't the smartest idea to mess with Tyrell before my runs, but the Junior Olympics was the only chance I had to see him. However, I had no idea that having sex before a race could have such a devastating effect.

It turns out that for runners, sex drains our energy and strength. I learned this the hard way. After four rounds of qualifying, I was predicted to finish in the top two in the 800-meter race. Piece of cake, right? Wrong. The pre-race sex left my legs weaker than before, and my mind was still wandering at that moment. As a result, I finished in eighth place. That was dead last in the finals. Disappointment overwhelmed me, as well as a sense of failure after finishing last in the race. It was a wakeup call for me to realize that I couldn't allow sex to hinder my success, not only on the track, but also in life. From that day forward, I made a commitment to myself to never let my sexual desires interfere with my goals and aspirations.

Looking back, I realize there was nothing remarkable about him. Perhaps I was attempting to replace the traumatic experience of being raped by my stepfather with a new memory of making love with someone I genuinely cared for. I yearned for that perfect love scene, just like Jason and Lyric under the tree in Jason's Lyric, or how Edward passionately held, kissed, and made love to Vivian in Pretty Woman. That vision, that version of intimacy and affection, was what I craved.

Over the years, I found myself in a revolving door of relationships, dating various men while searching for that elusive fairytale love story. From professional athletes to Caribbean men, from serious entrepreneurs to men from all walks of life, I explored every avenue. Some stayed around long enough for us to build a connection, but inevitably, the connection wasted away like the morning mist of a summer's sunrise.

After everything I had been through with my family, figuring things out with my business, and the uncertainty of my mental state, I thought giving dating a break was a good idea. So, when I uprooted my life and moved back to Florida, my intentions were only to focus on my two young children and my thriving business. With my heart guarded, I was determined to keep my head down and stay on track without anyone to distract me. However, fate had other plans when I sat beside a handsome boxer on a plane ride to Florida.

His name was Christian Romero. It wasn't just one feature that made Christian very attractive, though his eyes came close. A neatly groomed beard accentuated his jawline, and his dark hair was styled in a way that made it look effortlessly unkempt. His piercing brown eyes sparkled with a mischievous twinkle, as if he knew he was the object of my lustful desires. He greeted me with a warm smile that revealed a set of perfectly straight, white teeth. There was only one problem, though. He didn't speak any English, and I spoke not a lick of Spanish. Despite the language barrier, we still somehow flirted with the few words we knew in each other's languages. In fact, Christian and I were able to establish a connection between us that felt as natural as love can get.

As we spent more time together, I found myself drawn to Christian in a way that was different from anyone I had dated before. He brought new and exciting experiences into my life, providing a temporary relief from the monotonous routine I had grown accustomed to. Despite the challenges presented by the language barrier, we found ways to connect on a deeper level. Meeting his family was a special moment for me, as it made me believe we were moving toward a more meaningful relationship. Before I knew it, we were moving in together, and our bond felt strong and genuine. Christian was affectionate and attentive, always eager to meet my every need. Being with him made me feel desired in a way that forced me to be drawn into him. I was hooked on the rush of his love and the comfort he provided. Sort of like an addiction I couldn't shake.

However, as time passed, I began to notice troubling signs from him that made the hair on my arm stand to attention. He'd go mute and become emotionless out of the blue. Smoking an excessive amount of weed throughout the day became his thing. His moods were unpredictable and volatile. I couldn't quite put my finger on it at the time, but I started to believe that something was clinically off about him. I should have stepped off that train at the first crazy station, especially considering my past experiences with other abusive and manipulative men. Despite the warning signs, my foolish and naive inner me just wouldn't allow me to do so.

Like many of us stuck in a dead-end relationship, a creeping sense of low self-esteem can take root as time goes on in dysfunctional relationships. Persistent insecurity nags us and lingers in our minds, asking ourselves, "Are we actually deserving of love?" That's where I found myself dealing with Christian on random mornings and sleepless nights. It became unthinkable to pull away, and the cycle of hurtful behavior and attention only worsened the situation. But like many women, I was anchored in the belief that things would improve if I kept at it. I felt that if I were consistent in my loving behavior and continually tried to be a good partner, then things would get better.

One night, Christian and I decided to hang out after getting off work because I could feel my energy draining from my body. I just wanted a moment of peace to recharge in the arms of the man I loved. But as soon as I walked through the door, his usual charm was nowhere to be found as we immediately bickered over something insignificant. My patience was already thin, and his attitude only fueled the fire. I could feel my frustration bubbling up, threatening to boil over at any moment.

"I'm tired of this. Okay! I'm not dealing with this shit tonight," I said. With a sharp response, I made it clear that I was done with him for the night. Christian's presence only added to the chaos of the day, and I was in no mood to deal with it.

Well, that wasn't enough for him because as I turned to walk away, I could feel Christian's fiery eyes staring at the back of my neck. His words sliced through the air like sharp knives, taunting and belittling me in ways he had never done. Both in English and Spanish. I refused to engage, so that's when he turned his verbal abuse into a physical assault. His eyes darkened with a dangerous intensity. Instantly, my heart began racing with fear as I tried to get away. It was too late. With a sudden burst of energy, he lunged forward and landed a devastating blow to my jaw. The force of the impact sent me staggering backward, my feet slipping out from under me as I fell to the ground.

As I lay there, stunned and disoriented, I could hear the sound of Christian's fists battering my body with a furious intensity. His rage was real. Almost as if he was in the ring with one of his opponents he despised. Only here, there was no referee to stop the fight. I could feel each punch landing with sickening thuds, each blow robbing me of my strength and will to fight back. I screamed out in pain, begging him to stop, but he was deaf to my pleas, lost in a fury that consumed him.

In that moment, I realized that I was no match for his brutal strength and that my only hope was to survive his onslaught. As I huddled on the ground, my body battered and bruised, little did I know that my life would never be the same again.

"Christian, please stop! I love you, and I'm sorry," I softly said.

He looked down, staring at me like a deer stuck in headlights, and remained motionless on top of me. Fortunately, the brutal pounding stopped, but the damage had already been done. My head began to throb with a searing pain that made it difficult to articulate words, and my limbs trembled beyond my control as if they were on puppet strings. I felt a strange, prickling sensation coursing through me as if an electric current was surging through my veins. My vision was blurred and fragmented, with shards of light flashing before my eyes. Christian had struck me with such force to the head that it left a scar in my brain as a consequence, disrupting the normal electrical activity and communication between my brain cells. As a result, that night marked the first occurrence of a seizure in my life.

I was confined to a hospital bed for a few agonizing days, wracked by recurring seizures that left me lost and in despair. During that time, members of the church I was attending came to pray for me, offering me a small glimmer of hope and comfort through my recovery. It was the first time in a while that I felt some sort of love.

I would never return to Christian following that day, and although I managed to obtain a restraining order against him, I couldn't bring myself to press charges. That's the blessing and curse of being a loving person. Sometimes I was not too fond of the fact that I could have no hatred for anyone who hurt me or sought revenge on those that wronged me. Instead, I always left it up to God to decide what he would do with them. Besides, I knew Christian suffered from a mental illness and just needed help, not punishment.

Despite the trauma of the incident and the lack of support from authorities, I knew deep down that pressing charges on him was not the answer. As much as I wanted justice for what he did, I couldn't bear the thought of him being locked away in a cell, alone with his mental health neglected and untreated. It was a tough decision, but I knew that was the best way to move forward.

Admittedly, as I went about my daily routine, the memories of that fateful night lingered in my mind like a shadow, haunting me at every turn. The tingling sensation in my body and the flashes of light seemed to be a constant reminder of the violence I had endured. Despite this, I refused to let it consume me. Instead, I channeled my pain into my work, determined to create a better life for myself and my children.

As I reflected on the men who entered my life, and ultimately my body, I couldn't help but notice the similarities between them physically, mentally, and emotionally. It wasn't until I started therapy that I realized this pattern. During one session, my therapist suggested that my choices in partners could be linked to the trauma I experienced with my stepfather. At first, I couldn't fully grasp this idea. My focus was on my childhood and how it influenced my relationships. Despite having control over many aspects of my life, such as my health, finances, and career, I couldn't control who I was attracted to or loved.

By the summer of 2010, I put my medical recruiting aside to focus on my new business—medical equipment sales. In doing that, I was on-site at many of the facilities I had visited before, grinding! One day, while marketing my business at an assisted living facility, I encountered a tall, striking man with broad shoulders and a chiseled jawline that immediately caught my attention. His name was Paul Cinter. I had met him before that day, but our interaction had been cordial. The flirting progressed the more I visited the facility. So, on that particular day, when I walked in, something was different. His eyes glimmered with a spark, hinting at his adventurous and fun-loving spirit.

As we exchanged pleasantries, his smile felt warm and genuine, reaching his eyes and brightening his entire face. Despite our initial conversation being polite and casual, I could sense an unspoken attraction brewing between us that I did not feel before. Funny enough, I even noticed more details about him that I hadn't previously. Starting with his deep brown skin that seemed to be so smooth and flawless, making me admire his beauty even more. I estimated him to be at least 6'2 and weighing around 225 pounds with a powerful build that exuded confidence. The more Paul and I chatted, the more I was drawn in by his infectious laughter and easy charm. With Paul's assistance, I secured a contract with the facility to fulfill their medical equipment needs. As a result, Paul made it a point to see me every time. We flirted and started dating, and within two weeks of officially dating, we were intimately involved. Indeed, I wanted to take it slow because of the shit I had been through with the others, but I had no control over my feelings. Besides, it all felt natural.

Paul was unlike any man I had dated before. Unlike the controlling, chauvinistic, and abusive men of my past, he was considerate, emotionally stable, and caring. He was a great human being, raised in a loving family that instilled a sense of kindness and compassion. But despite his many positive qualities, something about him made me uneasy. Perhaps it was his frat boy lifestyle, something I wasn't used to. He always talked about his college days, reliving old memories, and laughing at inside jokes. He consistently drank alcohol and wanted to travel in packs, as if he couldn't imagine being alone. And while he was friendly to everyone, sometimes I couldn't help but wonder if there was something else behind his constant need for company.

In the beginning, I didn't expect much from Paul. I thought he was just another man passing through my life, a temporary fix to my loneliness. But I was wrong. He crept into my heart like a thief, and before I knew it, he made himself feel at home. At times, I felt like I was fighting a losing battle, desperately trying to keep him at arm's length, but it was useless. He had this magnetic energy that drew me to him. Deep down, I knew I wanted him, even if it meant risking everything. And yet, I couldn't shake the feeling that my children needed me more than ever, and I didn't let anyone, or anything, take my time away from them.

As time moved on, I finally found myself balancing the life of a mother and a businesswoman. I'm sure that's why Paul spoke so much about settling down, having kids, and making lots of money as business partners. Although those were soft melodies that I loved listening to, my heart wasn't ready to take the plunge just yet. I wanted to take it slow, slower than I had with anyone else before. However, in a moment of carelessness, I made a terrible mistake by having unprotected sex with Paul. I got too comfortable and safe.

"Are you crazy?" I scolded him.

"I know. I know. I'm sorry. We can take care of it," he apologized.

"You're damn right."

I calmed down and let Paul see that I was okay. It was all good. Besides, what was the worst that could happen? I knew I needed to take the morning-after pill because I was not ready to have another child, especially not at that point in my life.

"We have to get a plan-B pill," I told Paul.

"Yeah. Okay. I got you."

I was itching to head to the store immediately, but he insisted we wait until later that day. Hours slipped by, but I wasn't too concerned as I knew I had ample time to take the morning-after pill. Ironically, we were on our way to church when I brought up the pill. We passed several drug stores, their neon signs beckoning me to come in, but he made excuses for not stopping. "I can't make a U-turn there." "We'll be late if we stop." All sorts of bullshit. I tried to stay calm, hoping that nothing had happened.

After church, we returned to his place, and it happened again. He acted as if getting me pregnant was part of his grand plan, and I couldn't help but feel a chill run down my spine. His behavior was becoming sketchy, and the more I thought about it, the more uneasy I became. It became apparent that he didn't want me to get the pill because it wasn't a mistake. He had planned it all along.

As the days passed, I started hearing conflicting stories about who he was and what he did. The pieces of his life didn't fit together, and my gut instinct told me something was terribly wrong. He claimed to have a master's degree in civil engineering but never did any work as an engineer. He also explained how he used to work for the government but was laid off for an inexcusable reason, so he decided to start an assisted living facility. His friends were high-level government officials, such as FBI and CIA agents, and none of them were in the medical industry. I brushed it off, believing I was looking too much into it. Besides, nothing about his personality and how he treated me made me feel like my life was in danger.

Two weeks later, while at Paul's house, I began experiencing another violent seizure. This seizure was a recurrence of the previous one, which was initially triggered by a head injury sustained during a fight, resulting in brain damage. However, on that particular night, the seizure I encountered was further intensified by the added factor of stress in my life. Paul rushed me to the hospital, unaware of what was happening to me. While in the hospital, the doctor asked if I was pregnant. I had been through childbirth twice before that day, so I knew whether or not I was pregnant, so it was easy to answer no. However, I was wrong. It turns out that I was indeed pregnant after taking a test. And just like that, things changed in a matter of seconds. Before that positive test, a part of me was looking to walk away from Paul. Then in the next moment, our relationship became complicated, leaving us with some tough decisions to make. Paul and I sat down for a heart-to-heart conversation about the weighty matters crashing down on us. Important matters that should have been discussed beforehand. Was he ready to be a parent? Did I want to keep the baby? Did I even want to have a child with this man? We discussed our relationship, where it was going, and how we could make it work. Our conversation was long and exhausting, with each of us bearing our deepest fears and concerns.

Ultimately, we decided to keep the baby, and in doing so, I saw a softer yet sketchy side of Paul. He became very structured in his approach to me and the pregnancy, and we only saw each other on certain nights, but always at my home. Yet, another strange thing about Paul.

One night, we attended a function where many of the attendees were in the medical field. Doctors, physicians, nurses, facility owners, you name it. To me, it was a gold mine, a place where I could meet so many people to help catapult my business to the next level. However, Paul seemed to be entirely out of place. It was almost as if he were a blind man amongst the deaf. How was this man, who claimed to be well-known in the medical field, so uncomfortable? As the owner of a medical facility, I also wondered why he had no connections to anyone in the industry. I tried to give him the benefit of the doubt, thinking maybe he had formed his relationships before his government days, but the doubts still lingered. Who was he? And what did he want from me? Occasionally, he would ask me about my ex and why he mistreated and abused me. It was as if Paul didn't believe me or wanted me to prove something. Over and over, he'd pry further into my past relationship, opening wounds that I tried so hard to heal.

Then, one day, on the drive home from a professional gathering, he asked again.

"Damn man, I really don't understand how your ex left like that. Like something had to have happened."

The car was flying down the highway, the speedometer creeping up with every passing second. My heart raced as Paul's words began to annoy the shit out of me. His voice aggravated me with each passing moment. As he spoke, his foot pressed down harder on the accelerator. Before I knew it, we were going nearly ninety miles per hour. I could feel the tension in my body mounting as we came down the road.

On that drive home, I mustered up the courage to ask him the burning question that had been lingering in my mind "Why are you always asking me that? I told you already that some people are just assholes. What is it that you want me to tell you?" I knew he kept asking about my most recent ex-boyfriend because he thought I had done something to warrant his abusive behavior. Somehow, he'd find a way to blame me for all the hurt and pain that was caused by my exes. The car fell silent as I waited for his response.

We pulled up to my house, the tension intense, and a heavy weight pressed down on my chest, making it hard to breathe. Immediately, he parked my car, grabbed his bag from the trunk, and without saying another word, he got into his car and drove away. Once again, I was left alone, six months pregnant. And I just knew he wouldn't be returning because I knew the feeling all too well.

Days turned into weeks, and there was no communication. Eventually, I reached out to his father to inquire about Paul's well-being, hoping for any answers to the questions that continued to haunt me.

When I disclosed the news of my pregnancy to Paul's parents, their response fell flat and completely lackluster, leaving me with a hollow sense of disappointment. Paul's father casually mentioned that he had spoken to his son the previous day and earlier that day, assuring me that Paul was doing fine. Despite my attempts to express my anxiety about being unable to reach Paul regarding the pregnancy and feeling scared, his father appeared dismissive and uninterested. It was as if he was implying, "He's fine, don't bother me."

I became furious because Paul was alive and well, yet he chose to ignore me, leaving me to go through the pregnancy alone. I was infuriated with myself for allowing this to happen yet again. I wasn't some random person off the street who deserved to be treated this way. My actions were always rooted in kindness, love, and helping others. The situation was unwarranted and caused me to question my faith at times.

Paul's attitude toward me was one of complete indifference, so I shared this attitude by thinking, "Fuck him too! I don't need him." It was much easier saying it than it was believing it. That's for sure.

On April 27, 2014, I went into labor and clung onto the hope that Paul would finally come around. So, I sent him a text on the way to the hospital, and to my surprise, he showed up just as Kayla was being brought into the world. He stood off to the side, and after our baby girl was born, I handed her to him—all ten pounds of her. Just like Natalia and Gabe, Kayla wasn't going to wait for the full term either.

Holding her in his arms, Paul smiled as his eyes widened and gleamed with joy. He looked at Kayla and then to me, and for that moment, there was no animosity, tension, hate, or any negative emotion between us. Nothing but love with a dash of hope and forgiveness filled the room. But it's too bad that it wouldn't last long.

The next day, Paul made his way back to the hospital, and the nurse handed him the birth certificate to sign. As he scanned through the document, his eyes suddenly widened with fury, fixed on Kayla's name listed as Kayla Bailey-Center. The venom in his tone dripped like poison as he ranted, "No kid of mine is going to have your last name!" It was as if he was unaware of the fact that she came from my body! I was the one who had to carry her for thirty-seven weeks. And I was the one who had to do it alone. I didn't even know if I would ever see Paul again, let alone that day. Despite my best efforts to calm him down, he refused to listen to anything I had to say, and instead, he decided to storm out of the room in a fit of rage, leaving a trail of chaos behind him.

After Kayla and I left the hospital, I cried and sulked for a few days, feeling the weight of the burden that now lay upon me like a thick, heavy fur coat. I wondered how I had allowed this to happen to me, feeling as though this was not the life I had envisioned for myself. I had always dreamed of having a big family and a loving husband, not raising three children alone. However, I knew that this was the path that had been laid out before me, and like the long and winding path that my grandmother and aunt took to the market in Jamaica every Thursday without complaint, I would do the same. So, I held my head high and returned to doing what I did best. Grinding! Loving hard! And enjoying life. I refused to let the transgressions of others define me. Instead, I would be defined by how I chose to move forward in my life.

Then, one day, a couple of weeks after Kayla's birth, Paul's family contacted me, asking to see Kayla. I was a bit hesitant at first because

I didn't know their intentions. Regardless, my grandmother's spirit allowed me to do what was right and also bring Kayla around to meet them. On one occasion, I got to talking to Sonya, Paul's sister, and during that conversation, everything came to light and finally brought some clarity.

"I'm doing okay, but I just don't understand why he would leave me like that after seeing Kayla being born," I told her.

Instantly, her face became gloomy as if her soul had left her body. It was as if guilt was eating away at her, and she needed to get something off her chest. And she did.

"Well, here's the thing. My brother works for the government, and my parents will not tell you that because I don't think he's allowed to tell anyone. No one can know, but he's a CIA agent."

It all made sense. The random disappearance. Paul's ability to be cold and removed from the moment at the sudden drop of a dime was all too mysterious. Even the fact that Paul's friends were all involved in some sort of government position, except for him?! Strange. Even the way he asked me questions didn't seem as normal as other guys did. His were filled with more purpose and required details— almost as if he were writing a book or if he were some sort of therapist.

"So, what about the assisted living facilities he owns?" I questioned.

My mind was a jumble of confusion and frustration. What was the truth? But her answer cut through the fog of my thoughts like a beam of sunlight. "My parents own those," she said. "He doesn't know much about the business."

A wave of understanding washed over me, explaining why Paul had always seemed distant and disinterested at networking events. He didn't have the knowledge to engage with the doctors, physicians, and case managers who attended.

And then it hit me like a sudden gust of wind knocking the breath out of me. Paul had appeared in my life while Devin, Gabriel's father, was going through his trial. He had talked to me about my relationships, but it was clear now that he was much more interested in Devin's story and his involvement with the mafia. I felt uneasy as he asked probing questions like "How did you not know about what he was doing?" and "How did the relationship start, and why did it really end?" It was all becoming clear to me now—the pieces of the puzzle were finally fitting together.

There were many who believed I was somehow involved in Devin's criminal activities—money laundering, drugs, and racketeering. But the truth was far from that. Not only was I not anywhere near involved in any of Devin's shady dealings, but I also wanted answers my damned self.

Somewhere in between all of our interactions with each other, Paul must have recognized my innocence. Perhaps that's why he lost control of his feelings and fell in love with me, a love that brought Kayla into my life. But, who knows? Maybe it was all just a coincidence, and Paul had no idea about Devin's illegal activities. Maybe fate brought us together for another reason entirely. I guess I'll never truly know.

CHAPTER 14

REMAINING UNBROKEN

"I trusted love once again, and it found a way to fuck me over. Spiritually, I was drained and mentally twisted. Hell, I was downright furious at myself for continuing down this dark path of bad decisions."

When a woman anchors her entire existence to a man, her life begins to revolve around his every move. She can become so entangled in his world that she forgets her own dreams, her own ambitions, and even her own needs, relying on him for her happiness and validation, almost as a planet orbiting the sun, never straying too far from its gravitational pull. However, I learned that in the end, it's easy to find yourself trapped in a cage of your own making, unable to escape the commanding pull of a man who was never meant to be your whole world. That was certainly the case for me when I decided to marry Ricardo.

Before that night, when the darkness crept into my bedroom and awakened from a dream and into a nightmare, I had been through all sorts of shit with Ricardo. It was a marriage that I should have never allowed to happen. And although I couldn't undo any of the trauma that I had been through, I knew I didn't have to be defined by it. I could overcome it and remain unbroken.

During a time in my life when I felt lost and mentally drained, parties and clubs became my sole escape from the constant stress. Amid the cigarette smoke and the thumping beat of the music, I caught a glimpse of Ricardo weaving his way through the sea of people. Our eyes met, and for a moment, the world around us faded away, leaving only the two of us alone in that pulsating crowd. As if following a silent rhythm, we moved closer and closer to each other until we were face to face, like two strangers sitting across from each other at a coffee shop.

Before I knew it, Ricardo became a reliable go-to for years when it came to fulfilling sexual needs in between any relationship. A friend with benefits, as some would say. Through the years, Ricardo and I barely knew anything about each other outside our lustful interactions, and we never pushed for anything more than that, which was fine by me. Whenever I needed an escape from the pressures of life or a way to regain my edge, I could count on Ricardo to be there. He was always available, never hassled me, and never pressured me into anything more. Despite all the red flags, certain qualities kept me tied to him, like a boat struggling to stay afloat in a stormy sea. I convinced myself that I needed him, that he provided something essential that no one else could. But even then, deep down, I knew that it was only a matter of time before his true colors would shine through.

And they did. In a big way, too. He was the epitome of a piece of shit. Every warning sign, every gut feeling, was validated in a single moment. He was everything you warn your loved ones to avoid—manipulative, selfish, abusive. If my stepfather was a monster portraying the devil, then Ricardo was the devil dressed up as a monster, hiding in plain sight. Looking back at all the bad relationships and toxic men I had encountered in my past, it felt like a short journey on the path that led me to him—the epitome of waste. Love, I suppose, had the ability to cloud my judgment and steer me towards making some regrettable choices that lacked logic or reason. I willingly exposed myself to potential heartaches and disappointments, overlooking warning signs and making sacrifices for others that, in hindsight, I would now consider unwise. I guess love has a way of leading us to do foolish things, and upon reflection, I've come to realize that it holds true in my own experiences.

At some point during my interaction with Ricardo, before we got married, he began to share more about himself. Most of it was on a surface level, with nothing substantial to cling to. Funny enough, that was probably his way of opening up to me. Even funnier, I took it as something significant enough to keep me close to him.

He told me he was born and raised in Miami, where he lived with his mom and stepfather. He also claimed to have graduated from the University of Central Florida, where he played football and studied microcellular biology. I had no reason to doubt his story, so I never verified any of the details he shared. I didn't even conduct a background check on him.

I assumed that the foundation we had built over the years of knowing each other would account for something. Besides, what motive did he have to lie? We weren't even in a serious romantic relationship. Above all, I considered Ricardo to be a good friend. He knew that our interaction would be limited or nonexistent once I started dating someone seriously. Therefore, there was never any pressure for him to be anything other than himself with me. Nevertheless, I eventually discovered that he had always been incredibly convincing in everything he said.

Later on, in our developing relationship, I learned that he was involved in the music industry as an artist and producer. Everyone in his circle—his friends, family, and the community—knew him as Bishop the Rapper. A rapper? Similar to my experience with Paul, doubts about Ricardo's true identity started to arise. It seemed unlikely for someone with a degree in molecular biology to suddenly transition into the world of rap, at least from my perspective. Yet, I also realized that he was the type of man who made me question the rules I had set for myself in the first place.

By the time 2015 rolled around, I found myself entering a new tax bracket. I had officially become a millionaire, although not many people were aware of that fact. Truth be told, even I had only a limited awareness of my newfound wealth, as my focus was primarily on my work and what lay ahead. Like many individuals with significant financial resources, I began investing in assets that had the potential to appreciate in value, such as stocks, art, bonds, and, of course, real estate. The sense of accomplishment I felt was overwhelming when I took a step back and observed what I had achieved for myself. This included the acquisition of a magnificent 10,000 square foot home, which I later expanded into an impressive 16,000 square foot mansion. The house exuded a certain charm that unmistakably conveyed affluence. Little did I know that someone else was silently taking notice of it.

Soon after moving into the house, Ricardo came to visit, and as he walked around, his eyes darted around the room, scanning everything in sight. It was as if he was trying to calculate my net worth based on what he saw. He didn't know much about my financial status, and although I hadn't reached the peak of my success, the house was still enough to give off the impression that I had made something of myself. I took his gleaming excitement for him being proud of me or celebrating my win. The more he walked around the house, the more he opened his eyes to more than just a random visit. It became an opportunity to dive more darkly and fraudulently into my life.

At the time of Ricardo's new revelation of who I was, I was nursing a broken heart from my previous relationship that I had assumed was headed somewhere. However, that quickly ended when I discovered he was married with two kids. As Ricardo stood there, I couldn't help but wonder what he thought of me. Did he see me as a strong, independent woman who had worked hard to get where she was? Or did he only see someone he could take advantage of? I had so many questions at first, but his behavior soon answered them all.

The entire time I knew Ricardo, he assumed I was married, and even worse, he thought he was coming over to have sex with me while I was married. Like I said before, Ricardo and I didn't have much of a relationship outside of our sexual one. We never met at each other's place, always in public or at a hotel. I should have known right then that was a red flag, a warning sign that I chose to ignore at my risk. Any man willing to have sex with a married woman in her own home was not the man I should have found myself married to. At the same time, I wasn't innocent either.

So therefore, on that fateful day, I sat across from him, knowing it was time to come clean. The weight of my bold-faced lie had been heavy on my mind for far too long because that wasn't who I was. Telling him that I was married was my way of placing a barrier between him and me to avoid a romantic relationship that could never be. As much as I appreciated our intimate moments, I knew he wasn't the one for me. His rugged features and chiseled physique were attractive, but they didn't make up for the fact that we were fundamentally different.

Ricardo was a man of the moment, always seeking the next adventure and thrill. He lived for the rush of adrenaline, and while I admired his courage, it wasn't something I could sustain. I was a woman of stability who craved the comfort of routine and familiarity. Over and over, the thought of us being together in a real public relationship crossed my mind. And each time it did, I would scold myself and internally scream out, "Fuck no!"

There was no way I could look past our physical chemistry and show a glimmer of genuine interest. Still, he was the man that left me feeling beyond myself, and it felt so fucking liberating. If every woman could encounter a man that made her feel sexually free and weak at the same time…Ricardo would be the embodiment of that man.

"You know you should give me a chance to be with you," he said, his voice low and smooth like velvet.

I watched him repeatedly turn to weed as if God Himself had given it to him. He smoked joint after joint, becoming some sort of fake thug who reeked of rebellion. I knew I needed something more.

"I don't have any time for a relationship right now," I replied.

Days into our interaction, my emotions got the best of me as I sat down with my staff to plan our annual company trip. During the meeting, I listened to them excitedly talk about bringing their spouse on vacation and all the activities they could do for fun. The thought of being alone while everyone else had a partner by their side made my heart ache. I must have been desperate, because something allowed me to take a chance and asked Ricardo to join me on the trip, under the condition that we keep it discreet and mild.

From there, our relationship advanced swiftly. We traveled across the world, exploring various destinations, and creating cherished memories that solidified our bond. Before I realized it, Ricardo and I had transitioned into an exclusive dating relationship. Him and me? Together? I had never envisioned him as someone I could be with, as we were complete opposites, and he lacked the motivation to bridge that gap. He had a deep passion for rap music, and I couldn't stand to listen to it. I came from a close-knit Caribbean family, and he was an American man with a completely different upbringing. His idea of a good time involved going to the strip clubs with girls surrounding us, while I preferred the comfort of my home, sitting on the couch with a bag of popcorn and a glass of wine, watching a romantic movie. We were truly polar opposites in our preferences and interests.

Nevertheless, one thing we did have in common was our love for children. Ricardo was sometimes sweet, warm, and very interactive with my kids. He would talk to Natalia about life as a teenager and treat Kayla like the princess she was. Without having to say anything to him, I watched him step in and play a father figure to them all while also being a great dad to his very own. What I saw in him while he was with the kids allowed me to fall in love with him. Or, at the very least, fall in love with the side of him he portrayed to me. Before I knew it, he had moved into my home, making the idea of getting married more real than I ever expected it to get.

On the day of our wedding, the air was thick with tension, and the premonitions of family members didn't make it any better. My uncle Colin prophesied about impending trouble, while my aunt sensed something was wrong with Ricardo. Meanwhile, my uncle Kelvin ran a background check on Ricardo without even telling me, and what he found should have given me all the reasons to pause and consider. Still, blinded by love, I refused to believe that the man I was about to marry could be anything less than perfect. So, I determinedly pushed aside their concerns and refused to listen to their warnings.

As the hours ticked away, a cloud of uncertainty loomed over the wedding plans. I had gone to great lengths to ensure the prenuptial agreement was in place, even hiring an attorney to review it for Ricardo. However, his sudden change of heart turned the whole thing into a battlefield. That's because the day before the wedding, Ricardo and I got into a heated argument when he refused to sign the prenuptial contract, as we had previously agreed upon.

I stood firm, determined to protect my children's future and my hard-earned assets. I had been stepped on and manipulated throughout my life, but there was no negotiating regarding my kids or my finances. I refused to back down even in the face of mounting pressure from Ricardo and his family. Ricardo's mother said, "If a prenup is so important to you, why are you getting married?"

That comment struck a chord with me, and from that day forward, I embraced a strong dislike for her. It was particularly unsettling to know that she had moved into a house I owned and was living there rent-free, yet she could speak about me in such a manner. Nevertheless, I remained steadfast in my position, fully aware of what was at stake. Despite the turmoil, my intuition, and the lingering uncertainty, the wedding proceeded as planned.

As I stood at the altar with Ricardo, memories of past events shattered my mind, starting with the memory of Ricardo threatening to kill me, and out of fear, I jumped out of the car on a busy highway and found myself running through traffic in hopes of getting away from him.

If that wasn't bad enough, the warnings from my family members repeatedly echoed in my head. Even as I walked down the aisle, I could see their looks of sorrow and empathy.

My uncle's prophetic words rang in my ears like a church bell. "That man will bring troubles to your business and cause misery to your life." My uncle was so adamant that Ricardo wasn't the one for me that he refused to attend the wedding. That was a clear indication of his disapproval of the union. Yet, I had brushed off the warnings, ignoring the nagging feeling in the pit of my stomach, and instead stood right there with him before God to say, "I do."

Funny enough, later on, I discovered that while I was walking down the aisle, Ricardo was looking at me, whispering to himself, "This stupid dumb ass bitch."

After the wedding, it didn't take long to realize that Ricardo was not the man I had fallen in love with. The image of a stable and prosperous partner was shattered when I uncovered the truth about his financial instability, which he had cunningly concealed through lies and manipulation. He claimed to own a condo in downtown Orlando, but I later discovered it was all a fabricated story—a really sorry one at that.

The truth was, he didn't have much to his name. Despite that, I was still deeply in love with him, believing we would build a life together. I was willing to do anything for him.

Later in our relationship, I ended up purchasing a condo in both our names because I knew he'd always wanted one. However, he made sure to take credit for it, shamelessly parading around town, boasting about everything I owned as if it were his. Love certainly had a way of making me look stupid, and over the years, I've come to accept my past behavior as foolish.

His work ethic was non-existent, and he constantly needed guidance, like a child with ADHD. I found myself reminding him of the most basic tasks, such as changing a light bulb in the bathroom or taking out the trash. He barely spoke to me, growing increasingly distant both physically and emotionally. Each day, he would sleep until noon, only to spend hours glued to his phone, watching disturbing videos online—World star fights, women twerking, and random rap videos—always disregarding his family. Wherever he went, whether it was around the house or out on the streets, he always had a group of rowdy friends partying and causing chaos.

Before our wedding day, he was a master of surprises, whisking me away on spontaneous dates and getaways to all sorts of enchanting destinations. From romantic strolls along the beach to simply visiting a new restaurant, he always found new ways to keep me on my toes. But after we swapped our vows, everything changed. Date nights became few and far between, and he was hardly ever home. It felt like he had vanished into thin air, leaving me in the dark about his whereabouts and activities.

I'd ask him, "Where are you?" He'd always reply, "I'm at the studio." Whenever I mustered the courage to ask him what he was up to, he would offer vague excuses and totally disregard my questions. It was as though he had built a wall around himself, entirely shutting me out of his life.

At times, I felt like a stranger in my own home. But then, just when I thought I couldn't take it anymore, he would show up at the door with a bouquet of flowers, a warm embrace, and an apology. For a while, things would return to how they used to be—he would be attentive, affectionate, and present. But sooner or later, he would retreat into his world of secrecy and silence, leaving me alone once again.

Ricardo loved to live extravagantly, basking in a life of luxury beyond his means. He always seemed to have an insatiable appetite for spending my money, which he did with reckless abandon. He would boast about his lavish lifestyle by bragging about his possessions and the places he frequently visited—all of which was paid for with my money. If you ask those that know him, they'll tell you that he owned the fifty-eight-acre horse ranch and the downtown luxury condo with a sweeping view of the city skyline. That's what he wanted everyone to believe. He'd keep up appearances by posting pictures on social media of himself standing beside my cars or posing inside the state-of-the-art recording studio I built for him. He wanted people to believe everything was his, but in reality, it was all mine. He made it seem as if I had worked tirelessly to provide him with a life he could never have imagined.

The question that constantly came from family members, friends, and sometimes myself was, "Why did I stay in the relationship?" Although a great question, the answer was always the same: I don't know.

Despite all his flaws and the horror that he put me through, there were moments when his caring side showed itself, making everything else seem small in comparison. One of those moments was when I broke my spine in a freak accident. The pain was unbearable, but he waited on me hand and foot with the same level of detail and care as a home health aide or private nurse would have. He took charge of the house and the kids, ensuring I didn't have to lift a finger. It was like he suddenly "got it" and became the perfect caregiver, the ideal partner and, ultimately, the perfect man. When my oldest daughter Natalia faced a medical crisis, Ricardo stepped up to the plate as "super dad," taking her to doctor appointments, lab work, and treatments. He encouraged and affirmed her healing with unwavering support. He embraced my son Gabriel like his own, and when his own son came to visit, it gave me a feeling of a real blended family. But perhaps the most beautiful thing about him was his relationship with my daughter, Kayla. Though he wasn't her biological father, he was the only one she had ever known. They were inseparable until the demise of our relationship.

"We should have a kid," he said one day.

At the age of forty-one, I wasn't particularly enthusiastic about being pregnant, but his persistent and unwavering desire for a child made me consider it more seriously. It also didn't hurt that I had always loved kids and dreamed of having a large family. So, we made the decision to have a child together through in-vitro fertilization. The process was a difficult eight-month journey that left my body weakened and my hormones fluctuating. Despite the challenges, Ricardo showed remarkable compassion and understanding throughout the entire process. He was like my nurse of the year during my treatments and an incredible father figure to our other children. Finally, on December 12, 2018, my precious baby Ocean was born.

Even after we separated during the global coronavirus pandemic, he continued to visit the ranch to spend time with the kids and ease their anxiety about the breakup and the virus. Additionally, he had a calm demeanor that could ease my high-strung personality better than anyone else, especially during stressful times at work. He would whisk me away for a spa day or do something so romantically sweet that it made me forget everything else. Ultimately, I forgave him for his character flaws and overlooked the dangerous situations he put me in. It shouldn't have taken him raping me and nearly beating me to death to realize that I needed to leave him, but forgiveness had clouded my judgment.

There were several days and nights when I would find myself sitting in bed, surrounded by an eerie silence, and think to myself, "What the fuck have I done?" I knew deep down that it was time to let him go, even though we had only been married for a few months. Giving up seemed like the easy way out, but I couldn't ignore the memories of our intense physical connection that lingered in my mind, tempting me to hold on a little longer.

I had placed my trust in love once again, only to be betrayed. Spiritually drained and mentally twisted, I was filled with anger toward myself for continuing down this dark and destructive path of poor decisions. But as the veil of infatuation lifted, the truth became painfully clear. It turned out that everyone else had seen the reality of our situation long before I did, and it was an ugly truth to face. To make matters worse, I discovered that he had committed a murder at the age of fourteen, resulting in nearly eight years of imprisonment. It shattered the image of the man I thought I knew, and I realized I had no idea who I had truly married. I didn't blame him, though; I placed the blame squarely on myself. The sad part is that it only got worse from there.

Despite all my efforts to move on, he still found a way to torment me. During his visits to the ranch while we were trying to work things out, he would leave at ten o'clock at night and send messages pretending to care about how the kids were doing. Whenever I didn't hear from him, my gut told me something was wrong.

One morning, I needed to go to my house on the east side of the city to pick up some things for the kids, and I decided to make a stop at our hideaway condo where we would go to escape from everyone and just relax. My intuition kept tugging at me. I couldn't tell if it was because of my money or another woman, but something felt off. Immediately, I checked the bank account that he still had access to, and there it was—a large purchase of alcohol, mostly brands he didn't even drink. It was clear that he was throwing a party at the condo that I was paying for, with my hard-earned money, while he had only made $1.53 that year. No! That is not a typo. He earned $1.53 from his rap career.

When I would text or call him, he'd lie about his whereabouts and activities. I could always tell when he was lying because his voice would get low, and he'd mumble. I went to the condo, and as soon as I walked in, I was hit with a wave of heat, as if I were standing too close to a raging fire. He was in bed, wearing nothing but a tank top, having unprotected sex with another woman. He jumped up and freaked out the moment I walked in. I felt a burning sensation inside me, consuming my rational thoughts with a fierce desire to lash out. Fight!

"Get out of my fucking condo!" I screamed.

Suddenly, my breathing became shallow and rapid. The anger rumbled through my body and vibrated every nerve and muscle until I felt like I might fall apart. I was both mad and hurt, unsure of which was tormenting my mind and spirit more.

"Bitch, get out my face."

Ricardo always tried to make me feel like I was beneath him, undeserving, and simply unwanted. That did nothing to suppress the fire burning within me. I could not believe that this monster had brought a woman into my sanctuary, which I was paying for. My place? The thought of it made me want to tear the room apart with my bare hands. Despite all of that, I knew I had too much to lose and had so many people counting on me to ever let him break me.

"So, this is what you're doing now? To me?"

I stared at him in disbelief, not really looking for an answer, but what I saw in his eyes was nothing short of terror. Part of me wanted to attack them, but realizing I was thirty floors above the ground stopped me from doing anything. There was no telling what he'd do to me if I went belligerent. Ricardo had demons capable of doing anything at any given time, especially when I was upset about something. For all I knew, he could have easily pushed me off the balcony and not think twice about it. I could see it in his eyes, how he looked at her and then at me. It felt like he was deciding between which of us to save, and I didn't feel like the lucky one. He was already planning his next move, and I knew I had to leave before it was too late.

"Trisha!" he yelled from afar.

I quickly scrambled out of the condo, fearing what he might do to me. Or even worse, what I might do to him. As the tears poured out like a faucet, I got into my car and drove off. I had no idea where I was headed, but I knew I had to get away. I didn't even care about what would happen next.

Moments later, I pulled up to my ranch as my anger simmered just a little beneath the surface. However, that quickly changed when I noticed him following me like a shadow that refused to be left behind. When I exited the car, Ricardo came charging at me with the same intensity as he had done before. Quickly, I reached for my gun with the instant reminder of the assault he had committed against me just a couple of days prior. At that moment, with my right hand squeezed tightly against the steel, I thought of all the beatings and hurt I endured from all the men I never got to defend myself against. My stepfather, Ricky, Devin, Christian, Paul, and my own fucking husband. Days of profanity-laced threats had led me to this moment.

Pow! I fired a warning shot into the ground, desperately hoping it would prevent him from coming any closer. But instead of respecting the warning shot, he continued to approach me with a sinister grin on his face, resembling that of a hyena. My heart raced as he suddenly stopped in his tracks and sprinted out into the open field. The uncertainty of his intentions sent a wave of fear coursing through me. I had no clue what he was capable of, and the last thing I wanted was to stick around and find out. For all I knew, he could retrieve his weapon and direct it at me—the mother of his child. That's how heartless and cruel he could be.

I thought it was over. But boy, was I wrong. It was all just beginning. While in the house with my kids, I heard sirens from a distance quickly approaching. I was so lost and confused by the hurt Ricardo placed in my heart that I was oblivious to the fact that cops were outside, surrounding my house. Did he call the police on me? Are you fucking kidding me? That's all I could think about.

With the kids asleep, the police stepped onto my property and demanded that I come out with my hands up as if I were guilty of a crime. I did as I was told, and once the officer pulled me and bound my wrist with the heavy metal cuffs, I knew Ricardo had set this all up.

"Officer, what am I being arrested for?" I politely asked.

"Attempted assault with a deadly weapon."

I felt the blood drain from my body, leaving me completely cold and numb. I was so shocked that I couldn't even react to what I had just heard. Attempted assault with a deadly weapon? Me? That was it. That was exactly what my uncle Colin had prophesied when he said this wicked man would destroy me. All my hard work to build my empire while assisting others to make a living for themselves would vanish with the sound of a judge slamming his gavel, followed by the word "guilty." I was certain my life was over because Ricardo had convinced them that I had tried to kill him. The more I explained that I was protecting myself, on my own property, the less they cared. For some odd reason, the cops didn't care to hear it—except for one.

"I don't want to arrest you. Clearly, this guy is a piece of shit. But my boss tells me I have to because there's a gun involved," the man said to me.

And just like that, I was thrown in the backseat of the police car and sent off to jail. When I looked out, I saw my daughter standing at the window, her face a blur of sorrow as she watched me being taken away. At that moment, the full magnitude of my situation crushed me.

I recall going through the booking process, wondering if what was happening to me was real or just a terrible nightmare. Me, in jail? It seemed unfathomable that I could end up in such a place. But the cold and foul-smelling environment of the cell was a harsh reminder that it was real. I sat there, tears streaming down my face. I knew I had to be tough in jail and not show any weakness, but fuck that, I couldn't hold it in any longer. I was emotionally drained and spiritually empty. It was the first time I had felt that way, and sadly, it wouldn't be the last.

As I waited for hours to be processed, a woman walked into the jail, and her appearance alone suggested that she had done something serious. I saw her from across the room as I went through the humiliating booking process: fingerprinting, mugshots, and a strip search. The whole experience was embarrassing, and I kept thinking that it wasn't possible because I didn't belong there. But when I saw the woman, I felt even more out of place. She was a towering figure, with a strong and imposing build that spoke of power and strength. Her features were sharp and grim, with a fierce scowl etched on her face. Tattoos covered her skin, giving her a menacing look. Her eyes were cold and unyielding, piercing like daggers. Turns out, she had been arrested for murder. Not only did she murder a man, but she kept the body in her home for days. At that moment, I knew I didn't stand a chance. *Please, God, don't leave me with this woman*… I continued to pray in silence.

I was on the phone with my mother, listening to her pray for me, when suddenly the whole facility erupted into chaos. "Run! Right now!" the guard shouted. Sirens blared as the sound of footsteps flooded the hallways. But it didn't matter anyway, because my feet felt like cold hard bricks, and I remained frozen in place. Then, a guard pulled and rushed me down a corridor, then threw me into a cell. Not just me, but also the woman who was charged with murder. Oh, fuck! I screamed to myself. Just my luck. The door slammed shut, and I tried to remain as silent and lifeless as possible. I sighed quietly; my prayer had gone unanswered. It was just her and me. Alone. No one else. Just she... and I.

"No. That's a murder one. Get Bailey out of there. She can't be in there with her."

My mind raced as I tried to make sense of the chaos happening, but before I could process anything, a guard appeared before me like a guardian angel, pulling me out of my cell with urgency.

"Get down!" she commanded, and with no hesitation, I hit the ground, my heart pounding in my chest like a wild animal trapped in a cage. The suddenness of it all left me disoriented, unsure of what was happening around me.

As the chaos dwindled, I found myself alone in the cold, germ-infested room. Memories flickered through my mind like fragments of a broken film reel, tracing back to the day I made the fateful choice to be with Ricardo. The ensuing chain of events that led me to this confined and isolated space would torment me. At that moment, everything I had worked for over the years seemed to hang in the balance and could be taken away in the blink of an eye.

"Excuse me. Can I have a pillow and blanket?"

The guard chuckled momentarily and walked off, understanding that I was definitely out of my element. When she returned with the pillow and blanket, I asked what all the commotion was about earlier.

She told me they had arrested a guy who had entered the jail with a gun hidden in his ass. Once he made it in, the man pulled it during the search and held three officers hostage. That was just my luck.

The following day, I was relieved to know I had safely made it through the night. I was sure something terrible would happen, and the sad part was that I had accepted my fate. That's the only way I could go to sleep that night.

At 7:00 a.m., heavy metal doors opened, sounding like two thunderbolts clashing. Immediately, the guard removed me from my cramped, cold cell and placed me in a larger space filled with non-violent offenders. The room was brighter and more spacious, and although the people were in despair, they didn't seem to be walking around like corpses. I didn't say a word to anyone. Instead, I sat off to the side and stared into the unknown. From the silence, I could hear the TV playing in the background, with the voice of Joel Osteen, a well-known pastor, preaching. The more I watched, the more it felt like he spoke directly to me, delivering a message of hope and resilience in the face of adversity. His voice cut through the chaos and turmoil of my life, promising that this storm would pass, and that God would multiply all the good things in my life. It was the first time I felt something to spark a deep breath and smile.

Despite the small glimmer of hope that Osteen's words offered, my reality was a stark contrast. Ricardo's actions continued to threaten everything I had built for my children and my employees. He also jeopardized my state license for my business, and therefore, my ability to own the company. The divorce proceedings were already taking a toll, and now I was arrested and caught in a bitter legal battle. In a single night, Ricardo had taken over my ranch, changing the locks and the security codes. It was a cruel and heartless move, but it was only the beginning because he filed false reports with the Department of Children and Families, accusing me of physically abusing my children.

The allegations were absurd and unfounded. He even claimed that I pushed my daughter down a flight of stairs during her cancer battle and punched my oldest son in the face. The accusations were designed to hurt me, and he did just that. But the worst part was that they threatened my relationship with my children, my reason for living.

With determination burning inside me like a wildfire, I refused to give up despite the towering obstacles looming ahead. Ricardo's relentless pursuit to ruin me was beginning to take a toll. By allowing me to lose my license, he was essentially burning my company to the ground. That left me feeling like a soldier in a losing battle. I fought tooth and nail, pleading with his lawyers and family to have him drop the charges, but his heart remained hardened. Ricardo's words echoed in my head like a haunting melody, "Let that muthafucka burn to the ground for all I care."

Indeed, he wanted to watch me suffer, as if I was the one who caused him harm. But it wasn't just me that stood to lose everything. The livelihoods of my employees and their families hung in the balance. Every day, I could feel the weight of their anxiety as they wondered what would happen to them without their jobs. And even Ricardo's mother and family members would be caught in the crossfire of his decision to destroy my company. But no matter how hard he tried, I refused to give up the fight.

I was determined to break free from Ricardo's grasp and rescue my business, no matter the cost. I offered him everything, from a million dollars to monthly child support payments, a luxurious car worth $180,000, a condo worth $550,000, and all his jewelry. I even allowed his mother to stay in the house. But his heart was hardened, consumed by his own selfish desires. He was willing to sacrifice everything, including the future of our children, just to have his way.

However, I refused to lose hope and steadfastly put my trust in God. Miraculously, just in the nick of time, my prayers were answered, and my company was saved. Thanks to a friend who pulled strings to expedite the trial, we were able to resolve the case before I lost my accreditation. And to add insult to injury, the court exposed Ricardo's foolishness and lack of judgment for all to see.

During that stretch of our divorce, I faced some of the worst days of my life. His actions were despicable and often felt inhuman. He emptied the charitable organization's bank account before I could stop him. It was an account I had set up to help people in need, specifically students looking for scholarships and single mothers in need of aid. Whenever I thought it couldn't get any worse, he would do something else to prove me wrong. Ricardo told officials that I was forging documents for ownership of the ranch property, even though the original documents had given him zero percentage ownership. He was fighting for a property he could never afford, with monthly expenses totaling $50,000. One moment he would violently threaten me, and the next, he would plead with me, stalking me wherever I went. One night, he showed up while I was at a business dinner, confronting my new business partner and accusing him of lewd acts. He had blocked my car in, and it took everything in me to escape his grasp. He was a monster disguised as the devil.

Despite everything, Ricardo persisted in flirting with me, causing confusion as well as disgust. I detested the mere idea of him laying eyes on me, let alone speaking to me. He managed to reach out to me online, using fraudulent numbers in my phone, serving as yet another reminder that dealing with someone as senseless as him can lead to unpredictable outcomes.

Nevertheless, through it all, I found a way to maintain my strength and resilience in the face of adversity and hardship. It wasn't just for myself but for those who truly needed me. That's what my grandmother instilled inside my very being. In all my decisions, she was truly at the forefront of all my choices. Therefore, no matter when I was down, I refused to be defeated or subdued by difficult circumstances or traumatic events. I had to keep going on with my life despite the challenges that came along the way. Essentially, remaining unbroken meant holding onto hope, perseverance, and a sense of self in adversity, which sustained me through that horrific period with Ricardo, and just as it will tomorrow.

CHAPTER 15

HAPPY ENDINGS

"Nothing would prepare me for when the doctor told me that my firstborn, the child I had raised as a single mother while chasing my dreams, was diagnosed with cancer at just 15 years old."

I know this much: There are so many people who like to believe that I am different, that I somehow remain oblivious to the common problems of the world. It's not because of who I am, but more so because of the money I possess. However, I am no different than the next person standing in line at Starbucks. The truth of my life was woven into moments of shattered dreams and hopes, yet I never surrendered. I persevered through the hardships and remained a humble and loving woman.

The gravity of this sentiment truly hit me during a late-night phone call with a friend. We were casually chatting when I mentioned that I had to travel to Connecticut for a women's appreciation event at my alma mater, the University of Connecticut. At this event, the school administration planned to announce a new athletic facility to be named after me—The Bailey Athlete Success Center. It wasn't until he enthusiastically repeated it to me that the reality of it all washed over me like a sudden gust of wind. Instantly, I felt a powerful and exhilarating rush of adrenaline, anticipation, and joy all at once. It was as if a burst of energy filled my body with a sense of fulfillment. Are you kidding me? A building named after me at one of the most prestigious universities in the country?! It wasn't easy to comprehend at first, and often, it still isn't, but that moment allowed me to open my eyes to a level of humility that I didn't know I possessed.

That night in Storrs, I addressed hundreds, if not thousands of individuals gathered inside a massive dome to hear what I had to say. Tears rolled down my cheeks as I made my way up to the podium. My heart sprinted to an unfamiliar rhythm, and for a moment, my breathing came in short gasps. Shuffling feet and whispers of excitement filled the room, amplifying my nervousness. I could feel the weight of their expectations on my shoulders, and my mind raced with thoughts of the perfect words to inspire and motivate the audience with the triumphant story of my journey.

As I opened my mouth to speak, my eyes met with the sea of faces before me, patiently waiting. I lost myself in the moment, caught up in the intensity of the situation. But then, while looking into the eyes of everyone in the crowd, I met the gaze of my mother. Her eyes flared with admiration and pride that only a mother could possess, and at that moment, everything else faded away, leaving us alone in the dimly lit room. I could not even hear anything. It was as if time stood still, and transported me back to a simpler time, but this time, my mother was there with me.

My smile grew wider, and I was struck by a wave of emotions that threatened to consume me. It was a feeling I had never experienced—overwhelming joy and gratitude mixed with humility. Whatever I had planned to say next in my speech was overshadowed by my impromptu remarks for my mother, Gloria Tomlinson. In front of the large audience, I asked my mother to rise from her seat to a standing ovation, giving her the recognition that she deserved. In my speech, I thanked her for being my guiding light and always being there for me, no matter what. It was my way of giving my mother her flowers, so to speak, and the look of pride and love on her face was all the validation I needed.

It was a day I would never forget, a moment of pure, unadulterated love and appreciation between a mother and daughter. Additionally, I believe it's the moment that allowed me to become closer to my mother.

The truth is, she and I did not always have the best relationship growing up. In fact, there was a lot of turmoil between us that left us both on an emotional rollercoaster. I suppose the same could be said for many mother-daughter relationships. There were days when we had the type of relationship most couples get divorced over. Conversely, there is not a day, hour, minute, or second in my life where I would claim that my mother didn't love me.

Still, it doesn't change what I know to be true; she did not always know how to be a mother to me. However, I don't blame her because having been a young mother on my own, I understand that my mother was constantly struggling to figure out womanhood while trying to grasp the concept of it. Nowadays, my mother and I function in a space that contains more love than I ever knew we could have for each other. It can still be rocky at times, but because of our devotion to one another, we have learned to move on from anything that happens between us as quickly as water drying on the sidewalk during a sunny day.

As a mother, I have learned how difficult it can be to make choices for our children, hoping they will understand at that moment or later in life. I suppose some of my mother's decisions for me became clearer with time. For instance, she insisted that I attend the University of Connecticut, even though I didn't want to go there. That decision led me to where I am today. Similarly, she made me quit my high school job at Lee's Famous Recipe when I wanted to keep working. That enabled me to focus entirely on track and field. When I told my mother I wanted to be a teacher, she explained that my personality might not be suited for that role, as my lack of patience might lead me to give up too easily. As it turned out, she was right, and because of her guidance, I am where I am today.

As a child, it often felt like my mother didn't want me to have a life of my own. If it had been up to her, she would have homeschooled me, but we couldn't afford it. I was never allowed to do anything. She hated it when I talked on the phone or tried to go out with friends, so I had to sneak around to do anything. This caused many issues between us, and I held onto regrets for far too long. Ironically, my mother experienced the same thing with her own mother, which forced her to run away at every chance.

One occasion, I slipped through the window to hang out with my friends. It wasn't the first time, but when I did sneak out, my heart pounded from the thrill of rebellion. It was the only time outside of running on the tracks that I felt alive and somewhat free, even if just for a few hours. But my freedom was short-lived that day because I knew something was wrong when I crept back into my room. The air was thick with tension, and I could feel my mother's anger burning before I even saw her. To my surprise, Ms. Clark, our nosy neighbor, spotted me sneaking out the window and wasted no time telling on me.

My mother's fury was so intense that I could feel it. She grabbed me and beat me so badly that I saw flashing lights of various shapes and colors whenever I blinked. Her lashes felt like tiny needles piercing my skin until I thought I would break. But I remained tough, and through that beating, I kept repeating the same thing I always said to myself in those sorts of troubles: "You will never see me cry! You will never break me."

Those words gave me the strength to face adversity, pain, or any problematic situation. Eventually, my mother's fury ended, and she stormed out of the room. I was angry, numb, and emotionally hurt, lying on the floor, bruised, and battered...but unbroken. Despite all my feelings, I knew one thing for sure: I would never let anyone see my weaker side, including my mother.

Admittedly, my mother and I have grown strangely closer through all the ups and downs. In the past, I used to blame her for everything that went wrong in my life, all the mishaps, and the things I did not do well. I threw too many unfair expectations onto her shoulders. But now, I realize that she only wanted the best for me. At the time, I was living my life selfishly while being tormented by someone she considered her loved one. This created a rift between us that often left me feeling blind. Internally, I went through a severe battle to forgive my mother for her husband's transgressions. Like me, he had manipulated my mother for long enough to damage her emotionally and spiritually, even without her being aware of it. The hurt she kept buried inside somehow bled into our relationship, and I now understand it as her trauma rather than simply who she was. I am grateful for everything we went through because it gave me a deeper appreciation and love for her.

Though life has never been perfect, today I find joy in watching my mother play with my children. It evokes memories of the special bond I once shared with my grandmother. Perhaps that's why I can now see shades of my grandmother in my mother. Our relationship has grown and deepened, becoming something that I could truly cherish. She's not only a parent to me but also a dear friend. The way she showers me with love is a perfect blend of gentle and tough. It's unconditional and often selfless. Not only that, but it is a profound affection that nurtures and protects me, even at times when it can be overwhelming. I can always count on my mother to be there for me, whether I am celebrating an achievement or facing a challenging time. Her care and attention are unwavering, and I am grateful for her constant support. After all we have been through, there is no one in this world whom I trust more than my mother.

A parent's love for their child is unconditional, overwhelming, and all-encompassing of who they are. It's a deep and profound feeling of affection, protectiveness, and devotion that starts from the moment the child is born and continues to grow stronger over time. As a mother of five, I know this just as much as any other mother. And although loving my children comes naturally, it doesn't always come easy. There are times when a voice internally whispers, "Screw those kids." It's all in love, of course, because nothing means more to me than my children. But any parent deeply involved in their child's life can relate to that feeling, at least sometimes.

Nevertheless, throughout my years, one thing has remained constant—my love for my children. That love for them bleeds into everything I do and everyone I encounter. Sometimes, they'll come into my room laughing or playing around while I am working, and immediately a warm smile covers my face. I see a little bit of myself in each of them—physically, emotionally, and mentally. More than anything, I cherish the stories they tell me, which are always as colorful and animated as the ones before. Indeed, they are the apple of my eye, the prize of my soul, and the reason why I am even here today. Literally!

My oldest daughter, Kashena Smith, isn't my biological daughter. She's a first cousin I brought to America for a better life. Although I didn't give birth to Kashena, I love her like my own. I've watched her grow from a shy Jamaican girl to a beautiful, tall, brown-skinned queen. Sometimes, she and I behave more like sisters than mother and daughter. Even our conversations about dating and sex life take me to a space where I feel like I am speaking to one of my girlfriends.

As the pandemic swept through the world, Kashena and I found ourselves with a lot of time on our hands. With nowhere to go and nothing to do, we decided to try something new, like learning to ride a bike. As we stumbled and wobbled throughout the street, with occasional falls that left us laughing and brushing off the dirt, we bonded in a way I will always cherish. Despite the challenging times, this simple activity brought us closer together and gave us a moment of joy and adventure in the midst of chaos.

* * *

Navigating the delicate balance between being a parent and a friend is a challenge I face every day with my children, and with Kashena, there's no exception. While I cherish our close relationship, I also understand that my responsibility as a parent sometimes requires me to make difficult decisions for her—whether she likes it or not. Sometimes she resents me for it, but I am fine with it because it's a necessary part of raising a child. And I know that in the end, she'll understand and appreciate the choices I've made, just like I did with my mother.

And then there's my firstborn, Natalia, an independent and alluring soul who has a way of charming everyone she encounters. Like several of the women in my family, she is not one to waste words. In fact, Natalia was different from the other kids her age in that she was always quiet. She didn't fuss, cry, or cause any trouble. She was like a little angel, watching me with her big, curious eyes, full of wonder. She didn't start talking until she was about three. I can't help but blame myself for that, as I didn't talk to Natalia as much as I should have. I was always consumed by endless assignments and deadlines from school and work. However, when she finally did start speaking, it was in a small, clear voice, always to the point.

She is an extraordinary individual, gifted both creatively and intellectually. Interestingly, I see so much of myself in Natalia at her age. We both appreciate moments of solitude or being in the company of a select few, engaging in whatever brings us joy. Also, like me, Natalia is very aware of her spending habits. If I'm being honest, there are instances where it feels like she is the mature one, treating me as the child while assuming the role of a mother figure. Despite our shared similarities and slight differences, Natalia holds the key to my heart.

Natalia showed me a love I didn't know I needed when everything in my life felt hopeless. She was the one who saved me when I was at my lowest point. I was overwhelmed with everything—work, dating, family issues, and most of all, life itself. It was the first time I had ever considered ending my own life. Natalia and I were alone at home, and all she wanted to do was play because, like all kids, that's what she loved to do. Natalia couldn't comprehend that her mother was struggling with a deep sadness. But how could she? She was only five years old. And I was an empty shell, filled with darkness, ready to be discarded like yesterday's trash.

Then, as I sat there, lost in my own despair, I looked up and saw Natalia staring at me with eyes that held no judgment, only love, as if I were as perfect as all the princesses in the stories she had read. She smiled at me, ran her fingers through my hair, and reminded me that I had a little girl who needed me to be there for her.

One of the hardest things I ever had to face was watching Natalia go through the most challenging times of her life. I thought I had been dealt my fair share of hardships, but nothing would prepare me for when the doctor told me that my firstborn, the child I had raised as a single mother while chasing my dreams, was diagnosed with thyroid cancer at just fifteen years old. This was a cruel blow, especially considering she had already been diagnosed with Hashimoto's Disease the year before—an autoimmune disorder that causes the immune system to attack the body's tissues. No parent ever wants to watch their child suffer, and I thought I had been strong enough to deal with everything until I witnessed her go through that.

"Don't worry, Mom. Everything is going to be okay," she would tell me. During those times, Natalia encouraged me after seeing the dejected look on my face.

Before I discovered that she had thyroid cancer, our relationship was rocky, as is often the case with mother-daughter relationships during the teenage years. It's ironic, isn't it? I was trying to be the mother I believed she needed, making decisions that I thought were in her best interest. However, much like me when I was her age, Natalia struggled to understand and appreciate my ways. As a result, a disconnect started to form, and our relationship began to waver. It reached a point where it became turbulent, and there were even instances where it became physical. Those were not my proudest moments as a mother, and I felt like I had failed both as a mother and as a woman. I was trying so hard to guide her into becoming someone just like me, without realizing that she is her own person, an independent woman in her own right.

Looking back, I wish I had been more attentive to the signs that my daughter was struggling with more than just typical teenage rebellion. Instead of dismissing her behavior as simply hormonal, I should have taken the time to listen to her and understand what was really going on. Natalia was acting out in ways that I couldn't comprehend at the time, sneaking out of the house and experimenting with weed. She was also struggling in school. She couldn't wake up without significant effort, and her moods had become volatile. I reacted angrily and punished her by taking away her computer, trying to assert my parental authority. But despite my efforts, she found other ways to rebel, even hacking into top-level passwords to access restricted content. Honestly, I was angry enough to strangle her.

Even worse, I nearly reached a point where I wanted to give up because I couldn't handle it anymore. I felt numb and hopeless, and Lord knows how much I despised feeling that way because that's not how I truly felt. During that time, I didn't want anything to do with anyone because if I could not help my own daughter, then who could I help? Things got worse when my baby mistakenly put herself in the hospital one day after completely disregarding my direction. Her actions left her severely sick, yet I couldn't get past my anger for the situation that had taken place. My blood was boiling, I couldn't control my nerves, and my eyes were covered with red veins. I could barely think straight. That's when I did the unthinkable.

After the ambulance came to pick her up, I was still irate that I chose not to go to the hospital. I wasn't sure if that was my way of proving a point or if I was teaching her a lesson. Part of me didn't want to see her that way because it reminded me of my old self. So, I didn't go with her to the hospital. Still, the reality was, as a mother, I let her down at that moment by allowing her to be there alone. Very reminiscent of the day I was looking for my mother when I came out of my coma, wanting to have her by my side.

The doctor called and told me that I needed to be at the hospital or else they wouldn't be able to do anything for Natalia. Quickly, I grabbed my keys and purse and raced to the hospital, my mind a whirlwind of emotions. Fear, anxiety, and anger clashed within me like a violent storm brewing in the depths of my soul. The doctor's words kept echoing in my head, urging me to hurry, to not waste a single moment. The streets flew by in a blur as I pushed my car to its limits, desperate to reach my Natalia in time. I don't know what I would have done had she not made it because of my emotions. When I arrived at the hospital, my heart pounded dreadfully. The sterile halls felt overbearing, and my hand frantically shook as I inked my signature on the papers. As Natalia remained in the hospital bed, her body numb with pain, I couldn't see her, but I could totally feel her. Immediately, I felt myself slipping away from reality. The room around me began to fade into a blur as the beeping of the machines slowly got louder, and all I wanted was to get out of there!

Once I finished the final signature, I turned on my heel and walked away without saying another word. My anger had taken complete control over me, leaving me cold and empty. It was as if I was watching from a distance as my physical form wished to stay in the hospital, but the trauma and pain of my past made me cowardly hide away. I couldn't bear to face anyone, to let them see the pain and desperation threatening to consume me. Instead of focusing on my daughter's life, I left the hospital, remaining stuck on the anger that fueled me. That's a day I regret and a day I would never let happen again.

Today, my bond with Natalia is stronger than ever, always laughing and joking around as if in our own little world. I treasure the moments when she seeks my advice on topics ranging from love and aspirations to finances and current affairs. With her, I've come to realize that parenting is like a dance—a fluid and ever-changing art that requires adapting to the beat of life's music. Each child is unique and requires a distinct parenting style. It took some time for me to learn the delicate balance between giving Natalia enough space to learn and grow while also being there for her when she needed me most. It was like witnessing a butterfly unfold its wings, ready to fly and explore the world. However, I knew that as a parent, I couldn't be entirely hands-off.

When Natalia turns to me for guidance, I am always ready to offer the wisdom I have gained from my own experiences. I don't want to impose my beliefs on her, but instead, provide her with the tools to make her own informed decisions. Through my relationship with Natalia, I've come to appreciate the power of forgiveness and the significance of second chances. Mistakes are a natural part of life, but they can be corrected. Broken hearts can be mended, and beliefs that once seemed unshakable can be reevaluated with a fresh perspective. Natalia unknowingly taught me this invaluable lesson, and I am forever grateful for the wisdom she has imparted.

It's been said that a mother can't raise her son. She can only love him. As I reflect on the birth of my first son, Gabriel, I can't help but disagree. I think the circumstances and the season he was conceived have profoundly impacted his character. He has an uncanny ability to see into the future as if he were granted a prophetic gift. When I prayed to God for a child, I never could have imagined just how blessed I would be with Gabriel.

I tell anyone, if Gabriel approaches you with a dream or vision that he had, don't dismiss it as a childish imagination. He has a track record of accuracy, having already provided valuable insight into matters that concern our family and my business. I remember the day he told me about Bailey's having a storefront long before I had even spotted it myself.

In 2011, after starting my second business, I was working in a roach-infested, six-by-ten office on the first floor of a run-down building. I was working hard! Twenty-hours-a-day type of hard. There were days when Natalia and Gabriel would join me at the office, as it was the only way I knew how to navigate the challenging path of being both a dedicated mother and a determined businesswoman..

One day as we exited the building and headed to the car, Gabriel, just two years old, looked up at me and said, "Mommy, Bailey's is going to be in a large yellow building." Even at that age, he sounded more confident and prophetic than I could imagine anyone to be. Nonetheless, I coyly smiled, wondering how such a young boy could see so much potential in his poor old mother. Then, on his birthday, six years later, I closed on my first commercial property, which happened to be a large yellow building. It was just as Gabriel had told me. He would continue with his exceptional psychic-like abilities.

With a weeping infant cradled in my arms and Natalia and Gabriel standing at my side, I waited in a dreadful line at CVS. No matter what I tried, I couldn't soothe Kayla's cries. As a single mother raising three children, my patience wore thin all too quickly. Juggling the demands of both motherhood and running my own business was a constant struggle that didn't help, either. So, there I was, in the confines of CVS, when Gabriel glanced up at me and uttered, "Mommy, you should have one of these," his finger gesturing toward the pharmacy. He was onto something because a year later, I opened my very own pharmacy—a venture I hadn't even fathomed until he planted the seed in my mind.

Gabriel's confidence and charm seem to radiate from within like a natural-born leader. Even as a young child, he had a sharp instinct that proved to be invaluable. Now, as Gabriel grew, so did my anxiety about how to approach the subject of his father. It weighed heavily on my mind, and I constantly grappled with the right timing and words to use. Should I wait until he's older when he can handle the weight of such information? Or should I tell him now, during his formative years? It was like navigating through a dark and treacherous forest, unsure of which path to take.

I spent countless hours rehearsing different scenarios in my head, trying to anticipate every possible question and reaction. It was a conversation that required the utmost care and consideration, as it held the power to shape Gabriel's perception of himself and his family. But ultimately, I knew that I had to be the one to tell him. My responsibility as his mother was to be honest with him about his family history, no matter how difficult it may be. And so, with a heavy heart and a shaky voice, I sat down with him and began the conversation.

I found myself sitting next to Gabriel on the couch, the glow of the TV flickering across our faces. I took a deep breath and whispered, "Let's talk."

His prophetic intuition kicked in, and he immediately asked, "Is this about my dad?" My heart raced as I braced myself then nodded.

"Honey, your dad is in prison," I said slowly, deliberately. "He was with the wrong people, and they did something bad. And because he was with them, he was sent to prison too." The anxiety pulsed through me, but it was worth it because the burden of not knowing why his father was absent was finally lifted.

I seized the opportunity to teach him an important lesson about choosing the right friends. We talked about how friends can influence our decisions and lead us down the wrong path. I made sure not to condemn Gabriel's father, despite his actions. He was still his father, and I didn't want to taint their relationship any further.

He took in all the information maturely. Of course, he had questions, and I answered them because that's what he needed. He understood why his dad had not seen him, which I think relieved what may have felt like rejection for him. He now knew that he was wanted and realized he had to be more responsible and make the right choices. This was quite refreshing because we were battling his inability to sit still and focus on his work. Before that conversation, I had to review his grades closely and sit with him through every question in all his classes. However, once the weight of uncertainty about whether his father wanted him was lifted from his shoulders, an angel named Gabriel appeared before us. He transformed into a different boy.

As a mother raising a son without a father, I knew how important it was for Gabriel to understand the truth, no matter how difficult it may be. By being honest with him, I hoped to equip him with the tools he needed to navigate the world around him. Together, we could weather any storm that came our way. The barrier between mother and son was now bridged by a newfound closeness. We had shared a moment of vulnerability, and from it grew a bond that couldn't be broken.

Once in a while, a shooting star fires across the sky, and if you're lucky, you can make a wish that will one day come true. That's exactly how I got my Kayla. She is my baby girl, but from the moment she was born, her imagination was wild and vibrant. At just six years old, she declared that her wedding would feature the biggest cake ever, so enormous that it would fill up the entire room. Catching my breath between laughs, I tried to remind her that she needed to get through high school or even puberty before she got married. But that's Kayla for you—always bursting with creativity and personality. She's a natural comedian who loved putting on a show at any given moment, whether it was wearing my heels and a bright pink cartoon wig during my Zoom meetings or simply cracking a joke at the dinner table.

Kayla was the type of child who made people wonder where kids come from, and I couldn't help but see so much of myself in her. But what really set her apart was her unruffled nature; almost nothing fazes her. She is a beautiful soul, allowing me to learn much from her daily. When spending time with Kayla, every moment feels like an adventure. We have our special rituals, from relaxing in bubble baths to cozy Friday night movie sessions to sipping tea and saying prayers together. My daughter has an old soul in a young body, always surprising me with her wisdom and creativity. She's the one who comes up with the most absurd ideas that keep me young at heart. There was her brief stint of twenty-four-hour challenges, where she attempted to eat non-stop for a whole day. It only lasted fifteen minutes. Then, there was her determination to stay in the movie theater for a full day, which also ended after fifteen minutes. And who can forget when she tried to stay in my room for an entire day? Yup, fifteen minutes.

But it wasn't all for nothing. That summer, she tapped into her essence and began exploring her talents. Kayla recorded a few episodes of her own reality show, which we posted on social media. Watching the footage of her hosting tea parties with her friends, all of them oozing a fierce attitude, made me realize just how much spunk she has.

This little bundle of charisma and character always knows her worth, even when it comes to something as seemingly insignificant as water. I remember being on vacation in Jamaica, sipping my water when she approached me, asking if she could have some. But then, she paused and asked me what brand it was. I stared at her, wondering why it mattered.

"Kayla, it's water. What does it matter?" I asked.

She looked at me without a smile and said, "I only drink certain brands."

There are moments when I gaze upon Kayla, and my heart swells with joy, almost to the point of tears. It's as if she carries a piece of my grandmother's spirit within her that I can vividly see. Her generosity, even at such a young age, is nothing short of remarkable. Kayla would offer shelter to every homeless person she met and provide food to anyone hungry if she could. If Natalia wore a superhero cape during her cancer battle, then Kayla wears a cape of a different kind—that of a super-rescuer. She has a sixth sense when it comes to feeling the pain of others. I believe that's why she radiates so much personality with an innate desire to make everyone smile. And no matter what, she's taught me to believe everything will be okay.

For almost eight years, the thought of Paul lingered like a shadow in the depths of my mind. So, when he finally reached out, I felt a mix of anticipation and caution. I had always yearned for Kayla to have a relationship with her father, but I also had reservations about allowing him back into our lives for various reasons. The fear of potential hurt for both my daughter and I was one of the factors that made the decision difficult. Nights were spent wrestling with the pros and cons as I analyzed and reevaluated the situation repeatedly.

Ultimately, I decided that the blessing outweighed the risk because I wanted Kayla to know her father and have a bond that neither Natalia, Gabriel, nor I ever had with ours. As I watch them interact today, I feel my heart swell with a mix of emotions—relief, joy, fear, and hope. It's like watching two puzzle pieces finally fit together, each finding their place in the other's life. Paul had apologized, not just to me, but to Kayla too. I could see the sincerity in his eyes and hear it in his voice through his words and actions. It was as if he was trying to make up for lost time, to prove that he was worthy of being a father.

I understood that Paul's involvement in Kayla's life was more for her than it was for me. I couldn't be selfish. Besides, denying her access to her father wouldn't have done any good for either of us. Instead, it could have significant negative effects on her development and well-being. I saw how the absence of a father led to a lack of emotional stability, a decrease of self-esteem, and the tendency of behavioral problems in so many people. It happened to Natalia, Gabriel, friends, and countless others, including myself.

Today, as Kayla and Paul laugh and talk, my mind wanders to the future, thinking, "Will he keep his promise? Will he stick around this time?" Although I can't predict the future, I am satisfied to see the happiness on Kayla's face. The image of a father and daughter bonding will be one that she and I will never forget.

Oh, my Lord, I present to you my son, Ocean—a bundle of energy, athleticism, and rowdiness to turn your hours into minutes. He is my last child, and his name holds great significance. Just like the vast expanse of an ocean, he is powerful, mesmerizing, and awe-inspiring. Everyone loves the ocean, yet many are fearful of its depths. It encompasses more of the earth's surface than anything else, and that's precisely why I chose to name my son Ocean. His middle name, Mansa, is derived from the 14th-century Mali Empire's emperor, Mansa Musa. He was an African ruler who gained fame throughout Europe and the Middle East for his vast fortune of four hundred billion dollars.

Childbirth with Ocean was a traumatic experience that almost cost me my life. There were moments when I doubted if I would witness him grow up with his siblings. I had a complete placenta previa, which meant that my placenta had totally covered my cervix throughout the pregnancy and delivery. Consequently, I had to undergo an emergency cesarean section at 32 weeks. Following the birth, we spent 46 days in the hospital, navigating the challenges together. Despite the hardships, today I am grateful to God for sparing Ocean's life and blessing me with a bundle of joyful energy that everyone adores. Ocean has a unique way of mirroring my work ethic even at such a young age. I treasure the way he showers me with big, wet kisses when I need them the most. I am eagerly looking forward to witnessing his growth as his enthusiasm and curiosity bring a refreshing energy to our lives. Like Kayla, he possesses a beautiful and giving personality, and I can already discern that he may have a leaning toward athletics, much like me, Natalia, and Gabriel. Ocean is the only one among my children who has siblings from another parent, and he shares a bond with his responsible brothers, who possess strong character and sound judgment.

Through my love for Ocean, I have also gained a more powerful respect for forgiveness. I recognize that everyone carries their own baggage and that everyone deserves a chance to be forgiven. So that's what I did. In forgiving Ricardo, I chose to overlook his character flaws and all the times he showed his capacity for danger. Looking back at fragments of our time together, there were moments when I should have ended the marriage. I shouldn't have had to wait until he raped and nearly killed me before doing so. But I refuse to punish myself for that. Instead, I decided to prioritize myself and my children. I surrounded myself with people who uplift me, support me, and inspire me. All to remain unbroken.

Forgiveness became my way of dealing with Ricardo because I wanted my children to maintain their relationships with him. And because Ocean, our shared son, was still very young, I understood the weight of a father's absence on a child's life.

At the beginning of writing this book, I was still healing from a nasty and devastating divorce. The wounds of betrayal that came with it still had the Band-Aid wrapped tightly around it. To make matters worse, just when I thought I had gotten over it, I was swindled out of a million dollars by someone I had trusted. That relationship, or what I thought was a relationship, left me feeling foolish and exposed. I knew then I had to take it slow, find a better way to approach love, or better yet, find myself with someone who was nothing like the men I usually dated.

Despite my reputation as a woman who gave her all in love, my past experiences left me confused and vulnerable. Instead of seeking a deep connection, I settled for occasional sex and superficial texts, which left me feeling somewhat loved, but ultimately unfulfilled. I couldn't share this with my friends and family, who saw me as a successful woman with everything money could buy. But when it came to love, it seemed to elude me like a curse.

Nevertheless, coming out of the global pandemic, I fell for a decent man, a politician, who exemplified what it meant to be thoughtful, kind, and comforting. At that time, he was the remedy I needed to overcome the hurt I had endured. As much as I loved being with him, he was a man whose priorities didn't match mine. He was often unavailable and rarely chose me over his career. Although he was single, I sometimes felt like I was dating a married man. I never blamed him for his actions because I understood the shoes he was walking in. However, despite it all, I knew I needed better for myself, and leaving that relationship helped me to know exactly what I truly needed in a partner.

By now, you can tell that when it came to finding the right man, I failed miserably. Most of the men I had been with seemed to be cut from the same cloth, each causing me physical pain, stealing from me, and severely manipulating my emotions. But just as I was getting ready to give up on true love, he appeared in my inbox with a simple message: "Hey. How are you?" I had witnessed so many men sliding into my DMs, but one individual that did, caught my attention. As I scrolled through his page, there was something that pulled me in. It wasn't just one feature about the man that made him unique, but his ecstatic brown eyes, which told a story I was desperate to hear, did come close. The more we spoke, the more he transformed from being just a good-looking man I met on Instagram to someone who stayed on my mind rent free. A towering figure, his African heritage etched into his face, accompanied by a smile that illuminates my entire world. That's who he truly is.

I had gone through some extensive therapy to understand how the trauma in my life shaped my dating life. I couldn't understand for the longest time how and why I was going through some of these situations over and over again. On the other side of my EMDR therapy, I can say that I've come out a better woman who's able to see certain things in men I wasn't able to at first. No longer would I mistake lust and greed for love and passion. And at some point, I could look into the eyes of this man and feel he was a man I could let my guard down for. If anything, he was a man who could restore my faith in love. The gentle way he handles me, with grace and kindness, is something that I have never known. In every way, he touches my soul. Mentally, emotionally, spiritually, and sexually. It wasn't long before I knew he was the one I had been waiting for.

In some strange way, his vulnerability makes me feel safe. And his calming persona, acquired from his loving mother, puts me at ease, allowing me to embrace and adore the woman I see in the mirror every day. Admittedly, my past traumas often linger in my mind, threatening to derail my chances at happiness, and God, do I hate it. Yet, like a soldier on the battlefield, he stands tall against the fight, patient and understanding. In this battle of overcoming leftovers of my past fuckups, he holds my hand and walks by my side along this journey. I, in return, take his soul in ways he could never imagine.

Throughout this book, you may have gathered that I am a kind, forgiving, and hopeless romantic. It's evident in the movies I watch and how I love others. Love is a part of who I am. But it doesn't stop there. I also dream of love in an array of vividly expressed colors. For as long as I can remember, I have had an image of me riding off on a horse with the man I love, side by side. The horses would take us to my private jet, where we would take off into the sky and make love like we'd never done before. From there, we would land on a paradise island and live in a mesmerizing beach house surrounded by the beautiful blue water of the ocean, listening to the soothing sound of birds chirping and waves crashing against the shore. We would lie together, watching the moon and sun repeatedly switch shifts until the strands of our hair go from black to gray. Soon after, the pitter-patter of footsteps and cute giggles of children playing would fill the house. This is a dream that I have held onto so firmly that it became a memory.

Funny enough, I never dreamt of owning a massive property where horses could roam freely, but that dream became a reality when I stumbled upon the gem that would later be known as Serenity Ranch. The property in the heart of Orlando is not only a home but also a haven to escape the hustle and bustle of city life. It was sold out of bankruptcy, and without a second thought, I bought the property. Over six months, I expanded it to 58 acres with built-in stalls to house over sixty horses—four of which are my babies. These were the same horses I had dreamt of for years, and now they were mine to care for and love.

But that wasn't the only thing I had been dreaming of. For Christmas, in 2022, I decided to gift myself the one thing I had always desired—a private jet. I vividly recalled the time when I was removed from a flight simply for wanting to enjoy my snack, and that memory only intensified my longing to own an aircraft. The purchase of the jet brought me an immense sense of pride and fulfillment, knowing that a girl from Woodlands, St. Elizabeth, Jamaica, could turn her wildest dreams into reality. What made it even more surreal was the fact that I had already seen the jet in my dreams prior to experiencing it in actuality. It resembled the very aircraft that the man in my dreams and I embarked upon.

As my grand beach house in Jamaica, spanning an impressive 36,000 square feet, edges closer to completion, a swell of pride and admiration takes over me. The sight of horses gracefully galloping across my ranch and my private jet, poised for adventure at a moment's notice, feels like a surreal testament to my achievements. Yet, it is the presence of the man I've always wanted to be in love with, steadfastly standing by my side, that truly signals the realization of my dreams. The only thing left to complete this fairytale—a symphony of tiny footsteps and infectious giggles from a child who will one day call me Grandma. I eagerly await the moment when one of my beloved children turns this cherished dream into a cherished reality.

While writing this book, my mother would share stories with me that she had never told before. These stories included details about her relationship with my father. She didn't often go into specifics about what happened between them. Still, sometimes she finds herself giving me more information that helps me piece together the puzzle of their relationship, and ultimately, who my father truly was. My mother tried to connect me with a man she claimed was my father, but I didn't believe her because he didn't have certain physical features that I imagined my father to have—starting with our noses. I always thought that if my mother and I didn't share the same nose, it would have to be from my father. However, one day I took a picture with my brother Brian and realized we both had the same nose despite having different fathers. This realization allowed me to take the next step in connecting with the man I believe to be my father, who I hadn't seen in over forty years, and our reunion would start with a DNA test. Stay tuned.

Throughout the years, my relationships with my mom and sister have transformed, becoming stronger and more meaningful. As my mom aged, I saw her in a new light, and through therapy, I discovered that my sister had always been there for me. When we arrived in America, I relied on her to keep me safe from my stepfather. By going to pick Yolande up from school and staying by her side at home, it provided me with a sort of safety net. Later, when I struggled with childcare in a new city, she came to stay with me for a year to provide help. During different seasons of my life, she has been a source of encouragement. While my sister and I still have a lot to work on, nowadays I am more encouraged that our love will bring us closer together. Through our bond, I am positive that we will rebuild our relationship and heal from the trauma that we both faced together.

Now, my home is filled with love and joy, thanks to my mom, my cousins, and my own children. There is always an adventure to be had, and we cherish every moment spent together.

To remain unbroken is like taking huge rocks formed from past failures and traumas and using them as stepping stones to rise above your circumstances. It's the feeling of being battered and bruised but standing tall with a more resilient version of yourself. It is the triumph of the human spirit over adversity and the refusal to be broken by life's challenges. That is how I stand before you today, with my heart swelling with contentment and joy, like a beautiful butterfly taking flight on a warm summer day.

Nowadays, the world around me is so vibrant, with every color and sound clearer than ever before. Still, I know one day, the skies may darken, the winds may shift, and tomorrow may bring storms that threaten to tear me apart. And when that happens, I cannot promise that I will be as happy as I am at this moment, but I vow to my future self that I will not give up.

Like a soldier on the battlefield, I will fight to rise from the ashes of my struggles and soar even higher. I will search for light in the darkness and beauty in the chaos. Even when I stumble and fall, I will find the strength to stand up again with a fire in my heart that burns brighter than ever before. I know that with every challenge, there is a chance to grow and become something more meaningful.

So, I will fight, with every fiber of my being, knowing that with hard times come better days. That is how I have remained UNBROKEN!

UNBROKEN

Thank you for your order of **UNBROKEN**.
We value your feedback. Please consider leaving a review.

SCAN ME

Made in the USA
Las Vegas, NV
13 September 2024

d9ec86b5-3069-4441-b853-90dd7a43566dR01